The
EVOLUTION
of
AMERICAN
BICYCLE
RACING

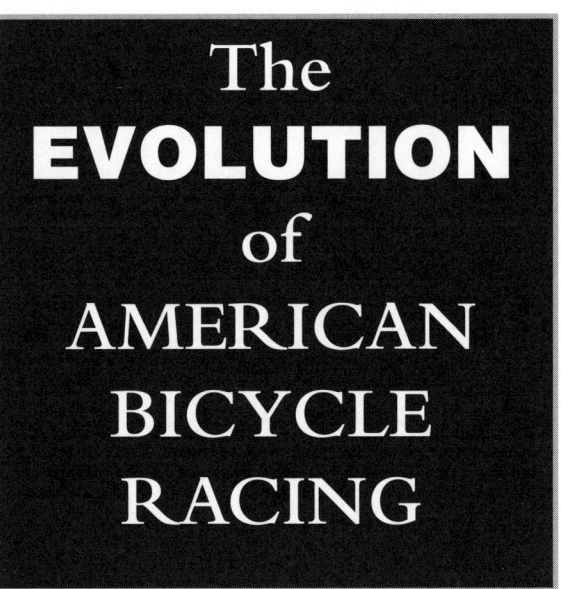

The
EVOLUTION
of
AMERICAN
BICYCLE
RACING

Lou Dzierzak

FALCONGUIDES®

GUILFORD, CONNECTICUT
HELENA, MONTANA

AN IMPRINT OF THE GLOBE PEQUOT PRESS

For Taylor, Claire, Emily,
and Jack

FALCONGUIDES®

Text design by Thomas Goddard

Library of Congress Cataloging-in-Publication Data is available.
ISBN 978-0-7627-3901-1

Manufactured in the United States of America
First Edition/First Printing

To buy books in quantity for corporate use
or incentives, call **(800) 962–0973**
or e-mail **premiums@GlobePequot.com.**

Contents

Homage is long overdue for America's cycling pioneers. To recall the great Major Taylor one needs to first pay tribute to his boyhood hero, A. A. Zimmerman. The torch is then passed to Frank Kramer, Alf Goullet, Jack Disney, yours truly, the Stetina brothers, Davis Phinney, Alexi Grewal, and Greg LeMond, to name only a few. After being applauded for his achievements, Sir Isaac Newton humbly replied, "If I appear taller than my contemporaries, it is because I stand on the shoulders of giants."

> —John Howard, three-time member of the U.S. Olympic cycling team and the first American to win a road race gold medal at the Pan American Games. Howard has twelve national championship titles in road racing, time trials, cyclocross, and off-road mountain bike racing.

It is indeed an honor to be included, or even mentioned, in this history of American racers directly preceding Greg LeMond and Lance Armstrong. Fortunately I had the opportunity to really know them all, after competing against them and with them on the same teams. This has made it all the more enjoyable to follow their international successes that my generation all dreamed about but could never begin to approach. Recalling these glory days of our cycling careers from twenty-five to thirty-five years ago, it's all too easy to forget how incredibly difficult and painful bike racing is. But I also remember the gears and cadences we rode. What is truly impressive to me is how much faster and fitter all the racers are today than the champions of my time.

> —Wayne Stetina, ten-time U.S. national champion and member of three Olympic teams, two Pan Am teams, and three Worlds teams

The Red Zinger and Coors Classic stage races were huge magnets that attracted a loyal and growing fan base, national television coverage, a feature-length film, and the greatest amateur and professional and women racers in the world. It sold $1 million in merchandise in just a year, was the only event to ever close a U.S. national park, and raced in Hawaii around a volcano and through California's wine country, state capitals, gambling towns, and the rarified air of the Rocky Mountain West. It nurtured names like Hampsten, Boyer, Carpenter, Mount, Phinney, Stetina, Howard, Alcala, Anderson, Grewal, Bauer, Kiefel, Roll, Carmichael, Longo, Twigg, and LeMond and hosted the winners of eighteen Tours de France. It changed lives, made careers, and no one died racing in it in thirteen years. It was the first in many cycling and national U.S. sports achievements, and I am proud that now the recounting of its grand and historical racing record can be found under one cover!

> —Michael Aisner, former Coors Classic race director

Acknowledgments

First and most important, you are holding this book in your hands because of the efforts of Scott Adams, my editor at Globe Pequot. From our first conversation to the delivery of the final manuscript, Scott has championed the idea, enthusiastically read my work-in-progress chapters, and offered well-timed words of encouragement. Thanks for everything, Scott. Robert Hurst and John Burbidge guided the book through the final stages. Their care and attention to detail has made this a better book.

The stories presented here begin with the generosity of Annette Thompson, curator of the Bicycle Museum of America, and Bob Williams, the track director of the National Sports Center Velodrome in Minnesota. Annette offered me access to the museum's collection of long-forgotten bicycling magazines, scrapbooks filled with turn-of-the-century newspaper reports, and Schwinn's business records. Bob graciously let me explore his thirty-year-old collection of racing publications. The yellowed pages of newspapers and magazines like *Competitive Cycling, Velonews, Cycling USA,* and *Winning Illustrated* provided the foundation for the book.

A book of history can't exist without the voices of the people who experienced the events the writer is trying to capture. I'm grateful for the many people who willingly responded to my telephone calls and e-mail queries. It was a thrill to listen to the best racers of the past tell their tales of close victories and frustrating defeats. Thanks to John Howard, Wayne Stetina, Ron Kiefel, and Tom Schuler for spending hours on the phone with me. Michael Aisner, race director of the Coors Classic, was a fantastic resource. I also want to thank Phil Liggett, Russell Allen, Peter Nye, Jeff Groman, Dave LaPorte, Jay Townley, Les Earnest, Phil Voxland, Zapata Espinoza, and Jonathan Vaughters for guiding me through bicycle racing's landmark events.

The photographs in this book bring the story to life. Barbara and Robert F. George and Cor Vos graciously allowed me access to their archives of historical photographs. A very heartfelt thank you for your contributions.

For every late night and lost weekend spent on the phone, paging through old magazine archives, and writing, my family was there to give me the freedom to focus. Thanks Mom, Dad, Bill, and Jane, for your support every step of the way. Taylor and Claire deserve much credit for keeping the archive in proper order, regardless of how many times I shuffled the deck. Finally, to Carey, words on a page can't begin to describe the gratitude I have for your support.

Foreword

There are more than 1,000 races listed on the international cycling calendar, and if you include the national races reserved for each country's riders, then you can at least triple this number. As a sport and pastime, cycling is likely the most popular in the world, as at some time in their lives everyone will have ridden a bicycle. But if you ask anyone to name a cycle race, you get only one answer: the Tour de France.

Its history, which dates back to 1903, is, to put it mildly, a colorful one, and even today, there are those riders who will go to any length to win it. Drugs, shortcuts along the way, sharp tacks on the route, demonstrations, and terrorist threats have all been part of this amazing race around France.

The Tour de France, long dominated by Europeans, has witnessed America's riders slowly earn a place in the peloton's incredible history. In 1973, as the chief international commissar of the Tour of Ireland, I invited John Allis, Stan Swain, Bill Humphries, and John Howard to enter the field as the first team of American riders to race in Europe. Surprising many, Howard won a stage and the team finished 6th. Eight years later, in 1981, Jonathan Boyer became the first American rider in the Tour. He finished 32nd, and his performance inspired other American riders to test their skills against the Tour's best.

In 1986, eighty-three years after the first Tour, America's racers claimed their right to wear the yellow jersey. For the first time an American professional team stood shoulder to shoulder with the best European riders on the Tour's first day. Davis Phinney, a member of that 7-Eleven team, captured the third stage. Even more astounding, Greg LeMond, Bernard Hinault's top lieutenant in 1985, became the first American to win the prestigious Tour de France. LeMond's come-from-behind victory in the final stage in 1989, which propelled him to an 8-second winning margin over Laurent Fignon and his second yellow jersey, remains one of the most thrilling races in Tour history.

It has been my privilege to follow every day of this great sporting event for radio, television, and newspapers since 1973. That was the year I thought I would get to see the race just once and never return!

In 2007 I will follow race number thirty-five, and it will be a fitting anniversary for me as the Tour de France will make its first-ever start from London. The Grand Depart, as the French call it, will spend the opening weekend in the capital and then progress to Canterbury before returning home to continue its journey to Paris, where it has always finished.

I have witnessed the first victories by English-speaking riders—Greg LeMond, Stephen Roche, and Lance Armstrong—and the domination by the great legends of the race like Hinault, Miguel Indurain, Eddy Merckx, and, of course, the insatiable American record holder, Armstrong.

When I started reporting the race, no English was spoken, and indeed, we were not made very welcome, as this was a race for the French. That has all changed now, as the field has become fully international and, sadly, the French are still waiting to find a new Hinault, the last Frenchman to win, in 1985.

They talk of Tour fever, a highly contagious disease that begins at the end of June and, once caught, is unlikely to be cured. It is easily recognized in the people who camp out on remote mountains for a week, get totally drunk, and can barely remember the passing of the race, yet go back again year after year.

Long ago I realized that the Tour de France is more than a cycle race; it is a way of life, and the eyes of the world are constantly upon it. It is also the greatest sporting event in the world, a race won not for the 1st prize (about £275,000) but for the privilege of saying: "I won the Tour de France." Everyone in the world will know what you mean.

Enjoy this great insight into La Grande Boucle. You will be all the better for it, but don't expect it to cure that fever!

—Phil Liggett
Hertfordshire 2007

Introduction

THE JUNE 29, 2006, edition of *USA Today* called Lance Armstrong "the greatest cyclist in American history." With an unprecedented seven consecutive Tour de France victories, two American professional titles, an Olympic bronze medal, and a world championship, he certainly has impressive credentials.

Whereas fans of baseball, football, and basketball have a sense of the past heroes of their sports, the explosion of interest in bicycle racing over the last decade has done little to honor the past. Football announcers compare the running styles of Shaun Alexander with Walter Payton. Baseball writers debate whether Ted Williams could hit Roger Clemens's fastball.

There's no question Lance Armstrong is one of the best racers in American history. But the best ever? Maybe not. From 1901 to 1922 Frank Kramer captured 18 national pro titles, a world championship, and more than 600 career victories. Kramer won regardless of the distance or the competition, foreign or domestic. His performances made the front pages of the country's best newspapers for decades. Promoters earned millions pitting Kramer against one challenger after another. In his time, Kramer was unbeatable.

Bicycle racing has a fantastic history filled with once-famous riders who have fallen into obscurity for all but the most hard-core racing historian. Lance Armstrong is just one rider in a long line of successful names reaching back to George Hendee and Arthur Zimmerman in 1892.

In the last thirty years, American bicycle racing has moved from an overlooked fringe sport to the center of media attention. Armstrong's performances are legendary, no doubt. But long before his rise to the top, the 7-Eleven racing team, the Coors Classic stage race, and Greg LeMond's come-from-behind 8-second victory in the 1989 Tour de France captured our attention.

This book isn't an exhaustive history of American bicycle racing. Instead, it's a selection of stories about the racers and landmark events that brought American racers out of obscurity at home and made them internationally respected competitors. Each chapter deserves to be its own book to truly explore the contributions of the racers, coaches, promoters, and organizations that moved racing forward.

At the turn of the twentieth century, six-day races were the most popular sporting events of the day. Only the coming of the World Wars would diminish the standing-room-only crowds that packed Madison Square Garden to watch cyclists fly around a velodrome.

After World War II racing's popularity faded as sports fans turned to baseball and other endeavors. In 1971 John Howard captured America's first gold medal at the Pan American Games in Cali, Colombia. A photograph of Howard crossing the finish line with arms thrust in the air appeared on the front page of the *New York Times,* signaling renewed interest in cycling. George Mount's 6th-place road race finish in the 1976 Olympics in Montreal was covered by newspaper reports and television broadcasts across the country. After decades away from the medal stand, were we finally ready to take the next step?

Watershed changes in the business of sports changed bicycle racing forever. For the first time companies were willing to support amateur and professional racing. In return they wanted their brands and products associated with winners. From 7-Eleven through Coors Light, Motorola, the U.S. Postal Service, and the Discovery Channel in 2006, America's best racers wore the colors of a corporate sponsor. Events like the Coors Classic, Tour DuPont, Tour of Somerville, Redlands Classic, Fitchburg Longsjo Classic, and USPRO championships in Philadelphia drew hundreds of thousands of fans to cycling.

On a parallel path, America's top racers looked across the Atlantic for another challenge. The competitive spirit demanded that the best racers compete against the best in the world, not just in the United States. With a much longer racing tradition, European race directors scoffed, questioning our ability to compete at their level. In 1972 twenty-year-old Mike Neel became the first American to compete in Britain's Milk Race. It was a miserable experience, but the line was crossed. One year later John Howard led the first American team to race in Europe. From then on American racers earned the right to compete shoulder to shoulder with the best from Italy, France, and Spain.

Although fewer in number than their male counterparts, America's female racers quickly earned the world's respect for their performances. In 1969 Audrey McElmury became the first American to win a world championship in fifty-seven years. Beth Heiden, Sheila Young-Ochowicz, Connie Carpenter, Sue Novara-Reber, Connie Paraskevin-

Young, and Rebecca Twigg followed McElmury on the international stage. Carpenter and Twigg kicked off the record-setting 1984 Los Angeles Olympics by finishing the first women's Olympic road race in 1st and 2nd place.

In the last decade the Tour de France has become the pinnacle of success for professional teams and racers. Twenty-four years before Lance Armstrong retired with his seventh Tour de France yellow jersey, Jonathan Boyer became the first American to enter and finish bicycle racing's signature event. America's progress to the podium was measured by the first team entered, the first stage win, and the first to wear the yellow jersey. In 1986 Greg LeMond became the first American to win the Tour. His 1989 come-from-behind victory over France's Laurent Fignon was arguably the most dramatic in the Tour's 103-year history.

Is Armstrong truly the greatest American bicycle racer? If you think Kramer's performances are too old to compare, what about Davis Phinney, who won more than 300 amateur and professional races from 1977 to 1993? Or Greg LeMond and his two world championships and three yellow jerseys? Who knows how many times LeMond would have won the Tour if he hadn't been wounded in a hunting accident. What if President Carter didn't boycott the 1980 Olympics? Track racers also deserve attention. Marty Nothstein won gold and silver Olympic medals, three world titles, and twenty-two national championships. What about Jack Disney, Steve Woznick, or Leonard Nitz?

There's no question Armstrong is one of the best. But his racing career stands on the shoulders of generations of racers who in their time were also called "the greatest cyclist in American history." Without multimillion-dollar sponsorship contracts and entourages to address their every need, these racers, their names long forgotten, competed with the same drive and passion Armstrong showed in leaving his competitors behind on a climb to Alpe d'Huez. To truly understand Armstrong's legacy, we should honor his predecessors.

TIMELINE

May 24, 1878 | First recorded bicycle race in the United States (C. A. Parker of Harvard University covers 3-mile course in 12:27).

1882 | George Hindee wins the first American sprint championship, on a high-wheel bicycle.

1885 | J. K. Starley of Coventry, England, invents the "safety bicycle."

1893 | League of American Wheelmen introduces first official world championships. Arthur Zimmerman wins both contested events.

1893 | High-wheelers used in competition for the last time.

November 30, 1894 | Ten thousand spectators fill Madison Square Garden to watch a single-day record sixty-eight bicycle races.

1901 | Frank Kramer wins first national championship. He defended his title for sixteen consecutive years.

1904 | American racers win three world championships in London.

1912 | Carl Schutte wins a bronze medal in the Stockholm Olympics. Seventy-two years will pass before an American racer will win again.

December 1920 | Amateur Bicycle League of America is founded.

1922 | Frank Kramer retires with 18 national championships and more than 600 career victories.

1933 | Nutley Velodrome in New Jersey draws 297,000 fans at thirty-five races.

1940 | Tour of Somerville is founded.

1949 | Jack Heid wins the bronze medal in the world amateur sprint championship, the first American victory in thirty-seven years.

1950 | Ted Smith becomes the first American racer to compete in the world professional road race championship. Suffered a flat tire and did not finish.

1960 | Fitchburg Longsjo Classic is founded.

1965 | Amateur Bicycle League introduces the first officially recognized national road championship. Michael Hitlner, twenty-four, wins first event.

1967 Nancy Burghart wins the women's national championship for the fourth time in six years.

1969 Audrey McElmury becomes the first American to win a world championship in fifty-seven years.

1971 The first major international stage race in the United States, the Tour of California, is won by Mexico's Augustin Alcantara.

1971 John Howard wins America's first gold medal in Pan American Games competition. A photo of Howard's victory appears on the front page of the *New York Times*.

1972 Mike Neel becomes the first American to race in Britain's Milk Race.

1973 John Howard, John Allis, Stan Swain, and Bill Humphries become the first American team to compete in a European race. Howard finishes the Tour of Ireland in 3rd place.

1973 Sheila Young wins a gold medal at the world championships in San Sebastian, Spain—the first American track championship in fifty years.

1973–74 OPEC oil embargo fuels bicycle sales in the United States.

1974 Jackie Simes wins the first U.S. national professional championship since 1936.

1975 John Howard wins the first Red Zinger Classic.

1975 Chaos ensues at the sprint competition at the Pan American Games in Mexico City.

1975 Amateur Bicycle League of America officials vote to change the organization's name to the United States Cycling Federation.

1976 Mike Neel becomes the first American to compete in the world professional road race championship and finishes 10th.

1976 George Mount finishes 6th in the road race at the Montreal Olympics.

1976 Connie Carpenter wins national championships in the pursuit and road race in her first year of competition.

1977 Eddie Borysewicz becomes the first paid full-time coach of the USCF.

1978	Greg LeMond wins a record-setting three medals at the 1978 junior world championships.
1979	Mo Siegel sells the Red Zinger Classic to race director Michael Aisner for $1.00.
1980	President Carter boycotts the 1980 Olympics in Moscow.
1980	The Red Zinger Classic becomes the Coors Classic.
1981	Southland Corporation forms the 7-Eleven racing team.
1981	Jacques (Jonathan) Boyer becomes the first American to enter the Tour de France. He finishes 32nd.
1981	The Soviet team comes to Colorado to compete in the Coors Classic. Greg LeMond wins the race.
June 6, 1982	The first U.S. professional criterium championship is held in Baltimore.
July 15, 1982	The Major Taylor Velodrome opens in Indianapolis, Indiana.
1982	LeMond finishes 2nd in the world professional road race.
1983	The National Off-Road Bicycle Association is formed. At the end of its first year, NORBA has 112 members.
1983	LeMond wins the world championship professional road race.
December 1983	Steve Tilford wins the first national mountain bike championship.
1984	Greg LeMond signs a three-year, $1 million contract to ride for the French La Vie Claire team, the richest contract in the history of cycling.
1984	The USSR boycotts the Los Angeles Olympics. American cyclists win an unprecedented nine medals.
1984	Marianne Martin wins the first Tour de France Feminin.
May 1985	The 7-Eleven team makes its European debut at the Etoile de Bessèges in France.
1985	Ron Kiefel of 7-Eleven wins the fifteenth stage of the Giro d'Italia. He is the first American to win a stage of the Giro.
July 1986	7-Eleven becomes the first American team to compete in the Tour de France.

July 1986	Greg LeMond becomes the first American to win the Tour de France.
August 1986	Bernard Hinault wins the Coors Classic.
1986	The world championships for road and track are held in Colorado Springs, Colorado.
April 20, 1987	Greg LeMond is seriously wounded in a turkey hunting accident.
1987	The Pan American Games are held in Indianapolis. The American team wins eleven medals, the most of any country in the Games.
1987	7-Eleven wins three stages at the Tour de France.
1988	Andy Hampsten becomes the first American to win the Giro d'Italia.
1988	Eddie Borysewicz quits as national team coach.
October 1988	Adolph Coors Company ends its nine-year sponsorship of the Coors Classic.
May 1989	One hundred fourteen riders from fifteen countries race in the first Tour de Trump.
July 1989	Greg LeMond wins the closest Tour de France ever raced. His margin of victory is just 8 seconds.
1989	Greg LeMond wins the world championship professional road race for the second time.
September 1989	LeMond signs a three-year, $5.7 million contract to ride for the French Z team.
1990	Saturn racing team is founded.
July 1990	Greg LeMond wins his third and final Tour de France.
1990	Ned Overend and Juli Furtado win the first-ever mountain bike cross-country world championship in Durango, Colorado.
September 1990	Southland Corporation announces the end of its ten-year sponsorship of the 7-Eleven team. Motorola becomes the team's new title sponsor.
1991	The Tour de Trump becomes the Tour DuPont.
1991	Lance Armstrong wins his first national road championship.

1992	Armstrong signs with Motorola.
Late spring 1992	Greg LeMond wins the Tour DuPont. It is his last major victory.
July 1992	Greg LeMond drops out of the Tour de France.
July 1992	Andy Hampsten becomes the first American to win the Alpe d'Huez stage at the Tour de France.
1993	Lance Armstrong races in his first Tour de France and wins the eighth stage. Motorola team manager pulls Armstrong out of the Tour.
September 1993	Lance Armstrong wins the world championship road race in Oslo.
1993	Motorola ends its sponsorship of its racing team.
1994	Marty Nothstein becomes the first American to win a world championship sprint title in ninety years.
1995	The USCF changes its name to USA Cycling. There are 35,000 members.
1995	Lance Armstrong wins the Tour DuPont for the first time.
June 1996	Lance Armstrong wins his second Tour DuPont.
July 1996	Lance Armstrong drops out of the Tour de France.
October 1996	Lance Armstrong is diagnosed with testicular cancer.
July 1997	The U.S. Postal Service team makes its Tour de France debut.
1997	Floyd Landis becomes U23 mountain bike national champion.
1998	Lance Armstrong returns to professional racing as a member of the U.S. Postal Service team.
July 1998	Bobby Julich becomes the second American to reach the podium in the Tour de France, finishing 3rd.
July 1999	Lance Armstrong wins his first Tour de France.
July 2000	Lance Armstrong wins his second Tour de France.
Late 2000	U.S. Postal signs Floyd Landis.
July 2001	Lance Armstrong wins his third Tour de France.

July 2002	Lance Armstrong wins his fourth Tour de France.
July 2003	Lance Armstrong wins his fifth Tour de France.
April 2004	The U.S. Postal Service announces the end of its eight-year sponsorship of the team. Less than two months later, Discovery Channel becomes the new title sponsor.
2004	Tyler Hamilton wins gold in the individual time trial at the Athens Olympics.
2004	The first indoor velodrome in the United States opens in the ADT Event Center on the campus of Cal State-Dominguez Hills.
July 2004	Lance Armstrong wins his sixth Tour de France.
Late summer 2004	It is announced that Tyler Hamilton failed a blood-doping test at the Athens Olympics.
April 2005	Lance Armstrong announces he will retire from professional racing after the 2005 Tour de France.
July 2005	Lance Armstrong wins his seventh and final Tour de France. He retires immediately afterward.
2005	For the first time in nineteen years, the United States hosts the track cycling world championships. The American team fails to win a medal.
July 2006	Floyd Landis wins the Tour de France after overcoming an 8-minute deficit.
July 2006	Landis's victory called into question after a failed drug test.

PART ONE

The Early Years of American Bicycle Racing

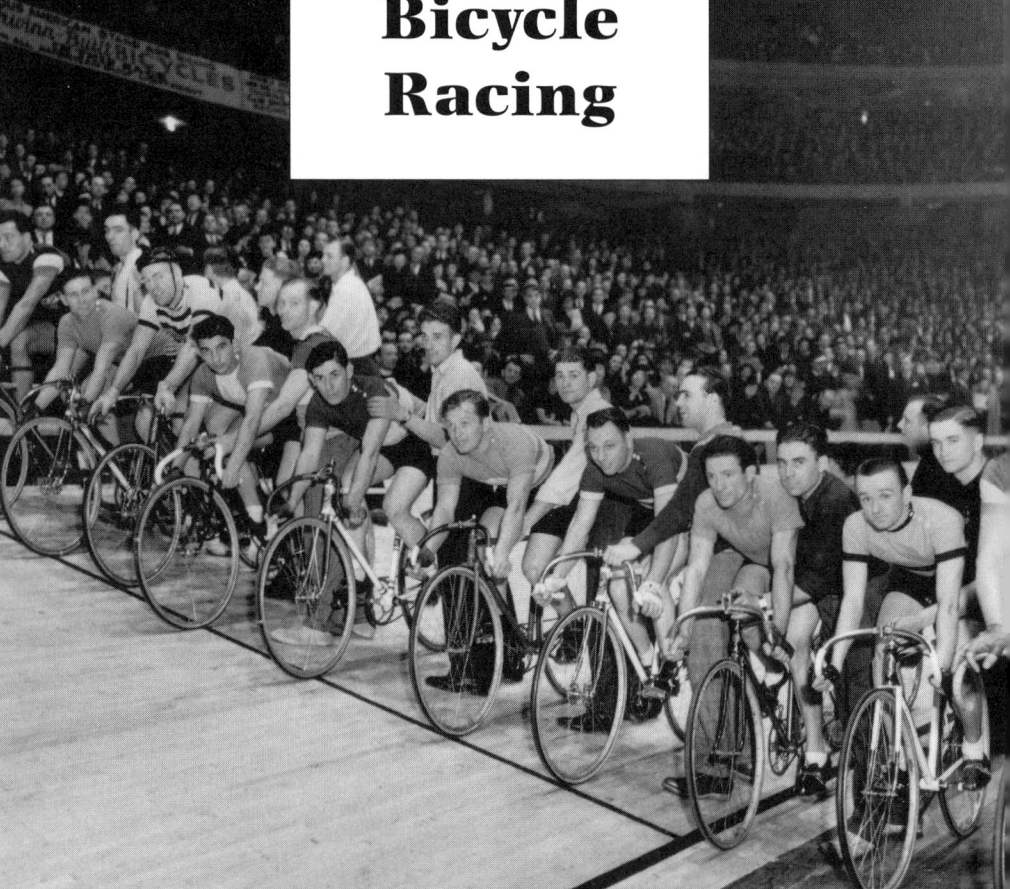

Six-day racers at the starting line in Chicago, 1929.
The stadium is packed with fans.

CHAPTER ONE

Bicycle Racing's First Stars

AT THE END OF THE nineteenth century, Americans moved from place to place on foot, by horse, and by train. By the late 1800s the bicycle offered people around the world a new form of transportation. Starting with high-wheel models, which have faded from contemporary memories, the bicycle evolved to its current form. A new industry was born. Hundreds of manufacturers in New York, Chicago, and across the United States could not keep up with the demand.

After initially riding for leisure recreation, bicycle riders moved quickly to competitive aspirations. Newspapers like the *New York Times* devoted front-page coverage to racers and events. Promoters offered financial rewards that far exceeded any other sport at the time. Spectators filled indoor auditoriums to watch their favorite rider race to victory. Bicycle racing was America's favorite sporting pastime.

Who Is the Fastest American Cyclist?

The competitive spirit lies deep in the human psyche. Recreational endeavors like bicycle riding could not avoid the question, "Who is the fastest rider?"

A race was the only way to accurately answer that question. C. A. Parker of Harvard University won the first recorded bicycle race in the United States on May 24, 1878, held at Beacon Park in Boston. Parker covered the 3-mile course in 12:27.

Four years later the first national championship was held. In 1882 fifteen-year-old George M. Hendee of Springfield, Massachusetts, won the first American sprint championship, on a high-wheel bicycle. Hendee defended the title over the next four years and dominated racing until he retired in 1895. In 309 races Hendee failed to win just 7.

In 1884 promoter H. E. Decker opened a bicycle-racing track inside the Hampden Park horse-trotting oval in Springfield,

Massachusetts. Over a three-day competition, all existing American and European bicycling records were shattered. The record for the mile fell from 3:20 to less than 2:30. Nine thousand people attended the first day, but word spread of the record-setting performances and the crowd doubled on the second day.

Bicycling enthusiasts flocked to events not only to watch but also to enter the races. A popular race in Chicago drew hundreds of entries. In 1893, 325 people entered; two years later the number grew to 515. Promoters avoided the mass crashes that marred many events with large fields by sending riders away from the starting line at fifteen-second intervals.

In the 1895 event more than fifty riders were injured in crashes along the course. The organized start turned to chaos at the finish line. In order to establish a formal finishing order, riders shouted their names into a phonograph as they crossed the line. When the judges listened to the phonograph recording, Homer Fairmon was declared the winner.

Although events were well attended, interest in road racing as a spectator sport suffered because of the distances involved and inability of fans to watch the race unfold. Promoters responded by moving racing indoors to board tracks.

On November 30, 1894, 10,000 spectators filled the first Madison Square Garden (replaced in 1904) to watch a schedule of sixty-eight bicycle races, a record number for a single-day event. The amateur racers competed for a silver plaque awarded by the *New York Times* that was on display in the lobby. Charles Murphy set a new record in the 2-mile scratch race. He also won the mile indoor championship and the 5-mile "scratch" race, where all racers start from the same position rather than staggered positions.

Early Heroes

The heroes of bicycle racing are connected like the links on a bicycle chain. One follows the next over the course of history. Arthur Augustus Zimmerman followed George Hendee as the object of racing fans' adoration. Riding as an amateur or professional, "Zimmy" was difficult to beat.

In 1892 Zimmerman won seventy-five amateur races. His rewards included fifteen bicycles, fifteen rings, fifteen diamonds, fourteen medals, two cups, seven shirt studs, eight watches, one city lot, six clocks, nine pieces of silverware, two bronze sculptures, two wagons, and one piano. In 1893 the League of American Wheelmen and the International Cyclists' Association introduced the first official world championships, for amateurs only. Zimmerman won both the 1-mile and 10-kilometer races. Records show Zimmerman won 101 victories that season. He turned professional in 1894 and negotiated lucrative contracts to race in France, England, Ireland, and Germany. At an exhibition race in Sydney, Australia, 27,000 fans watched him ride. With one hundred victories to his credit, Zimmerman created his own brand of shoes and clothing.

George Banker, one of Zimmerman's competitors, won the world's pro title in Vienna in 1898, making him America's second world cycling champion and first professional racing champion. Major Taylor made it two in a row by winning the 1-mile sprint in 1899.

Disputes over the blurred lines between amateurs and professionals caused controversies and hard feelings over winnings. In 1893 the racing committee of the League of American Wheelmen created a division system titled Class A, Class B, and Professional. Class A amateurs could not accept any prizes or expense reimbursements from the races they entered. Class B riders could accept prize money and collect fees from sponsors.

The Class B riders quickly hired managers and trainers and became businessmen who made a great living as racers. By 1895 a substantial number of racers in the Class B designation moved to professional events. Disagreements between the League, promoters, and racers over Class B definitions remained unresolved until the designation was eliminated in 1896.

By 1896 there were 1,200 bicycle builders in New York and eighty-three bike shops in a 1-mile radius that served 692 professional track riders. At the turn of the century, bicycle racing was the most popular spectator sport in the United States. The League of American Wheelmen had 100,000 members. It wasn't uncommon for a highly contested race to draw 20,000 spectators. During the same period 2,500 people might be found in the stands of a baseball game.

Racers and spectators traveled a circuit of outdoor tracks across the eastern United States. Velodromes in New York and Newark were packed every day of the week, and tracks in Boston, New York, Hartford, and Providence attracted a steady and profitable stream of racing fans.

Major Taylor

Like Arthur Zimmerman before him, Marshall Walter "Major" Taylor was one of America's dominant racers. Taylor was born on November 25, 1878, and at age thirteen he worked at Hay and Willit's bicycle shop. He ran errands, cleaned the store, and practiced his trick riding in front of the store during the afternoon. The shop owners pressed Taylor to enter a 10-mile road race the shop sponsored. Coming from far behind, Taylor won his first race. He would win 158 more before retiring. Taylor earned the "Major" moniker from the military jacket that shop owner Tom Hay gave him to wear when he performed his cycling tricks.

With the advice of Louis D. Munger, a manufacturer and retired racer, Taylor made his professional racing debut at a Madison Square Garden six-day race. It was one of the few races Taylor would lose early in his career.

After George Banker won the world's pro title in Vienna in 1898, Major Taylor read about Banker's success and in 1899 traveled to Montreal to the world championships. Eighteen thousand fans watched Taylor defeat five other riders and win America's second consecutive world championship title.

In the last year of the nineteenth century, Taylor mastered every sprint distance on the track. He set new records in the quarter-mile, third-mile, half-mile, two-thirds-mile, three-quarter-mile, 1-mile, and 2-mile races. One of the most popular and successful racers at the turn of the century, Taylor was one of the first black athletes in professional sports. His name frequently topped the headlines of *New York Times* racing coverage.

On July 15th, 1982, the Major Taylor Velodrome opened in Indianapolis, named in honor of this great racer. When the velodrome opened Taylor still held three records for distances that were no longer contested: the quarter-mile, three-quarter-mile, and 1-mile riders-paced records that he set in Philadelphia in 1891 when he was only thirteen years old.

Frank Kramer

Frequent newspaper reports about Major's financial success inspired Frank Kramer to leave the amateur ranks for the professional racing circuit. Riding for the Harlem Wheelmen bicycling club, Kramer won the amateur national championship in 1898. He repeated the achievement a year later.

In 1899, in his first year of professional racing, Kramer finished 1st eighteen times, 2nd eight times, and 3rd nine times. Over the next two years, the rivalry between Kramer and Major Taylor filled the indoor tracks with enthusiastic fans.

In 1900 Taylor switched allegiance from the League of American Wheelmen to the National Cycling Association (NCA) and beat Kramer to win the NCA title in a final match race. During the 1901 season Kramer dominated the racing schedule, winning forty-nine races, finishing 2nd thirteen times, and settling for 3rd in seventeen events. In a thirty-day span from July 8 to August 5, 1901, Kramer and Taylor faced off in thirteen meets. Kramer claimed his first national championship by defeating Taylor at the Hartford Velodrome in front of 4,500 fans in early August. In his heat against Kramer, Taylor finished a full length behind. With the win, Kramer took the points lead in the NCA competition. When the season ended and the national championship was awarded, Kramer had beaten Taylor 22-20.

Kramer held the national championship for the next sixteen years. After losing to Freddie Spencer in 1917, Kramer recaptured the title in 1918. He won his last championship in 1921.

The fans supported Kramer at every race. In October 1909 Kramer received the largest ovation recorded at the Newark Velodrome after he won his ninth consecutive national title. He addressed the applause with an American flag draped over his shoulders and a bouquet of flowers in his arms.

When he retired on July 26, 1922, at the age of forty-two, 20,000 fans in Newark showed up for his final lap. Over his career he captured 18 national pro titles, a world championship, and more than 600 career victories. On July 31, 1922, the *New York Times* called Frank Kramer's record "one of amazing endurance and stamina, not to mention success . . . one of the most marvelous in athletic history."

Track Stars

John M. Chapman was the most important race promoter of his day. In 1911 Chapman and his partner, Frank Mihlon, built a 0.6-mile track in Newark. Constructed of thin pine boards attached to a sturdy wooden frame, the facility had 12,000 reserved seats, bleachers, and

Telephones
HEmlock 3200
Main Line
HEmlock 6786

City Offices
COMB HOTEL
in Francisco

BLAKELEY AND SAUNDERS
N. C. A. Representatives
- - OPERATING - -

PACIFIC SIX DAY BICYCLE RACING ASSOCIATION
- - CIVIC AUDITORIUM - -
SAN FRANCISCO, CALIF.

MAR. 28th
1934

Mr. Russell Allen,
3245 Hill St.,
Huntington Park, Calif.

Dear Russell:

We are enclosing contract for the May
race. Kindly sign both copies and return the
original to us, keeping the carbon copy for your
own records.

If you have not already paid your $1.00
registration fee for the National Cycling Association, please also send your $1.00 to us, together
with this contract immediately, so that we can get
your card for you at once. It is necessary for you
to give your age, your height and your address. (Also weight)

Partners for the May race will be announced
May 5th.

Sincerely,

BLAKELEY AND S

By:

ECS/G

**Racing as independent
businessmen, track racers signed
appearance contracts.**

I hereby make application for participation in the
Six Day Bicycle Race to be held from May 13th to
May 19th, 1934, inclusive, in the Civic Auditorium,
San Francisco, California.

It is understood that I will receive the sum of
ONE HUNDRED TWENTY FIVE ($125.00) DOLLARS under the
following terms and conditions:

In the event that I am injured, which will necessitate
my withdrawal from the race before 10 P. M. Wednesday,
May 16th, I will receive one-half (1/2) of the above
contract. In the event of my injury, which would
force me to discontinue in the race at any time after
10 P. M. Wednesday, May 16th, I am to receive the
full amount of my contract.

It is further understood by me that in the event I
finish the race with my partner in the first four
teams, I am to receive an additional Fifty ($50.00)
Dollars bonus.

_____

Accepted:

BLAKELEY AND SAUNDERS

By:

Size of Jersey_____
Trainer Suggested_____
Wheelmen Suggested_____

room for another 3,000 fans in the infield area.

To fill the seats, Chapman negotiated a ten-year contract with Frank Kramer. In return for racing in Chapman-promoted events, Kramer received a five-figure annual income. On the strength of Kramer's performances, Chapman became a very wealthy man.

Freddie Spencer became Chapman's next protégé. Under Chapman's control Spencer won five world records, three six-day races, and three national pro sprint titles. Anxious to strike out independently and compete in Europe, Spencer contacted European promoters to negotiate a racing contract. Noticing the foreign stamps on his rider's correspondence, Chapman kept the letters, negotiated a new contract with Spencer that provided a small raise, and prohibited him from racing in Europe.

Chapman then signed a contract to bring Holland's Pete Moeskops, the reigning world sprint champion, to race at Newark. The winner of the professional sprint title from 1921 to 1924, Moeskops was not expected to be challenged in 1925. Moeskops and Spencer raced each other in four separate races, each time in front of 18,000 fans rooting for their hometown champion. Chapman's manipulation of the competition worked profitably in his favor when Spencer won all four matches. Freddie Spencer received a new set of steel-shafted golf clubs from Bobby Jones. Uninterested in golf, Spencer won sixty-five straight sprint matches after a frame-builder modified the club shafts and turned them into seat stays on his track bike.

Track racing's popularity began to fade in the 1930s. On August 4, 1930, a fire destroyed the 30,000-seat New York Velodrome. The lease on the Newark Velodrome expired the same year, and in 1931 Chapman, one of the best promoters of his era, suffered a stroke. The loss of a strong promoter and two important racing venues and the coming of World War II ended track racing's hold on American sports fans.

The Six-Day Grind

 The goal of a six-day race was easy for spectators to understand. The winner was the rider who covered the greatest distance in the time allotted for the race. The rider who stayed on the track the longest, often as much as twenty hours per day, had the best chance of winning. To maintain a competitive field and fan interest, promoters required riders to cover at least 1,350 miles to qualify for a portion of the prize purse. Six days was the maximum number of consecutive days a competitive event could be held without violating religious rules concerning the Sabbath.

Before each race 200 workers spent a week building an 18-foot-wide oval track by nailing flat boards to a frame. The League racing rules called for the track to be a tenth of a mile in circumference.

New York's first six-day race was held from October 18 to 24, 1891, a time frame that included a seventh day for the final award ceremonies and celebrations. Racing against fourteen other competitors, William "Plugger" Martin covered 1,466 miles in 120 hours on a high-wheeler.

At a race in 1893, promoters allowed riders to race on high-wheelers, also called ordinaries, or on a new style of bike called the safety. After three days the competitors saw that the best chance to win came with the new safety style. Although there was concern about the physical toll on riders bent over on the new low handlebars, the bikes were clearly faster than the ordinaries. Albert Schock's 1893 victory on a safety bike marked the last time high-wheelers were used in six-day competitions.

PETER NYE, JEFF GROMAN, MIKE TYSON/WWW.SIXDAYBICYCLERACE.COM

Wearing the stars-and-stripes jersey, Bobby Walthour races for the lead at the Chicago Coliseum, 1936.

Initially, tracks were slightly banked at each end. In 1893, when safety bikes became the norm, the banks grew steeper, and by 1896 the tracks were banked all the way around the oval.

A scorekeeper assigned to each rider counted laps and posted distances on a large scoreboard. An electrician named Frank Martin invented a system for tallying laps. As the rider completed a lap, the scorer placed a ring on a steel rod attached to an incandescent lamp. When all ten lights were lit, the scorer added another mile to the rider's total distance.

Promoters sold general admission seats on the main floor and on balconies. Higher-priced tickets were available closer to the track. The infield area was reserved for track officials, riders, and their supporters. Bands set up in the infield to entertain the spectators and play rousing music to pace the racers.

At the turn of the century, still years

before six-day racing reached its zenith, bicycle racers could earn more money than all but a few professions. In 1896 the riders assembled at the Hotel Bortholdi near Madison Square Park to divide the prize purse. A sixteen-pound bag containing double eagle gold coins sat in front of the race promoters. Teddy Hale, the winner, carried his winnings away in his hat. His reward also included $1,000 from a chain manufacturer, $500 from a tire maker, and more than $2,000 for endorsing other cycling-related accessories.

On each of the six days he raced alone, Hale consumed four pounds of roast chicken, one pound of boiled rice, one pound of oatmeal, two bowls of custard, toast, jelly, tapioca, and at least two pounds of fruit. On each day he also drank four quarts of beef-flavored tea, four quarts of chicken-flavored tea, and milk.

Since staying on the track was the key to finishing in the money, riders ate and drank while riding. When Albert Schock's safety bike gave him a wide winning margin over his competitors' ordinaries, he stopped for twenty-two minutes to eat pork chops, toast, and tea for breakfast.

In 1897 six-day racing came to Madison Square Garden. The arena had an oval pine board track measuring 10 laps to the mile. A black stripe was painted 18 inches from the bottom edge of the track to warn the riders who ventured too close to the infield. Another stripe at the upper edge let riders know they were dangerously close to the top edge. A wooden fence prevented riders from flying off the top and crashing into the crowd.

Ten thousand fans filled the Garden on opening day in 1897. The 142-hour race began at midnight on Sunday evening and ended at 10:00 on the following Saturday night. Race fans paid 50 cents for tickets, but on the final day ticket prices doubled to $1.00 for regular admission and jumped to $1.50 for box seats closest to the track. Spectators often stayed overnight to watch the race unfold. Officials and building managers asked people to leave on Wednesday so the seating areas could be cleaned and made ready for the weekend rush.

Waiting for the starter's pistol to fire, the racers needed their managers and handlers to hold them steady on the steeply banked track. With the crack of the gun, the pack started a seemingly endless series of laps. The riders moved slowly at first, sizing up the competition and conserving their energy for sprints and the finish six days later. They often rode twenty hours a day. When they wanted to rest, the riders retreated to one side of the Garden, where accommodations were set up. They slept on cots, changed in small tents, and used oil stoves to cook their meals or keep themselves warm when they were off the bike. Race officials occupied the infield and a track announcer kept the fans informed using a giant megaphone hanging from a metal tripod.

Race officials closely monitored the physical health of the riders. On the fifth day of the race, the New York chief of police brought surgeons into the Garden to check the temperature and pulse rates for each rider. Despite the energy-sapping fatigue of riding in circles, the doctors reported the riders were all in good condition.

Endurance racers suffered physically by the end of the competition. Trackside physicians frequently treated cramped muscles, sore joints, congested lungs, and digestion problems. Crashes and collisions caused by exhaustion were common occurrences. Trainers kept their riders awake with smelling salts or handed them peppermint oil–soaked sponges that the riders put in their mouths. Newspapers published extensive daily reports on the races including sensation-alized speculation about riders using cocaine and strychnine as stimulants.

Saturday night, 142 hours after the start of the 1897 season-opening race, Charlie Miller crossed the finish line in 1st place. Miller, from Chicago, covered 2,093 miles, 67 miles more than the 2nd-place rider. Over the course of the race, Miller spent all but ten hours on the track. He slept on a cot for four of those hours. The other six hours were spent maintaining his racing bike and eating. His menu over six days included three pounds of rice, a pound of oatmeal, twenty quarts of milk, and three gallons of hot coffee. Miller earned $3,550 for the victory. Not all of the winnings came from the promoter. In addition to the $1,200 1st prize, Miller received $1,000 for appearing at the event, $550 from his bike manufacturer, $200 from the seat builder, $500 from the tire manufacturer, and $100 from the handlebar company. The last-place rider took home $75.

In February 1898 the annual report of the National Racing Board of the League of American Wheelmen announced that bicycle racing was more popular than any other form of entertainment in the United States. The report stated that eight million spectators spent $3.6 million on tickets to attend 2,912 racing events in the 1897 season. Nine thousand riders competed for prizes with a value of $1,645,020. Promoters earned over $1 million for their work. Interest in racing continued to grow.

One year later Miller returned to Madison Square Garden for another six-day race. On December 5 to 10, 1898, he covered 2,007 miles and celebrated his second victory by getting married at the end. The crowd enthusiastically greeted the bride and groom. Miller dressed for the occasion. One leg of his racing tights was white, the other pink. His coordinat-ed shirt reversed the matching colors. There was an American eagle embroi-dered on the back of his jersey and an American flag worn like a sash around his waist.

Miller's second victory marked the last time solo riders competed in six-day events at Madison Square Garden. In 1898 state officials in New York and Illinois passed laws that created limits for riding time, and thereafter riders could only race twelve out of every twenty-four hours. Billy Brady, a Madison Square Garden promoter, adapted by creating two-man teams. One man rode while his teammate slept, ate, and recovered.

When the riders switched positions, the transfer maneuver became one of the most recognizable elements of six-day racing. After his rest period the returning rider would enter the track and ride around the top. Once in position, the rider would sweep down the bank and grab his partner's hand. The tired rider's last act before leaving the track was to throw the refreshed rider forward. Promoters called the new two-man racing format the Madison after the venue where it was created. The first Madison was held on February 12, 1899, and was won by Charlie Miller and Frank Weller, with 2,733.4 miles.

The rhythm of a six-day race had a recognizable ebb and flow. After the fren-zied excitement of the start, the pack set-tled into the long monotonous days of holding their position relative to their competitors. The last twenty-four hours challenged the mental and physical capacities of the riders, when race strategy called for staying on the same lap as the leader and preparing for the final sprint. For the leaders the last mile separated winner from follower. Riders often took strychnine, which was then prescribed for debility and anemia, to give them a competitive edge in the final sprints.

For the next thirty years, six-day racing was king. Velodromes opened across the country, and racers traveled by train around the East Coast and as far as Chicago, Salt Lake City, and San Francisco. Madison Square Garden hosted two major events each year, usually in March and December.

The eighteenth annual six-day race was held on December 5, 1910. At 12:01 Monday morning Senator Timothy D. Sullivan fired the starter's pistol and sent fifteen teams on their way. Campaigning politicians and attention-seeking celebrities were often on hand to start the races in this manner.

On December 9, 1912, fifteen teams left the starting line. Forty-eight hours later all fifteen were still on the same lap. It was the first time in six-day racing that the field did not lose riders to early fatigue, crashes, and injuries. Between 9 and 10 p.m. on the first day, in front of a full house of raucous fans, the pack circled the track 223 times—22.3 miles. By contrast, from 7 to 9 a.m., when the attendance was lowest, the racers only covered 13.7 miles, largely due to the fact that when spectators weren't present the riders often rode without holding the handlebars so they could eat and drink. Shortly after midnight on December 11, the pack, including stars Bobby Walthour and Floyd MacFarland, passed the 1,000-

mile mark faster than ever before to set a new forty-eight-hour distance record.

During his career Floyd MacFarland won four of the eleven six-day races he entered. He also won more than 200 times in other racing disciplines and distances. When his racing days were over, MacFarland managed the Salt Lake City Velodrome and promoted six-day racing events in the United States and Europe. As general manager of the Cycle Racing Association, MacFarland and his competitor John M. Chapman tangled for the best riders and best races.

In 1914 MacFarland won the rights to promote the Madison Square Garden six-day events. He paired New Zealand's Alfred Grenda with Alf Goullet against riders from five other countries. Grenda and Goullet's 2,759.2-mile winning record for a 142-hour six-day race remains unbroken.

MacFarland's rising career as a promoter ended tragically on April 18, 1915. During a sparsely attended practice session at the Newark Velodrome, MacFarland argued with David Lantenberg, a concessionaire who was hanging posters on the guardrails to promote his confections and refreshments. The argument grew loud enough to draw the attention of 150 people scattered around the track. Witnesses said MacFarland grabbed Lantenberg's arm to stop him from hanging another poster. Lantenberg responded by striking back. With a screwdriver in his hand, Lantenberg swung his fist at MacFarland's head. The point of the screwdriver pierced MacFarland's skull near his left ear. Unnerved by the fight, Lantenberg tried to make amends by driving MacFarland to the hospital. MacFarland suffered a mortal wound and died at 9 p.m. with his wife, Frank Mihlon (president of the Cycle Racing Association), and his racing friend

Frank Kramer at his bedside. Chapman regained control of bicycle racing and was named president of the National Cycling Association.

The best six-day racers started fast and kept a steady pace to separate themselves from the second-tier riders. The leaders would frequently lap slower riders. Knowledgeable spectators followed the riders' positions and encouraged the leaders when they lapped the field. At 10:12 p.m. on December 7, 1928, the Italian-American combination of Franco Georgetti and Freddie Spencer set a six-day record when they caught and lapped the pack. It marked the 430th lap "stolen" in the forty-fifth international cycling six-day.

At 3:30 a.m. on August 4, 1930, a three-alarm fire brought firefighters to the New York Velodrome. After ten years entertaining 20,000 fans at events, the velodrome was lost. One month later the Newark Velodrome's lease expired and that track was dismantled. Two major tracks were gone—bicycle racing suffered and began to lose its popularity.

Postwar Revival of Six-Day Racing

World War II brought a halt to almost all professional sports when athletes enlisted in the war efforts. Six-day racing would never return to its prewar success. The first postwar six-day event was held in 1948 to limited financial success and disinterested spectators.

On September 28, 1961, Madison Square Garden hosted the seventy-fifth international six-day race. Fifteen teams started the race. On the last lap three of the seven remaining teams were tied for distance with 2,359.2 miles. Swiss riders Oscar Plattner and Armin von Buren won by accumulating 1,224 points in 142

hours (points were awarded for short sprint competitions within the overall race in an effort to hold fan interest and keep the riders lively). Ted Smith, the last American in the race, was forced to retire because of a painful case of boils.

The riders performed at a high level, but spectator interest and attendance had dropped dramatically from prewar levels. Although 14,000 fans attended the last night, midweek ticket sales were dismal. New fans didn't understand race strategies like their older counterparts. The promoters lost more than $25,000 and the track was dismantled the day after the race ended. Six-day racing was lost to history.

Twelve years later Charles Ruys and his partners planned a series of six-day races across the country. The Los Angeles Pro-Bike '73 International Six-Day Race was held in May 1973. The organizers spent $35,000 on a portable 160-meter cedar plywood track with 21-degree banking on the straights and 58 degrees on the turns. Assembly of the track was completed just five minutes before the event was scheduled to begin. The field included thirteen Europeans, ten Americans, and a single rider from Canada. Six of the competitors had just a few months of track experience. The new track and the riders' lack of experience took its toll. In less than fifteen minutes, there were six crashes involving nine different riders.

The 13,000-seat Los Angeles Sports Arena attracted only 2,000 spectators for the six afternoon and seven evening sessions. The event was a financial disaster. Ruys and his backers tried again in Detroit six months later. Legal entanglements prevented them from transporting the new portable track from Los Angeles to Detroit. Herbert Schuman, a renowned

German track builder, was hired to build another track. The Detroit Six was held inside the Coliseum at the Michigan State Fairgrounds on September 26 to October 2, 1973. Twenty-one riders received $20 per diem and competed for a $2,250 purse. Ruys worked tirelessly to recruit new sponsors. The promoters distributed 2,000 posters and 10,000 flyers to fill the seats. Snowstorms hampered attendance on the first and last nights. Fewer than 1,000 people attended each evening session. The Detroit Six lost more than $75,000, and six-day racing ended in the United States.

Contemporary reflections on sports early in the twentieth century often focus on baseball. To our eyes, Babe Ruth, Lou Gehrig, and the Yankees appear to have dominated the headlines. In reality, six-day racing was far more popular. Madison Square Garden—actually three different buildings carried that title—was the place to be for promoters, riders, and spectators.

More than one hundred velodromes across the country hosted six-day events, and the professional racers made a very good living. The best riders in the world demanded and received appearance fees for just showing up at an event. Even the lesser-known, anonymous riders in the pack could earn more than $5,000 in a six-day grind. When the average American earned $15 per week and $750 per year, six-day riders were the best-paid athletes in the world. Alf Goullet, reportedly paid $1,000 per day for a six in 1926, said, "The race is the most grueling contest in athletics because of its sheer monotony."

"Just Let Us Race"

Throughout the history of six-day racing, legal, political, and business issues threatened to disrupt the riders' opportunity to

ROBERT F. GEORGE

In 1973 promoters tried to rekindle interest in six-day races by holding events in Los Angeles (pictured) and Detroit.

earn a living. The first legal intervention prohibited solo riders from competing in six-day events. Spectator interest in six-day racing actually increased when two-man teams were introduced in response.

In 1901 New Jersey Chief Justice David D. Depue ruled that bicycle racing at the Vailsburg track in Newark was illegal. The chief justice's order read: "That an exhibition of a worldly nature that brings together on Sunday a large concourse of people, occasioning noise that unreasonably disturbs others entitled to a quiet Sunday at their homes is illegal. Races on Sunday, wherein prizes are awarded to the winners are in violation of the statute and any places where such practices are permitted habitually is indictable as a disorderly house." The ruling was one of many legal and political challenges promoters and racers faced before stepping onto the track. In response to Justice Depue's ruling, promoters started their six-day grinds at 12:01 a.m. Monday morning and scheduled the finishes at 10 p.m. Saturday night.

On the political front, the Greater New York Board of Aldermen discussed prohibiting six-day racing in Madison Square Garden in 1904. The government officials considered the long races "injurious to the competitors and are brutal exhibitions." American six-day racers felt they were the best athletes in the world and ridiculed the aldermen's uninformed judgments. Newspaper accounts often sensationalized the races, editorializing about the long hours, lack of sleep, and rumors of drug doping. In fact, riders didn't object too strenuously since the exaggerations resulted in larger crowds and ultimately bigger paychecks.

Disputes between governing bodies, promoters, and racers frequently led to calls for strikes and the formation of a riders' union to protect their rights. In 1916 the National Cycling Association (NCA) and the newly formed Federation of American Cyclists battled to a standoff. The Essex Trades Council placed the NCA, managed by the promoters who controlled the Newark Velodrome, on a list of unfair businesses. Frank Mihlon, president of the NCA, claimed the trade organization did not have any jurisdiction and ignored the union's demands:

> We are of the opinion that the general public, and particularly the patrons of bicycle racing in this city, are not in sympathy with this latest move on the part of belligerent riders and the Trades Council, who are attempting to force us to surrender our connections with the National Cycling Association and be governed by a body created by the riders' union and known as the Federation of American Cyclists.
>
> If we employed bicycle riders at so much a day and had a scale of wages for the various classes, then we would feel that organized labor would have the right to take action in the event the wages were not commensurate with the work done by the riders or if the hours of their labors were not according to the ideas of organized labor. But it is absurd to think of paying cyclists a uniform wage and the riders

have never suggested such a thing, as it would not be satisfactory to them and it would also kill the spirit of competition.

Calling the NCA a failure, the organizers of the Federation of American Cyclists fought to control racing schedules and rules. The riders wanted their federation to be the official governing body but failed to overcome the NCA's powerful influence with promoters and track owners.

Five years later the struggle between promoters and riders reached a flash point when two independently promoted six-day races were scheduled one week apart. The first race, promoted by the New York Velodrome Company, was scheduled for the week of November 21 to 27 at the 22nd Regiment Armory. The NCA, still recognized as the governing body for competitive cycling, did not sanction the race. The second race, to be held at Madison Square Garden on December 5 to 11, was sanctioned by the NCA.

Riders who entered the New York Velodrome Company's event faced disqualification and lost income. Elder statesman Alf Goullet acted as a spokesperson for the riders: "We have no desire to break away from the National Cycling Association but we do not consider that we are being treated fairly in this matter and we insist upon the protection of our rights." Goullet, Freddie Spencer, and twenty other top riders released a statement to the press to present their point of view:

> The undersigned twenty professional riders, who have always abided by the rules of the National Cycle Racing Association, protest against the unjust criticism heaped upon us by the promoters of the bicycle racing track in Newark, who claim they constitute the N.C.A because we refuse to

bow to their wishes and repudiate contracts which we legitimately entered into to ride the six day race in the Twenty-second Regiment Armory, New York the week of November 21 to 27. We are threatened with suspension if we ride in the race and for no other reason that we can see than that we refuse to give the Newark promoters preference.

The Newark promoters fear open competition in the cycling sport and whenever there has been any danger of opposition they have been using a club on the riders. This we now resent. We feel that we are within our legal and moral rights in competing on any track or for any company under the rules that govern the sport of cycle racing. We feel that we have as much right to increase our earnings as a boxer or ball player.

. . . We are fully decided to ride in the race at the Twenty-second Regi-ment Armory, sanction or no sanction. The undersigned represent the best six day riders in the world and we are going to let the public judge for itself.

In 1922, after eighteen months of controversy, debate, and acrimony, the National Cycling Association and the Amateur Bicycle League of America (ABLA), another organization competing for the right to represent riders' interests, signed an agreement that recognized the rights of both organizations. The NCA recognized the right of the ABLA to control all amateur road racing in the United States. Amateurs were required to register with the NCA for all races promoted on a track.

The Racers Take Control

In December 1920 amateur racers, frustrated by feuding governing bodies and inconsistent racing rules and regulations, convened a series of meetings to take control of their sport. Delegates from a dozen clubs representing 2,500 amateur racers reorganized the Interclub Amateur Cycle Road Racing League and launched the Amateur Bicycle League of America (ABLA). D. J. McIntyre, former leader of Interclub League and a member of the New England Wheelmen, was elected president.

The Amateur Bicycle League sanctioned amateur national title races from 1920 to 1930, before the Depression put the events on hold for several years. Despite the terrible financial struggle people faced during the Depression, bicycle racing still thrived. In 1933 the Nutley Velodrome in New Jersey drew 297,000 fans over thirty–five scheduled events.

Successful promoters like John Chapman and Floyd MacFarland kept professional racing at the forefront. Chapman signed the best riders to contracts that kept their racing schedules under his control. Just before the 1928 Olympics in Amsterdam, Chapman kept Willie Honeman from competing by declaring him a professional racer.

During the 1934-35 racing season, Honeman competed on indoor tracks in France, still under Chapman's control. A Parisian sports shop created a silk stars-and-stripes jersey for the American rider to wear racing against European competitors. At the time, the United States did not have a formal national championship jersey and the design was adopted. From that point on American racers coveted the stars and stripes. Honeman became the first three-time winner of the professional sprint title, capturing the championship from 1934 to 1936.

The Amateur Bicycle League of America's first sanctioned women's national championship was held in Buffalo, New York, in 1937—fifty-five years after the first men's championship title was awarded. A small field of fewer than fifteen women raced half-mile, 5-mile, and 25-mile events. Points were awarded to the top five finishers in each race.

Fifteen-year-old Doris Kopsky Muller of Belleville, New Jersey, trained for the national championship race by entering men's races as a member of the Belleville Bicycle Club. Doris received a china tea service for her first race victory, in a 10-mile race at the National Capital Sweepstakes. She became the first American woman national champion. She also received a gold medal with a diamond chip embedded in the center.

The World War II Era

On Memorial Day 1940 Fred Kugler, a professional racer and bike shop owner, started a race in his hometown, Somerville, New Jersey. Kugler's son Furman, a junior champion and up-and-coming racer, won the first Tour of Somerville. Later that year Kugler, his fifteen-year-old sister Mildred, and their training partner Harry Maismyth traveled to Detroit, Michigan, to compete in the national championships. On September 1, 1940, all three captured national titles. Furman won the senior division championship, Mildred the girl's title, and Harry the junior championship, which at this point was for riders under age seventeen. A year later Furman defended his Tour of Somerville title. Furman's friend Carl Anderson won in 1942. World War II put the race on hold from 1943 to 1946. When it resumed in 1947, tragedy had changed the name of the event. Furman Kugler and Carl Anderson were killed in the war, and the race was renamed the Kugler-Anderson Memorial Tour of Somerville. Over the next sixty-six years, the Kugler-Anderson Memorial's winners' list has contained the names of some of America's best riders.

THE BICYCLE MUSEUM OF AMERICA/NEW BREMEN, OHIO

An ABLA program from 1949.

The Tour of Somerville

In 1940 Fred "Pops" Kugler, a professional racer and bike shop owner in Somerville, New Jersey, was frustrated to learn that bicycle racing was illegal on the town's Main Street. Kugler worked around the prohibitions and launched the 50-mile Tour of Somerville on Memorial Day 1940.

Kugler's son Furman, a junior champion with a promising future in racing, won the first two tours. Carl Anderson, his friend, won it in 1942. Furman Kugler was killed in Okinawa in 1945 and Anderson lost his life fighting in the European theater. In honor of the two men, the official name of the event became the Kugler-Anderson Memorial Tour of Somerville.

Held each year on Memorial Day, the Tour of Somerville holds an important place in American racing. Look down the list of sixty-three men and thirty women who have won it and you will see the history of American bicycle racing unfold. The best riders of their time—Jack Heid, Art Longsjo, Jack Simes, Ron Skarin, Wayne Stetina, and Davis Phinney—put their names on the winners' list.

In 1951, the eighth annual event, the Amateur Bicycle League of America awarded $3,000 in donated prizes. Winners celebrated their victories when they received furniture, carpeting, and appliances. In 1953 Hugh Starrs received a new Chevrolet.

On May 30, 1961, twenty-one-year-old Bob McKown, a pipe organ repairman, established a national bicycling record at Somerville. McKown, in front of 18,000 spectators, completed 43.5 laps over the 1.1-mile circuit in 2:16:06, shat-

tering the year-old record of 2:30:07 set by Michael Hiltner. Over the Tour's history the American record for the 50-mile distance was broken more than a dozen times.

In 1974 Ron Skarin established a new national record for the 50-mile distance. Skarin, a future Olympic medalist and 7-Eleven team member, covered the course in 1:54:01, breaking the 1:56:10 mark set by Jack Simes in 1967. Riding for the Teledyne-North Hollywood Wheelmen team, Skarin averaged 26.4 mph during his winning ride.

A women's event, the Mildred Kugler Women's Open, was added in 1976. Mary Jane Reoch finished the 20-mile race in 1st place.

In 1982 7-Eleven was a title sponsor, and once again records fell. Gary Trevisiol of Sudbury, Ontario, lowered the American record for a 50-mile criterium to 1:46:56. Dave Boll set the previous record, 1:47:18, in 1976. For the women, the Tour of Somerville was the third race in the *Self* magazine race series. Sue Novara-Reber captured the 20-mile race in 46:39.

The next year Canadian Steve Bauer lowered the record and narrowly defeated Davis Phinney at the finish line. As the top American finisher, Phinney was awarded the 1983 national criterium championship. As a member of the 7-Eleven team, Phinney returned in 1984 and won the race. In a rare twist, siblings Matt Eaton and Sophie Eaton finished 1st in 1985.

The women's race continued to build its own history.

In 1986 the United States Cycling Federation held the women's national

ROBERT F. GEORGE

Sue Novara was a national and world champion track racer who won the women's Tour of Somerville four times. She later became head coach of the U.S. women's cycling team.

championship race at the Tour of Somerville. Peggy Mass received $1,000 of the $4,500 prize purse. The same year, the United States Bicycling Hall of Fame opened in Somerville, and the Tour became part of the Hall of Fame's annual induction ceremonies.

At the end of the '80s, when races like the Coors Classic, Tour DuPont, and USPRO championships attracted much of the media attention, the Tour of Somerville remained an elite event for international as well as American racers. In 1988 the Soviet team, including 1987 world individual and team pursuit champions, came to race. Roberto Gaggioli, an Italian riding for Coors Light, won the race on Memorial Day and went on to win the USPRO championship in Philadelphia.

When the Tour of Somerville celebrated its fiftieth anniversary in 1990, the purse had grown to $20,000. Among American racers, winning the Tour was seen as a major achievement. Eric Heiden, Connie Carpenter, Rebecca Twigg, and Greg LeMond raced in the Tour, although none on this exclusive list ever won it. In 1988 George Hincapie won the junior competition.

At the fifty-ninth annual event in 2002, Jonas Carney defeated riders from twelve other countries to win his fourth Tour of Somerville. The three-rider finishing sprint was so close, race officials had to review the photographic record to formally award Carney the victory.

Like 7-Eleven and Coors Light in the past, new teams came to the Tour to claim their place in the competitive ranks. In 2006 the new Toyota-United team put Juan Jose Haedo on the winner's podium. Haedo outgunned racers from the Kodak Gallery-Sierra Nevada and Colavita-Sutter Home teams to claim his victory in a 350-meter field sprint.

WINNERS OF THE KUGLER-ANDERSON MEMORIAL TOUR OF SOMERVILLE

1940 - Furman Kugler
1941 - Furman Kugler
1942 - Carl Anderson
1943 - World War II
1944 - World War II
1945 - World War II
1946 - World War II
1947 - Donald Sheldon
1948 - Donald Sheldon
1949 - Frank Brilando
1950 - Richard Cortright
1951 - Francis Mertens
1952 - Ernest Seubert
1953 - Hugh Starrs
1954 - John Chiselko
1955 - Pat Murphy
1956 - Jack Heid
1957 - Arnold Uhrlass
1958 - Art Longsjo
1959 - Rupert Waitl
1960 - Michael Hiltner
1961 - Robert McKown
1962 - Richard Centore
1963 - Olaf Moetus
1964 - Hans Wolfe
1965 - Eckhard Viehover
1966 - John Aschen
1967 - Jackie Simes
1968 - Siegi Koch
1969 - Jackie Simes

1970 - Robert Farrell
1971 - Edward Parrott
1972 - Roger Young
1973 - Ron Skarin
1974 - Ron Skarin
1975 - Rory O'Reilly
1976 - Dave Boll
1977 - Dave Ware
1978 - Jocelyn Lovell
1979 - William Martin
1980 - Steve Bauer
1981 - Wayne Stetina
1982 - Gary Trevisiol
1983 - Steve Bauer
1984 - Davis Phinney
1985 - Matt Eaton
1986 - Marc Maertens
1987 - Paul Pearson
1988 - Roberto Gaggioli
1989 - Graeme Miller
1990 - Matt Eaton
1991 - Brian Moroney
1992 - Jonas Carney
1993 - Gary Anderson
1994 - J-Me Carney
1995 - Jason Snow
1996 - Julian Dean
1997 - Brett Aitken
1998 - Jonas Carney
1999 - Eric Wohlberg
2000 - Jonas Carney
2001 - Eric Wohlberg
2002 - Jonas Carney
2003 - Jonas Carney
2004 - Victor Repinski
2005 - Kyle Wamsley

2006 - Juan Jose Haedo

MILDRED KUGLER WOMEN'S OPEN WINNERS

1976 - Mary Jane Reoch
1977 - Karen Strong
1978 - Sue Novara
1979 - Karen Strong
1980 - Karen Strong
1981 - Karen Strong
1982 - Sue Novara-Reber
1983 - Sue Novara-Reber
1984 - Sue Novara-Reber
1985 - Sophie Eaton
1986 - Peggy Mass
1987 - Henny Top
1988 - Susan Elias
1989 - Susan Elias
1990 - Jan Bolland
1991 - Karen Bliss
1992 - Laura Charameda
1993 - Marianne Berglund
1994 - Jeanne Golay
1995 - Jessica Grieco
1996 - Jessica Grieco
1997 - Karen Bliss-Livingston
1998 - Karen Bliss-Livingston
1999 - Laura Van Gilder
2000 - Tina Mayolo
2001 - Christina Underwood
2002 - Laura Van Gilder
2003 - Sarah Uhl
2004 - Melissa Sanbom
2005 - Laura Van Gilder
2006 - Tina Pic

The Chain of Champions

With previous champions like Freddie Spencer and Willie Honeman retired, Jack Heid became the next American racer to capture the public's attention. Born on June 26, 1924, in Manhattan, Heid spent much of his childhood watching six–day races in Madison Square Garden. He started his own racing career at eighteen and won the Garden state championship in August 1942.

After serving as a Navy mechanic for three years, Heid returned to racing in 1945 and won the Northern California state championships. The next year, Heid raced in twenty-three events in distances from 1 mile to 100 kilometers. He won thirteen and finished 2nd in four and 3rd in three. The performance earned him the BAR—Best All Rounder—awarded by the Bicycle Racing Stars of the Nineteenth Century Association.

In 1948 Heid competed at the Olympic trials in Milwaukee, Wisconsin. Racing on an asphalt track at Brown Deer Park, Heid won the 1,000-meter sprint in 1:15. His performance raised hopes for an American medal at the London Games. Heid's time was just two-hundredths of a second slower than times recorded on the Herne Hill track in London. At the Olympics Heid raced the kilometer and the match sprint but finished out of the medals in both. He suffered a flat tire at the start of the kilometer. After making repairs, he raced again and finished 7th. After the Olympics Heid remained in Europe and raced as a professional in Denmark, Belgium, Holland, England, and France. In 1949 he won a bronze medal in the amateur sprint at the Ordrupp Velodrome in Copenhagen, becoming the first American rider in thirty-seven years to win a medal in a world event. Heid returned to the United States in March 1951. After a five-year hiatus, he was reinstated as an amateur and won the Tour of Somerville in 1956.

Three-Time Winner

Ted Smith of Buffalo won the first of three consecutive senior national championships in 1945. By winning the 25-mile road race event, Smith narrowly edged Heid for the 1947 national championship by just one point. Smith joined Heid as a member of the 1948 Olympic team by winning the 135-mile Olympic qualifying road race by more than 3 minutes. Like Heid, Smith finished out of medal contention.

In 1950 he was the first American racer to compete in the world profes-

Ted Smith (left) poses with Doris Travani and junior Don Clausen, the other two 1948 national champions.

Frank Schwinn Jr. presents the Ignaz Schwinn trophy to Ted Smith.

sional road race championships. He suffered a flat tire 160 kilometers into the 248-kilometer course and did not finish. Service in Korea with the Army Air Corps kept Smith off his bike until 1956.

Disney and Longsjo

In the 1950s national championships were decided in a single weekend. Several track events, ranging from half-mile to 10-mile to sprints, points races, and pursuit events, were used to crown the national champion. (A pursuit event is one in which two cyclists begin the race on opposite sides of the track. If one cyclist manages to catch the other, the successful pursuer is declared the winner; otherwise, the first one to complete the required distance is declared the winner.)

From 1954 to 1958 Jack Disney wore the stars and stripes jersey. Disney was a member of three Olympic teams and won silver at the Pan American Games. Disney won his second consecutive national championship on August 29, 1955, at the Flushing Meadow bicycle track. He finished 1st in the half-mile, mile, and 5-mile events. In the fourth event, the 10-mile road race, Disney couldn't maintain the pace set by Arthur Longsjo of Fitchburg, Massachusetts. Although Longsjo won the race, Disney had accumulated enough points to win the overall championship. Longsjo finished 2nd overall.

Living in California, Disney held a day job and raced as a hobby. In 1956 the Olympic trials were held in San Jose. Twenty-four hours before the trials were scheduled to begin, Disney remained at home. Don Furgeson, Disney's friend and a fellow racer, cajoled Jack's mother, Laurine, to convince Disney to come to the trials. In an all–night road trip, Disney's mother, sister, and future wife took turns driving to deliver him to San Jose at dawn. After a short nap and breakfast, Disney raced through thirteen heats to earn the sole sprinter's spot on the Melbourne Olympic team. Disney would go on to win seven national sprint titles.

While Disney dominated the West Coast, Arthur Longsjo, originally an Olympic-level speed skater, was making a name for himself in the

THE BICYCLE MUSEUM OF AMERICA/NEW BREMEN, OHIO

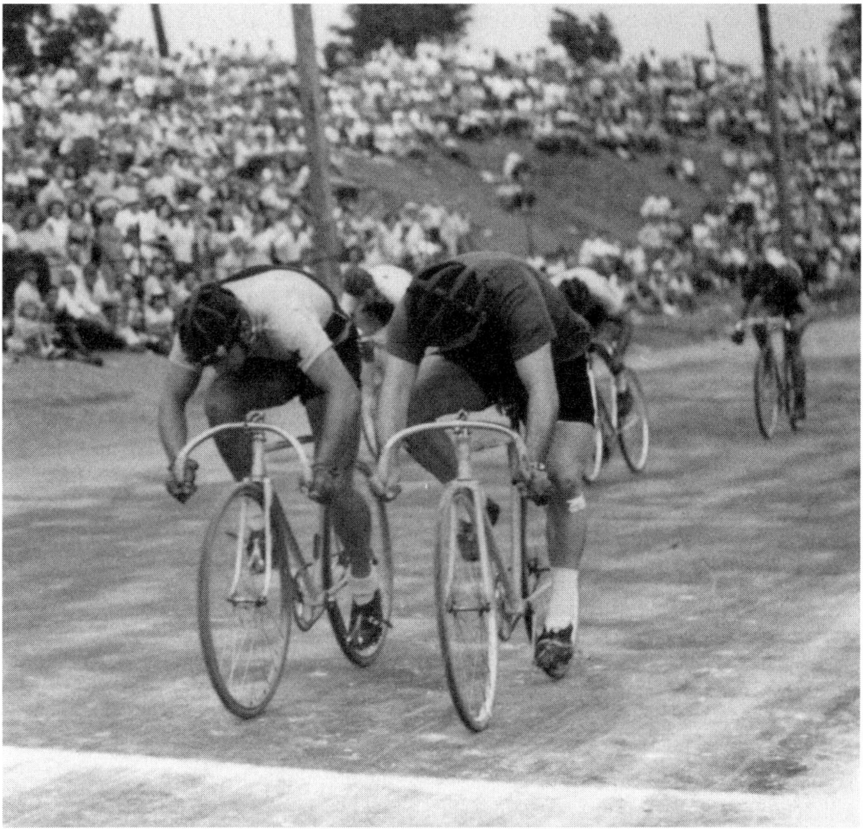

The 1948 Amateur Bicycle League of America's national championships were held in Kenosha, Wisconsin. Ted Smith (left) defeated Gus Gatto in the 1-mile final.

East. In 1954 Longsjo won his second Massachusetts state championship and finished 4th in the Tour of Somerville and the national championship events. Longsjo's win at the 1958 Tour of Somerville earned him a 1-inch replica of the Kugler-Anderson Memorial trophy, two watches, and a share of the $3,787 prize purse.

Longsjo joined Disney on the 1956 Olympic team and rode on the 4,000-meter pursuit team. He became the first American to compete in the Winter and Summer Olympics in the same year.

In July 1958 Longsjo decided to race in the four-day Tour du St. Laurent stage race instead of attending the national championships. After becoming the first American to win the race, Longsjo moved on to capture the Quebec-to-Montreal title. Longsjo slept in the passenger seat on the drive back home. On the way, the driver lost control of the car trying to swat a bee. Longsjo suffered major head and internal injuries and died later that day.

The Fitchburg Longsjo memorial race was founded in 1960, organized by Longsjo's teammate Guy Morin. Morin defeated a dozen riders to win the first race. For the next twenty years, results at Fitchburg documented the evolution of American racing.

Fitchburg Longsjo Classic

 In the late 1950s Arthur Longsjo was making a name for himself as a cyclist. His racing career moved quickly to national championship races and Olympic trials. In 1956 Longsjo became the first person to compete in the Winter and Summer Olympics in the same year, which he did as a cyclist and a speed skater. After the Olympics he continued to capture victories on his racing bike. Returning home from a record-setting win at a Canadian race, Longsjo was killed when the car he was riding in crashed. Three cyclists and three speed skaters served as pallbearers at his funeral.

Starting in 1960, America's top racers came to Fitchburg, Massachusetts, to memorialize Longsjo's racing prowess and stake their claim as top cyclists. Wayne Stetina captured three titles in the '70s, more than any other racer.

In 1980 the United States Cycling Federation changed the name of the race from Fitchburg Classic to the Fitchburg Longsjo Classic to honor its place on the racing calendar. Ninety-five racers entered that year but only 35 finished. Bruce Donaghy outsprinted Eric Heiden to win the 50-mile race in 1:53:14. Heiden slipped to 5th but had something to celebrate when his sister Beth captured the

15.73-mile women's event.

In 1991 the Longsjo Classic expanded to a four-day stage race, opening with a tough road stage circling Mount Wachusett—where Longsjo used to end his regular 180-mile fixed-gear training rides. After four days of racing, Stephen Swart was declared the winner. But officials reviewing each stage's results discovered an error in their calculations, and Davis Phinney was handed the victory.

In 1992 Lance Armstrong, twenty years old and a member of the U.S. national team, won the second-stage circuit race and held a commanding lead entering the road stage. Armstrong and his Olympic teammates (Bob Mioske, Tim Peddie, Darren Baker, and Chann McRae) used the Fitchburg race as a training ride for the Olympics. Halfway through the road stage, Armstrong, Baker, and two others broke away from the pack. Baker and Armstrong remained in front for the final sprint. With the overall win sewn up, Armstrong let Baker, an Olympic alternate, cross the line first.

Saturn, one of the strongest domestic teams at the time, found its riders on the Longsjo Classic's winner's podiums as the '90s came to a close. Frank McCormack and Dede Demet won in 1998. It was McCormack's second win at Fitchburg.*

*McCormack's brother Mark won the race in 2004. Alan McCormack, no relation, won in 1982.

McCormack received $1,300 for the victory, Demet just $400.

In 1999 the prize purse increased from $5,000 to $25,000. Local companies provided consistent financial support for each race stage. Saturn and U.S. Postal were added to the sponsor list. Saturn's Bart Bowen avoided a major crash at the end of the road stage and captured the overall title. Lyne Bessette, a Canadian member of Saturn, won the first of four consecutive victories in 1999.

WINNERS OF THE FITCHBURG LONGSJO MEMORIAL CLASSIC

MEN

1960 - Guy Morin (Can)
1961 - Arnie Uhrlass (USA)
1962 - Richard Centori (USA)
1963 - Rob Parsons (USA)
1964 - Paul Ziak (USA)
1965 - Franco Poutenzieri (USA)
1966 - Sam Watson (Ire)
1967 - Guiseppi Marinoni (Can)
1968 - Robert Simpson (USA)
1969 - Jocelyn Lovell (Can)
1970 - Doug Dale (USA)
1971 - Bobby Phillips (USA)
1972 - (2) Giuseppi Marinoni (Can)
1973 - Steve Woznick (USA)
1974 - Bill Shook (USA)
1975 - Wayne Stetina (USA)
1976 - Tom Doughty (USA)
1977 - (2) Wayne Stetina (USA)
1978 - (3) Wayne Stetina (USA)
1979 - Tom Schuler (USA
1980 - Bruce Donaghy (USA)
1981 - Steve Pyle (USA)
1982 - Alan McCormack (Ire)
1983 - Louis Garneau (Can)

1984 - Russ Williams (GBr)
1985 - Jeff Slack (USA)
1986 - Patrick Liu (USA)
1987 - Roberto Gaggioli (Ita)
1988 - Graeme Miller (NZ)
1989 - Jeff Slack (USA)
1990 - Tom Post (Ned)
1991 - Davis Phinney (USA)
1992 - Lance Armstrong (USA)
1993 - (2) Davis Phinney (USA)
1994 - Frank McCormack (USA)
1995 - Mike Engleman (USA)
1996 - Tyler Hamilton (USA)
1997 - John Peters (USA)
1998 - (2) Frank McCormack (USA)
1999 - Bart Bowen (USA)
2000 - Henk Vogels (Aus)
2001 - Eric Wohlberg (Can)
2002 - Chris Horner (USA)
2003 - Victor Rapinski (Bel)
2004 - Mark McCormack (USA)
2005 - Jonathan Page (USA)
2006 - Shawn Milne (USA)

WOMEN

1999* - Lyne Bessette (Can)
2000 - Lyne Bessette (Can)
2001 - Lyne Bessette (Can)
2002 - Lyne Bessette (Can)

2003 - Katie Mactier (Aus)
2004 - Sue Palmer-Komar (Can)
2005 - Sue Palmer-Komar (Can)
2006 - Sarah Ulmer (NZ)

* First year of women's race.

PART TWO

The Rebirth of American Bicycle Racing

Sheila Young captured the sprint national championships in 1971,'73,'76, and '81. She also won world championships in 1973, '76, and '81.

CHAPTER TWO

Champions of the Road

ON AUGUST 29, 1964, JACK SIMES III, grandson of racer Jack Simes, won the national bicycle racing championship by winning three of the four senior events. Simes won the 1,000-meter race and needed a victory in the 10-mile road race to earn enough points to pass Alan Grieco, his best friend and training partner.

Held at Kissena Park in Queens, the road race started with forty riders. Riding almost side by side for the entire race, Simes and Grieco attacked with 1.5 laps to go on the quarter-mile banked asphalt track, which acted as the "road" during this era. Simes finished in 23:12.9, a half length ahead of his friend. Five thousand spectators were on hand to watch Simes break Jim Rossi's five-year reign as national champion. Nancy Burghart, of Jackson Heights, New York, recaptured her women's title from rival Edith Johnson. Burghart also won in 1962.

Through the late '50s and early '60s, racers like Bob Tetzlaff and Bob Parsons had long, successful road racing careers that received little attention in the national media. Parsons won the "unofficial" national road championship in 1964. A year later the Amateur Bicycle League introduced the first officially recognized national road championship. The first road course covered 11 laps up and down the Santa Monica foothills. Michael Hiltner, twenty-four, rode the last 3 laps alone to win the first road racing national championship.

Bob Tetzlaff, with thirty years of racing experience, won the 1966 championship in Northbrook, Illinois. Riding in the rain, Tetzlaff finished the 105-mile course in 3:59. A flat tire with 8 miles to go threatened his lead, but a veteran rider gave up his wheel and Tetzlaff recovered to take the title.

Bob Parsons added his name to the official records, winning the championship in 1967. The same year, Nancy Burghart of New York won the women's national sprint, 3,000-meter pursuit, and 23-mile road race events to win the national championship for the fourth time in six years. In 1963 Edith Johnson beat her for the title and in 1966 a crash took Burghart out of contention.

In 1969 the Amateur Bicycle League had just 3,000 members.

Road Racing Returns to the Front Page

After decades of infrequent, single-paragraph race reports buried deep in the sports pages, the media spotlight returned to covering American bicycle racing in the early 1970s. Fueled by a new generation of kids and an energy crisis, sales of bicycles set new records year after year. As more recreational riders took to the roads, news about the exploits of American racers attracted their attention.

The 1970s was a watershed decade in American bicycle racing. The governing body moved from a loose-knit, contentious old-boy network to a nascent professionally managed organization renamed in 1975 the United States Cycling Federation (USCF). Internationally, American racers ended decades of futility by winning medals and finishing high in events traditionally dominated by Europeans. At home the competition for national road and track championships created new legends and new heroes and moved race coverage from newspapers to cable and broadcast television.

The photograph of John Howard's wide smile and raised arms as he celebrated his victory at the 1971 Pan American Games graced the front pages of newspapers across the country (see the Pan American Games sidebar). In 1972 Sheila Young raced in the world championships in France and brought home a bronze medal. A year later in San Sebastian, Spain, she became the first American woman to win a gold medal at a world championship track race in fifty years, and her performance was noted in *Sports Illustrated.* Young and her teammate Sue Novara found their pictures on the covers of national magazines like *Ms., Newsweek,* and *Womensports.* American men, led by John Howard and John Allis, broke through European skepticism to race in the Tour of Ireland and Britain's Milk Race.

In 1974 professional racing returned to the United States for the first time since the mid-1930s. Although beginning with only a handful of riders, by the end of the decade professional racing was firmly established.

In 1975 the Celestial Seasonings Red Zinger Classic made its debut in Boulder, Colorado. Known as the Coors Classic after sponsorship changed hands in 1980, the stage race became one of the most significant American events in modern racing. In its first five years, the Red Zinger/Coors Classic became the launching point for a generation of racers and teams that would dominate the sport for decades to come. Race director Michael Aisner's mastery of public relations and promotions brought media attention and sponsorship dollars to racing, and American sports fans began to follow the career arcs of Greg LeMond, Davis Phinney, Andy Hampsten, and Connie Carpenter. 7-Eleven, America's first professional racing team, used the Coors Classic to draw millions of new fans.

At the 1976 Olympics in Montreal, George Mount's 6th-place finish in the road race fueled hopes that American cycling's long Olympic medal drought would end in four years.

By the end of the decade, the USCF had hired its first full-time head coach and secured the largest corporate sponsorship in its history. Bicycle racing was working its way back to prominence.

JOHN HOWARD

In 1969 John Howard won the Silver Dollar City roller coaster road race. It was one of his first competitive events.

A Name to Follow

In 1968 John Howard earned a spot on the U.S. Olympic team. The same year he outdueled Bob Parsons to win the national road racing championship. In the next few years, Howard's performances on the domestic and international stage would force American media to take notice. Like all emerging sports, bicycle racing needed a face to follow. John Howard served that role with a vengeance from 1970 to 1975, showing young racers how to win.

The Business of Cycling

In 1971 Ernest Seubert assumed the presidency of the Amateur Bicycle League of America. He led an organization with fewer than 5,000 members and a $25,000 budget.

More an old-boy network than a business operation, the Amateur Bicycle League was a divided group of cycling clubs and power brokers jockeying for position. Rumor, innuendo, and fractured communications distracted the clubs from reaching consensus on any issue.

Seubert introduced a bimonthly newsletter that was sent to district representatives, board members, and regional and state cycling publications. Under Seubert's direction, committee chairmen were required to publish and distribute reports at quarterly meetings.

Al Toefield, the previous president, had started a program to change the way the Olympic team was created. Seubert continued Toefield's work and established a development program that used points awarded in regional races as the basis for team selection. In the past, district officials' recommendations carried more weight than race performance in the selection process.

Bringing professional management and oversight to American racing governance was a slow process during a period when bicycle sales set new records with each passing year. During Seubert's term, the Amateur Bicycle League of America's budget exploded, growing from $25,000 in 1971 to $200,000 four years later.

In 1971 the ABLA began a program of commercial sponsorship of bicycle clubs. By 1973 the total dollar value of club sponsorships reached $45,000. By 1975 it reached $75,000. Ten percent of the sponsorship funds were used by the ABLA to send riders to the world championship events.

In 1974 Follis became the first company to sponsor two clubs simultaneously. In 1975 Schwinn entered the sponsorship arena, providing financial support for the Paramount, Wolverine, and Somerset Wheelmen bicycle clubs. Frank Schwinn, the company's third-generation president, made the decision to sponsor three teams to get national exposure for the company. At the time, Schwinn's Paramount was the only American competition bicycle on the market. Schwinn had provided road and track racing bikes to the U.S. Olympic team since the 1930s.

Despite the increases, the ABLA missed opportunities to create relationships with corporations to bring long-term financial support to the organization.

The Growth of International Competition

The Tour of California

In 1971 California hosted the first major international stage race in the history of American bicycle racing. Raleigh Bicycles was looking for a way to promote its brand in the United States and worked with Peter Rich, a former racer and owner of Velo-Sport Cyclery in Berkeley, to organize the race. A field of seventy-nine international riders started the eight-day, ten-stage, 685-mile race on August 28 at the Bear Valley resort near Lake Tahoe.

On the third day the peloton raced from Santa Rosa to Davis. Flying down a downhill section of the course in a shoulder-to-shoulder pack, the racers leaned into a sharp curve. A pickup truck traveling in the opposite direction reached the apex of the turn just as the lead pair was approaching. Tom Baker sideswiped the truck, lost control, and crashed. John Howard collided with the truck head-on. The chase pack of sixty riders avoided the chaos in front of them. Fortunately, injuries were limited. Baker suffered a broken leg. Howard, bruised and scraped, completed the stage.

Mexico's Augustin Alcantara won the first Tour of California and a check for $1,385. Top American finishers included John Allis in 4th place and David Brink in 5th. John Howard managed to finish 6th despite his collision with the truck.

The Tour of California received little media attention, and Rich lost thousands of dollars promoting the first major American stage race. Other races like the 1972 Grand Prix and the Tour of Baja California joined the Los Angeles Six-Day as heavily promoted cycling events that failed despite high hopes of raising interest in international-caliber racing. The Mexican stage race drew only sixty riders and three five-man teams.

Despite the financial struggles, the Tour of California did not go completely unnoticed and inspired promoters to organize future races like the Coors Classic and Tour DuPont.

Racing across the Atlantic

In 1972 twenty-year-old Mike Neel became the first American to compete in Britain's Milk Race. Bill Squance, the controller of the race, had initially rejected an American team's request to enter the race. Squance didn't believe American racers were capable of competing in international events. He did agree to give Neel a spot on an international team of riders from Scotland, Ireland, Australia, and Canada.

The 1972 Tour of Britain Milk Race covered 1,100 miles in twelve days. Four miles outside of Brighton, where the race began, a pack of sixty-nine of the top amateur cyclists in the world entered a highway cloverleaf. Because they were riding shoulder to shoulder, seven or eight across, the corners couldn't accommodate the crush of riders. In a moment, almost all of the riders had crashed, throwing frames, wheels, and riders in all directions. Mike Neel was caught in the chaos. Ten minutes after the race started, Neel was picking himself off the ground and looking for help to repair his punctured front tire.

With repairs made, Neel and three members of the British Provinces team worked together to get back into the race. The group was 3 minutes down on the lead group when Neel noticed a crack in his frame. As he applied the front brakes to slow down, the frame snapped, the front wheel collapsed, and Neel was thrown over the handlebars. Another support crew trailing Neel treated his injured forearm and gave him a replacement bicycle. Far behind and riding a misfit bike, Neel continued and finished the first stage 1 hour and 1 minute behind the leaders. He started again the next day and finished the third and fourth stages, with each day taking a physical toll. He left the race at the end of the fifth stage and returned to the United States.

The Tour of Ireland

One year later American riders delivered a much stronger performance when Raleigh backed a four-man American team's entry into the Tour of Ireland. In the first few years of the '70s, bicycle sales in the United States reached record levels, and Raleigh, headquartered in Nottingham, England, wanted a piece of the American market.

Phil Liggett, the chief international commissar of the 1973 Tour of Ireland, extended invitations to John Allis, Stan Swain, Bill Humphries, and John Howard, the current American national road champion. With Raleigh's support, they were the first American riders to race in Europe as a team.

Eager to prove themselves against nineteen other four-man teams, the Americans started strong in the eight-stage race. Howard and Allis led a breakaway on the first 97-mile stage, and by the end of the second day Howard was in 3rd place, Allis in 5th.

The pack endured cold rain on a 95-mile stage over the Iron Mountains to Athlone on the Shannon River. Fifty miles into the stage, Howard attacked with three other riders on a steep climb. On the descent the racers reached 60 mph. Flocks of sheep standing on the side of the roads unnerved Howard, but he remained in the four-man lead pack. Howard sprinted to the finish, winning the stage by a bike length.

JOHN HOWARD

In the 1973 Tour of Ireland, John Howard captured a stage and finished 3rd overall. It was the first podium finish by an American in a major international stage race.

On the final stage, a 30-mile criterium in Dublin's Phoenix Park, Howard crashed on a wet corner. The Dutch team (with rider Math Buckx in 4th place) accelerated, trying to take advantage of Howard's mishap. Back on his bike and in the race, Howard surged forward and finished in 3rd place overall. His teammates also had respectable finishing positions: Allis 5th, Swain 46th, and Humphries 47th. The American team finished 6th in the team competition.

Based on the performance, Phil Liggett, hired to organize the 1974 Tour of Britain, told the team to send their best six riders to the Tour, including Howard and Allis, and offered to pay their expenses. Raleigh again paid the team's airfare to England and provided race support. The American team finished 9th of 11 teams and Howard was 31st of 59 finishers. American riders had earned the right to compete in Europe.

Americans at the World Championships

 On the world stage the performance of American racers failed to match their successes in domestic events. For years the United States cycling governing bodies did not support international racing. From the point of view of racing officials, winning the national championship or a spot on the Olympic team was the pinnacle of success for the American racer. Riders who wanted to test their skills against Europe's best riders often paid their own travel expenses.

The lack of support contributed to years of finishes far from the podium. When there was good news to report, the hero was usually a woman. For decades the performance of American women far exceeded that of their male counterparts. Long before Greg LeMond and Lance Armstrong captured headlines, Audrey McElmury became the first American to win the world road race title.

Early Worlds

In 1893 the League of American Wheelmen and the International Cyclists' Association introduced the first official world championships. The event was only open to amateurs. Arthur Zimmerman of Asbury Park, New Jersey, won both the 1-mile and 10-mile races. Records show that Zimmerman, the dominant racer of the era, won 101 races that season. In these first world championships, held in Chicago, American riders won nine

of the ten medals offered.

In Vienna six years later, George Banker became the second American to capture the world's cycling championship. He became the first rider from the United States to carry the title of world professional champion.

Inspired by Banker's success, Major Taylor went to Montreal in 1899. Taylor, one of the best riders of his era, beat five others to win the 1-mile sprint. America's winning streak stood at two.

In 1904 American riders dominated the world championship event held at London's Crystal Palace. Bobby Walthour Sr. won the world professional motor-pace championship (drafting behind a motorcycle, a race form that didn't last long), Iver Lawson won the world professional sprint championship, and Marcus Hurley won the world amateur sprint championship. Hurley, a member of the New York Athletic Club, defeated English riders Alfred Reed and J. S. Benyon to capture the world's amateur 2-kilometer race. The *New York Times* reported that Hurley's time, 11:07.25, was slow because the three competitors loafed until the final 300 yards. In the final sprint, Hurley beat Reed by an inch. Lawson, of Salt Lake City, won the professional 2-kilometer world championship. Lawson and Hurley faced each other in the final of the 1-kilometer event. Lawson won, earning another world title.

Americans won four of the five international championships on the competition schedule. No other country could match that record over the previous twelve years of international championships.

Formal records list Lawson as the first American to officially hold the world championship title. Although Banker and Taylor won in 1898 and 1899, both riders refused to compete in a race that included an amateur racer.

Frank Kramer followed Zimmerman and Taylor to become America's best racer. From 1901 to 1916 Kramer reigned as the American national professional champion. When the Newark Velodrome hosted the world championships in 1912, Kramer added his name to the list of American world champions. It would be almost forty years before another American would win a world championship medal. World War II interrupted world championships from 1939 to 1945.

Jack Heid of Rockaway, New Jersey, competed in the 1948 Olympics in London. After the Olympics Heid stayed in Europe and raced with teammate Al Stiller in Belgium. In 1949 Heid traveled to Copenhagen and won the bronze medal in the world amateur sprint championship.

There was a span of thirty-seven years between Frank Kramer's gold medal in 1912 and Heid's bronze. Another nineteen years passed before an American won again. Jack Simes rode at the 1968 Mexico City Olympics and finished 12th in the kilometer time trial. Simes finished far out of the medals but was the fastest American to date in Olympic cycling. At the end of the Games, Simes joined a group of riders who traveled to the world championships in Montevideo, Uruguay.

Simes raced in the kilometer, his best event, and won the silver medal.

America's First World Road Race Champion

Women's road, sprint, and pursuit events were added to world cup competition schedules in 1958.

In July 1969 Audrey McElmury prepared for international competition by setting the women's national hour record on the Encino Velodrome in California. She finished 162 laps covering 24.8 miles (39.872 kilometers). (Her record stood until 1987, when Carol Lewnau covered 40.116 kilometers on the Major Taylor Velodrome in Indianapolis.) One month later McElmury won the 3,000-meter pursuit and overall national title before traveling to Brno, Czechoslovakia to compete in the 1969 women's world road race championship.

To prepare, McElmury's training routine started at 7:15 a.m. at Maylen's Gymnasium in San Diego. After ninety minutes of weight training, she returned home to attend to the regular household chores of a mother and housewife. Later in the afternoon she would run up a hundred-step flight of stairs at her local beach. She alternated climbing the stairs with fast and slow repetitions. Managing all aspects of her physical conditioning, McElmury followed a strict diet of organically grown foods and homemade yogurt. Ten hours of sleep every night helped her body recover.

In Brno a field of forty-three riders, including four Americans, raced for 5 laps over an 8.7-mile course featuring a 2.5-mile hill near the halfway point. Living and training in San Diego, McElmury was not used to riding in the rainy conditions, but she had come too far to let the weather affect her performance. On the

4th lap McElmury broke away. Negotiating a turn at the base of a downhill, she lost control and crashed. McElmury got back on her bike and after several minutes of hard solo riding recovered the 30 seconds she had lost to the lead pack.

With 5 miles remaining on the 5th lap, McElmury attacked again. This time she rode alone to the finish, 70 seconds ahead of Bernadette Swinnerton of England. McElmury became the first American to win a world championship in fifty-seven years. Her victory surprised race officials, and she waited patiently in the rain while they scrambled to find a copy of "The Star-Spangled Banner" to celebrate her victory. A year later she finished 7th in the world championship in Leicester, England. Before her victory, eight Americans competing in track events had won world championships—but all before 1913.

McElmury inspired a new generation of American men and women. In the next twenty years, eight Americans won world titles: Beth Heiden, Sheila Young-Ochowicz, Connie Carpenter, Sue Novara-Reber, Connie Paraskevin-Young, Rebecca Twigg, Gibby Hatton, and Greg LeMond.

After McElmury's victory the gap between world championship podium appearances narrowed quickly. In 1972 sprinter Sheila Young won a bronze medal in Marseilles, France. McElmury finished just out of the medals in 4th place. One year later Young won the gold medal at the world championships in San Sebastian, Spain. It was the first track championship for the United States in fifty years.

Until the end of the 1970s, American men struggled at the international level. Financial support from the USCF was virtually nonexistent. In 1975 team mechanic Steve Aldrich donated $1,000 worth of equipment to the riders, and individual supporters offered contributions to cover expenses. Progress came in small steps from year to year. Skip Cutting's 5th-place finish in the pro sprint championship was the best result for an American male in 1975. In 1976 Mike Neel turned pro and finished 10th in the world professional road race in Ostuni, Italy. It was the first time an American man had ever finished the event. One year later Mark Pringle's 10th-place finish in the amateur road race marked another best-yet.

In 1978 the junior world championships in Buenos Aires offered a glimpse into the future of American men's racing. Greg LeMond set a world championship record by winning three medals in the same event. LeMond captured gold in the 120-kilometer road race and a silver in the 3,000-meter individual pursuit. The third medal came when LeMond and teammates Jeff Bradley, Greg Demgen, and Ron Kiefel captured the bronze medal in the 70-kilometer team time trial.

American women captured their second world road championship in 1980. Racing in France, Beth Heiden won the women's 53.6-kilometer road race in 1:45:15. Teammate Heidi Hopkins finished 5th in the road race, and Sue Novara won the match sprint title for the second time. Jacques Boyer's 5th-place in the pro road race was the highest American finish to date.

September 1982

September 1982 was a watershed month in America's pursuit of legitimacy in international racing.

Connie Paraskevin became the third American to win the women's sprint championship when she defeated 1981 champion Sheila Young-Ochowicz. Rebecca Twigg captured the United States' first-ever world pursuit gold medal; Connie Carpenter finished 2nd, giving the women gold and silver in two events.

Jacques (Jonathan when he was in the United States) Boyer and Greg LeMond were new members on the French Renault-Gitane team in 1982. Boyer, who had spent years in Europe, was hired to ease LeMond's transition to France. Instead of the intended close bond, the two Americans had a tenuous relationship. Both riders were part of a nine-man team USPRO officials named to compete in the 1982 world championships. Still very early in its history, USPRO—the governing body of professional bicycle racers in the United States—had limited funds and resources, and some of the American riders paid their own way to Goodwood, England. Only six of the nine invited riders joined the team. John Eustice, George Mount, David Mayer-Oakes, and Eric Heiden joined Boyer and LeMond at the start. In his second season as a professional, LeMond was coming off a win at the Coors Classic and strong finishes at the Mediterranean Tour, the Tour of Corsica, and the Tirreno-Adriatico.

On September 5, 136 professionals stood ready for the 275-kilometer race. The course covered 18 laps around a 15.28-kilometer circuit through Sussex County. The riders started an uphill climb on the last 2 kilometers of the course. On the final lap only thirty-five riders remained in the lead group. While six members of the Italian team rode in support of Giuseppe Saronni, Boyer and LeMond rode as individuals rather than teammates.

On a 10 percent grade 1 kilometer

Greg LeMond won three medals at the 1978 junior world championships in Buenos Aires. With teammates Ron Kiefel, Greg Demgen, and Jeff Bradley, the 70-kilometer team time trial team finished third.

from the finish, Boyer launched a solo attack, the first time an American rider was to be found in the lead of a world professional championship race. In the last 500 meters, Boyer had a 20-meter lead, but LeMond and Saronni countered, quickly catching and passing him. LeMond could not match Saronni's aggressive finishing sprint and crossed the line 5 seconds behind. LeMond's silver medal was the first for an American male in a world professional road race championship. Boyer, who finished 10th, complained bitterly that LeMond should have supported his attack instead of passing him. Headlines and follow-up stories in American cycling magazines debated the finishing sprint for weeks. George Mount, in 52nd place, was the only other American finisher.

In the women's professional race, Connie Carpenter and Rebecca Twigg finished 5th and 6th.

In 1982 Rebecca Twigg became the first American to win a gold medal at a world championship pursuit event. Over her long career she also won the silver medal in the first women's road race at the 1984 Los Angeles Olympics.

Three weeks later, on September 20, LeMond answered any question about his abilities against European riders by winning the ten-day Tour de l'Avenir. His winning margin of 10:18 was the largest in the history of the race.

LeMond Wins the Worlds Road Race

When Greg LeMond won the amateur world championship in 1979, Cyrille Guimard, director of France's Renault-Gitane team, was watching. Impressed by the young American's competitive spirit, Guimard and Tour de France winner Bernard Hinault recruited LeMond to join their team.

Four years later, in 1983, LeMond became the first American to win a professional road race world championship. At the start of the race, LeMond was considered one of the riders to watch.

His 4th-place finish in the Tour of Switzerland and victories at the Tour de l'Avenir and Dauphiné Libéré earned him the respect of the European peloton.

At the time, it was still rare to find English-speaking riders on European professional teams. LeMond and Boyer from America, Phil Anderson from Australia, and Irishmen Sean Kelly and Stephen Roche shared a common perspective as outsiders working for acceptance. Before the 1983 world championships, LeMond and Anderson trained extensively together, following mileage and route plans drafted by Guimard.

During the race rider loyalties shifted from the professional teams that paid their salaries back to their home countries. The camaraderie between LeMond and Anderson carried over to the race. The field of 117 riders included defending champion Saronni and the thirteen riders of the Italian team. Against this formidable competition, Anderson and LeMond rode patiently and waited for the right moment to make a move to the front.

With 2 laps remaining LeMond was in a lead pack with three other riders. Two riders dropped off, unable to maintain the pace. LeMond and Spain's Faustino Ruperez began the bell lap with a 72-second lead over the thirty-eight-rider chase group. On the first climb of the last lap, LeMond increased the tempo, testing Ruperez' willingness and ability to respond. By the top of the climb, LeMond had created a 38-second lead. On the descent Stephen Roche and two other riders joined Ruperez, but they could not close the gap. LeMond rode the last 11 kilometers unchallenged and finished 1st, 1:11 ahead of the four riders chasing him.

LeMond, who rode a production Gitane bicycle in the race, received the first rainbow jersey awarded to a professional American rider. The spoils for his victory also included a Union Cycliste International (UCI) gold medal and a heavy brass cowbell.

After finishing 2nd in the 1983 world road race and winning the silver medal in the first Olympic women's road race, Rebecca Twigg recaptured the world 3,000-meter pursuit crown in Barcelona, Spain. Twigg, who won the event in 1982, rode a Raleigh with a disc rear wheel that was considered state of the art at the time.

The World Championships Return to the United States

The Newark Velodrome hosted the world championships in 1912. Seventy-four years later the world's best racers returned to the United States.

In 1983 Southland Corporation, the parent company of 7-Eleven, approached the USCF about the recently awarded 1986 world championship event. Southland executive Bill Scott presented Southland's offer to pay a $100,000 rights fee for the event, pay a $150,000 rights fee to the UCI, and commit $1.5 million to event expenses. In return the USCF would grant all rights to Southland. As the title sponsor, Southland hoped to recoup its investment by selling television rights, secondary sponsorships, and merchandise. In order to seal the deal, Southland also agreed to pay $250,000 in administration costs the USCF estimated would be required to manage the event.

With an agreement in principle in hand, contract discussions were put off until the 1984 Olympics were over. When negotiations resumed, a new Southland manager had replaced Bill Scott. While planning moved forward, the contract discussions became increasingly difficult and strained. There was a collective sigh of relief when the contract was signed on January 22, 1985.

Over the next eighteen months, event preparations strained the relationship and the capacity of both partners. Southland was surprised when its attempts to sell the television rights to the event were greeted with skepticism by the major networks. Without any prior events with which to compare, network officials could not accurately estimate the size of the audience or potential ratings. The race schedule also presented a challenge—the amateur and professional road races were scheduled on the same weekend as the opening of the NFL season and the finals of the U.S. Open tennis tournament. Even a delayed broadcast of the Little League baseball World Series was viewed as a competitor to world championship bike racing coverage.

When the time came, Colorado Springs was ready. Seven hundred racers from a record-setting sixty-two countries arrived for the nine-day world championships. Amateurs and professionals competed in sixteen track and road events.

A look at the historical medal totals revealed just how far behind American racers had fallen in international competition. Through 1985, Italy's 236 medals led all nations. With just 64, the United States ranked 12th. After a dismal period from 1946 to 1976, American performances had improved steadily, and the team had captured at least two medals every year since 1980.

At the time, *Bicycling* optimistically predicted the American team would win ten medals. Other observers were more skeptical—or realistic, depending on the source—and wondered if three or four medals were even possible.

Americans won five medals, second only to the East German team. Five medals but no gold. Gold medal favorites Connie Paraskevin and Rebecca Twigg-Whitehead lost to old rivals. Paraskevin finished 3rd in the women's sprint behind Erica Salumiaee of the Soviet Union. France's Jeanne Longo defeated Twigg-Whitehead in the 3,000-meter pursuit. In the women's road race, Twigg-Whitehead raced to a 100-meter lead but crashed less than 2 minutes from the finish line. Jeanne Longo finished 1st and Twigg-Whitehead's teammate Janelle Parks, a third-year member of the national team, finished 2nd.

In the men's track events, Leonard Nitz won the bronze in the amateur points race. The tandem team of Kit Kyle and David Lindsay replaced the original team of Nelson Vails and Scott Berryman

after Berryman crashed in an individual match sprint round. The replacement team took silver, losing to Czechoslovakia in the final. Men's team pursuiters Dave Lettieri, Steve Hegg, Carl Sundquist, and Leonard Nitz were hampered when, on the day of the race, the UCI rejected the specially built aerodynamic bikes they planned to ride. Substituting bikes used in 1984, the team could only manage a 7th-place finish.

Greg LeMond, after becoming the first American to win the Tour de France, fell ill in Colorado Springs. He finished the world championship professional road race as the top American rider, in 7th place.

In the end, years of hard work by the USCF, sponsors, and volunteers paid off. There were winners and losers, but overall the American team performed well. Track events held at the four-year-old Southland Velodrome were packed almost to capacity each night.

The weather was the one detail no one could control. A marketing campaign to entice spectators from Denver to Colorado Springs had started two months before the event, and USCF organizers estimated 50,000 fans in 15,000 cars would travel to the Air Force Academy grounds to watch the road races. Early Saturday morning racers woke up to learn the temperature outside was 33 degrees. Even worse, it was raining. Cold weather, fog, and persistent rains kept spectators away. The 82 women entered in the road race suffered miserably. By the second 9.5-mile lap on the 38-mile course, some competitors showed signs of hypothermia and fell almost 20 minutes behind the leaders.

Even the most optimistic media reports of 20,000 fans were met with skepticism from vendors and sponsors who spent millions of dollars preparing for the event. The USA Network's planned television coverage was grounded when its helicopters couldn't fly in the foggy conditions. USA Network broadcast just one hour of highlights.

After the landmark performance at the Los Angeles Olympics in 1984 brought attention from potential sponsors and new audiences to bicycle racing, the U.S. teams could not maintain the momentum. The much anticipated return of the worlds to the United States did not end with a performance to match the Olympics.

A year later in Vienna, Rebecca Twigg (formerly Twigg-Whitehead) recaptured her individual pursuit title. There were few other reasons to celebrate. Observers questioned the team's commitment to international competition.

LeMond Wins Again

In 1989 Greg LeMond joined a very exclusive club of international racers. Only four other riders—Stephen Roche, Eddy Merckx, Louison Bobet, and Georges Speicher—had won the Tour de France and world championship professional road race in the same year.

The 262.5-kilometer race was held in Chambery, France. A record 190 riders started the race. Laurent Fignon, who had finished a crushing 2nd to LeMond in the Tour de France, twice tried to break away from LeMond, the second time with 1 kilometer to go. Each time LeMond—riding a new carbon fiber bike outfitted with Mavic components—quickly retook the lead, as he raced to his second rainbow jersey.

France's Jeanne Longo dominated the women's road race, winning for the fourth time. American women continued to make strides to reach the standard

McElmury and Heiden had set for them. Inga Thompson finished 4th, Sally Zack 11th, and national champion Juli Furtado 35th.

At the world track championships in Lyon, Janie Eickhoff saved the American team from a complete medal shutout by winning the bronze medal in the 30-kilometer points race on the second-to-last day of track competition. She saved the American track team from going without a medal for the first time since 1971.

American Women Dominate in Japan

In 1990 the world championships were held in Japan for the first time. The U.S. team returned home from that competition celebrating its best performance to date.

American women dominated their events, winning all but one of the contested medals. Ruthie Matthes won the silver in the women's road race. Connie Paraskevin-Young won her fourth world sprint title, beating teammate Renee Duprel in the final. The women's team time trial squad of Phyllis Hines, Maureen Manley, Eve Stephenson, and Inga Thompson brought home the silver by defeating the defending champion Soviet team, with the team from the Netherlands taking the gold.

Mike McCarthy's bronze, the first-ever medal for an American male in individual pursuit, was the sole medal for the men's team in Japan. (McCarthy would go on to win gold in the (pro) pursuit at the worlds in Valencia two years later.) The team time trial squad of Lance Armstrong, Nate Reiss, Nathan Sheafor, and Jim Copeland appeared to be in position to bring home a sixth medal, but leading the 100-kilometer event at the halfway point, the four riders experienced mechanical problems and finished in a disappointing 7th place.

The five medals equaled the team's effort at the 1986 event in Colorado Springs. The 1990 team's total included a gold medal, compared to 1986's three silver and two bronze.

Each year the list of winners in world championship events records the names of the best riders of the day. Racing observers reading farther down the finishers' lists often find the names of future champions. The 1990 amateur road race showcased one of America's next elite riders.

Seven laps into the 174-kilometer amateur road race, eighteen-year-old Lance Armstrong was chasing a solo attack by Switzerland's Fabian Jekker. Although the pair could not sustain the break, Armstrong stayed in contact with the lead group. He slipped to an 11th-place finish but the world noticed that a new American rider was on the rise.

In 1992 American women continued to compete shoulder to shoulder with the best European teams and came home with another gold. The women's team time trial squad of Jeanne Golay, Bunki Bankaitis-Davis, Eve Stephenson, and Jan Bolland averaged 46.57 kph over the 50-kilometer course to defeat the defending champion French team by 13 seconds. For the men, Mike McCarthy took gold in the professional-class individual pursuit. He was the first American to win the title.

America's Best Worlds

At the 1993 world cycling championships in Oslo, Norway, American riders recorded the team's most successful world championship since the race began in 1893. For the first time in the history of the worlds,

the track events used an open format, with amateurs and professionals racing against each other. The U.S. men and women won two golds, two silvers, and three bronzes, finishing 2nd in total medal count, just one behind Germany. The team also set a new medals record, surpassing the previous total of five medals won by the professionals and amateurs in 1982, 1983, 1985, and 1986. Amateurs won six of the seven American medals.

Rebecca Twigg defeated Marion Clignet in the 3,000-meter individual pursuit, earning her seventh world championship medal. The bronze medal was awarded to the fastest time of the remaining six riders in the semifinal round. Janie Eickhoff rode against Australian Kathy Watt, the 1992 Olympic individual pursuit champion, and won her fifth career world championship medal.

The women's team time trial riders, Dede Demet, Jeanne Golay, Eve Stephenson, and Jan Bolland, started the race as defending champions but struggled when Bolland's legs cramped 15 kilometers into the race. The team held on to finish 2nd behind the Russians. Laura Charameda placed 3rd in the women's road race. It was the first medal for Charameda but the third consecutive medal for U.S. women in the event. Ruthie Matthes and Inga Thompson won silver medals in 1990 and 1991.

Armstrong Follows LeMond to the Podium

At Altenrhein, Switzerland, in 1983, twenty-two-year-old Greg LeMond won the first of his two world championship titles. Ten years later Lance Armstrong capped off a career year by winning the 1993 world professional road race in

Oslo. Already that season Armstrong had won the CoreStates USPRO championship and Triple Crown million-dollar prize, and followed with a stage win at the Tour de France.

The men's professional road race was the final event of the competition in Oslo. Cold sheets of rain drenched the riders, and the slippery pavement caused multiple crashes. Lance Armstrong crashed twice, on the 1st and 14th laps. After 6 hours and 17 minutes, a wet but jubilant Armstrong crossed the finish line 10 seconds ahead of a ten-man chase group including Tour de France champion Miguel Indurain. The race started with 171 riders, but only 66 finished. At twenty-one, Armstrong became the third-youngest rider to win the world championship professional road race.

1994 to 2006

By 1994 American racers were no longer overlooked in international competition. USCF's director of coaching, Chris Carmichael, hired coaches and introduced training programs that improved the American teams' competitive performances. Craig Griffin, the national endurance track coach recruited from New Zealand, instituted a training program that resulted in the first-ever team pursuit medal. Marty Nothstein, America's best sprinter, reached higher levels under the guidance of Andrzej Bek, a bronze medalist for the Polish Olympic team. After Henny Top came on board in 1991, the women's team accumulated thirteen medals in the next two years, including four golds. At the 1994 world track championships in Palermo, Italy, the team finished 3rd in the medal standings, winning two golds, two silvers, and a bronze. Marty Nothstein became the first American to win a gold medal in the

keirin (a specialized form of motorcycle-paced track racing popularized in Japan) and match sprint in the same world championship event. His sprint gold medal was the first for the United States in eighty-two years. (Donald McDougall won the amateur title and Frank Kramer the professional title in 1912.) Nothstein and Gibby Hatton, his coach, are the only Americans to win keirin medals at world championship events.

The United States' 4,000-meter pursuit team also delivered a record-breaking race. Carl Sundquist, Mariano Friedick, Adam Laurent, and Dirk Copeland stunned the prerace favorite Australians and won the silver medal (Germany took gold). Both the American and Australian teams appeared to cross the finish line simultaneously. The teams had to endure an hour-long delay before the results of the photo finish were announced. The silver medal marked the first team pursuit medal for the Americans.

The results from the 1997 world championships in San Sebastian, Spain, were mixed. For the third consecutive year, the United States failed to win a medal in the road race. Already that year Marty Nothstein had won five world cup titles and three national titles. At the start of the world championships, he was the number-one-ranked sprinter. In Spain he became the first American to win medals in five consecutive world championships. But after winning world titles in the keirin in 1994 and 1996, Nothstein only managed a bronze in 1997.

At the 2003 UCI road world championships in Hamilton, Canada, the United States' road team (Fred Rodriguez, George Hincapie, Mark McCormack, Floyd Landis, Levi Leipheimer, Chris Horner, and Bobby Julich) failed to live up to its own expectations. With 10 kilometers remaining in the race, the American riders, who had lost Bobby Julich to a mechanical problem, were still in contention. When the lead group attacked and headed for the finish, they could not respond. Rodriguez finished in 18th place. George Hincapie finished 37th, Floyd Landis 60th, and Chris Horner 76th.

In 2005 the United States hosted the UCI Track Cycling World Championships for the first time since 1986. The track competition was held at the ADT Event Center in Carson, California. on March 24 to 27. The seventy-eight-rider field included seven members of the 2004 American Olympic cycling team.

Marty Nothstein, America's most successful track sprinter, competed in a world championship for the last time in 2005. His racing resume included an Olympic gold and silver medal, three world championships, eight world championship medals, four Pan American gold medals, seventeen world cup victories, and thirty-five U.S. national championships. In 1994 Nothstein became the first American to win a world championship sprint title in ninety years. He also won a world championship in the keirin the same year. But Nothstein's last world championship did not end on a high note. His 10th-place finish in the Madison, combined with Erin Mirabella's 13th-place finish in the women's point race, illuminated the struggles the American track team was experiencing.

Once on the cusp of becoming a perennial international force, the track team has faltered in recent years. It has been hindered because it has operated without a full-time endurance coach and adequate financial support. Jennie Reed's bronze medal in the women's keirin was the only top-three finish for the 2004 American track team. At the 2005 world track championships in Carson, California, the American team could not capitalize on its home-field advantage. The championships ended without a single medal going to an American. Jennie Reed's 6th place in the keirin was the Americans' best showing.

The 2005 world championship road races were held in Madrid, Spain. Fred Rodriguez and his American teammates failed to respond to a lead pack breakaway, and Rodriguez finished in a pack 25 seconds behind the winner, Tom Boonen of Belgium. American women had better success, with three riders in the top ten of the individual time trial. Kristin Armstrong captured the bronze medal while Amber Neben and Christine Thorburn followed in 5th and 8th places.

After eleven years of close calls, disappointments, and unfulfilled expectations, Sarah Hammer brought the American team back to the top step of the winner's podium. On the first day of the 2006 UCI Track Cycling World Championships in Bordeaux, France, Hammer defeated Olga Slyusareva of Russia to win the gold medal in the individual pursuit. Hammer's performance earned the first American gold medal since Marty Nothstein's keirin title in 1996. She also became the first American woman to win the event since Rebecca Twigg took the pursuit title in 1995.

The Numbers Skyrocket

Mirroring the growth in bicycle sales across the United States, Amateur Bicycle League of America registrations reached 8,621 in 1973, a 70 percent increase from 1972. Senior men paid $5.00 for an annual license, women and juniors $3.00. With more than 1,000 letters arriving each week, the ABLA established an office address and hired a part-time clerk to handle the inquiries.

In 1973, for the first time in its fifty-three-year history, the Amateur Bicycle League of America created national road and track teams. The ABLA's international committee selected the riders. John Howard, John Allis, Rick Ball, Emile Waldteufel, Wayne Stetina, Mike Neel, and Ron Skarin were named to the road team. Gary Campbell, Steve Woznick, Dave Chauner, Bob Phillips, Roger Young, Ralph Therrio, and Jeff Spencer were selected for the first track-specific team. Led by Wayne Stetina, the American team won the Tour de L'Estrie stage race in Canada. Stetina, who won the National Prestige title by winning four consecutive U.S. Bicycling Classic events, would soon replace Howard as the dominant road racer with a run of national championship titles.

Ernie Seubert, the ABLA's president, called the 1973 national championships "possibly the best in the history of the League." More than 400 road riders competed in Milwaukee. The national championships were cosponsored by the Bicycle Institute of America and The Travelers Insurance Companies. The additional financial support from Travelers allowed the League to increase the amount of expense money each racer received.

Otto Wenz and the Milwaukee Wheelmen hosted the event for the second consecutive year, paying the ABLA $1,000 to bring the event back to the Midwest. The road races were held on a 4-mile loop through downtown Milwaukee, Lake Park, and along the Lake Michigan Parkway.

In the senior road championship race, three-time Olympian John Allis led a breakaway with 20 laps to go. At the halfway point, 5 laps later, the lead group of fourteen riders had created a 60-second gap over the main field. In the last 300 yards, Greg Meeker and Bob Schneider held a slight lead. Rick Ball sprinted past Schneider on his right, while John Howard did the same on the left and finished a wheel length ahead of Schneider to win his second national title. Howard finished the 120-mile course in 4:45:50, averaging 25.9 mph.

Although the Trexlertown Velodrome was the center of attention in the late 1970s, in the early '70s many national track championships were contested on this track in Northbrook, Illinois. The 1974 national track champions include (left to right) Steve Woznick, Sue Novara, Dana Scruggs, Ralph Therrio, Gibby Hatton, Bruce Donaghy, Amy Johnson, and Italo Bastianelli.

Almost the same number of track riders went to the twelve-year-old Northbrook Velodrome in Illinois to race for fifteen stars-and-stripes jerseys. Fans were charged $1.00 for admission and filled the stands for all events. The record number of competitors required numerous heats to narrow the field. Officials discussed plans to add qualifying limits in the next year.

Sheila Young dominated the women's sprint, beating Sue Novara, the defending champion, for the 1973 title. Sheila's brother Roger won the men's national sprint championship over Jack Disney. Steve Woznick won his second national championship in the kilometer.

The Wolverine Cycling Club of Detroit, Michigan, dominated the 1973 championships. Wolverine riders, including Sheila Young, won six of the seventeen national championship events. Sisters Eileen and Carole Brenneman of Michigan finished 1st and 2nd in the 32-mile women's road race.

America's steady improvement on the international racing scene took another step forward in 1973 when Mike Maaranan and Bill Lambert attended a two-week course offered by the Union Cycliste Internationale. The pair graduated in the top third of their class and became America's first two international commissaries, qualified to officiate at Olympic and world championship events.

In late 1973, four riders sponsored by California's Montrose Cycle Club became the first American team to finish the longest amateur stage race in the world. Team manager Tom Snedden and mechanic Augustus Pintado supported Charlie Dixon, Dan Nall, Laurie Schmidtke, and Rich Hammen. The team received a $100 food allotment from ABLA officials.

Informed that the 1973 Tour of Mexico would be a six-stage event, the team was surprised to read a local newspaper announcing a twelve-day, 1,100-mile race. The Montrose team finished 14th of 22 teams entered and all four riders completed the race. Rich Hammen finished 43rd out of 82 starting riders.

CHAPTER THREE

The New Professionals

The Shimano Team

IN MAY 1974 SHIMANO, a Japanese bicycle parts company, announced plans to financially support American racing. The company planned to send eight professionals to compete in the Montreal world championships and offered to support the riders as they trained for the event. Shimano thus became the largest supporter of American racing.

Shimano already sponsored three European teams and was involved with the U.S. Grand Prix. Bob Hansing, in Shimano's West Coast office, reported that the company was concerned about the state of professional racing after the failure of the Los Angeles and Detroit six-day races in 1973.

Jack Simes, John Vande Velde, Skip Cutting, Tim Mountford, Doug Downer, Tom Sneddon, Bill Kund, and Clif Halsey were named to the first Shimano professional team. Each of the first group of competitors had extensive racing experience and credentials. Mountford was the national sprint champion for amateurs in 1969. As an amateur, Cutting won more than one hundred medals in international meets. In 1974 Vande Velde held the American record in the 4,000-meter at 4:53.2, and he was a member of the American four-man 4,000-meter pursuit team.

Simes Wins the National Professional Championship

In 1974 the Shimano riders competed for the first national professional championship in almost forty years. The three-race series began in June and ended on August 7 in Northbrook, Illinois. Competition was fierce and financial incentives kept the racing at a high level. The 1st-place rider in each event received $600, 2nd place $500. Jackie Simes, five-time amateur national champion, won the first round of the Shimano

National Professional Championship at the Encino Velodrome in California on June 22, 1974. Simes also finished 1st at the second race in Kenosha, Wisconsin, and at the finale in Northbrook.

Simes won the first U.S. national professional championship since 1936, when Bill Honeman held the title. At the end of the Northbrook race, Honeman presented Simes with a bouquet of flowers and a check for $600.

In 1975 Shimano continued its sponsorship of American professional riders by signing Skip Cutting, Tom Sneddon, and Clif Halsey to three-year contracts. Jack Simes and Bill Kund were also offered contracts, to create a five-man team that was eligible to enter European races.

The Rebirth of Track Racing

 At the turn of the twentieth century, track racing was one of the most popular sporting events in the United States. By the peak of its popularity in the 1920s and 30s, the best racers of the day were more popular and earned more money than Babe Ruth.

Velodrome racing waned when two World Wars pulled the country's attention away from sporting endeavors. While major league baseball returned and thrived, bicycle track racing could not rekindle its position as the top spectator sport in the United States. Hampered by the cost of building and maintaining velodromes, track cycling could not attract sustained corporate support. Racing's governing bodies, first the United States Cycling Federation, then USA Cycling, put track cycling far down the list of funding and coaching priorities.

For forty years track racing struggled to draw consistent corporate support and to explain often-confusing track disciplines to spectators who were following road events. American results in international and Olympic track racing competitions reflected the second-tier status track racers received at home. After a strong beginning, the story of American track racing is filled with choreographed press conferences proudly announcing a new race series or event that would "reinvigorate the sport."

In the mid-1970s two new velodromes and several highly publicized domestic and international track-racing events were launched to bring riders and spectators back to the high-banked tracks.

The Dick Lane Velodrome officially opened on Sunday, March 23, 1975, in East Point, Georgia. Promoter Dave Chauner spent the month of March holding racing clinics and training officials to operate the new $200,000 facility. The inaugural event, called the Pepsi-Cola Meet of Champions, pitted Steve Woznick, the U.S. amateur sprint champion, against Jackie Simes, the U.S. professional champion. Two thousand spectators came to the only operating velodrome in the southeast portion of the

United States to watch Woznick and Simes. The racers split the first two heats and Woznick came from behind to edge Simes by a few inches at the finish to take the third heat and the overall win.

Chauner stepped away from his promoter's duties and joined partner Roger Young in the 100-lap Madison against the team of Simes and Woznick. With 20 laps left in the race, an exploding tire shocked the crowd of spectators. Losing control, Simes and Woznick collided, slammed to the track, and slid in a tangle of bikes and bodies toward the infield. Woznick recovered but Simes stayed down, a growing puddle of blood surrounding his head. An ambulance crew responded, and fortunately his injuries were limited to bruises and a deep cut on his scalp.

In May 1975 the Amateur Bicycle League of America announced a nine-race series called the U.S. Open Track Series. Racers competed for points in 750-, 1,500-, and 7,500-meter disciplines. The ABLA awarded $1,200 in U.S. savings bonds to the series winners.

Bob Rodale, publisher of *Prevention* magazine, donated land and financial resources in 1974 to begin building the Trexlertown Velodrome of Lehigh Valley, Pennsylvania. Jackie Simes received a salary from Rodale Press to serve as the velodrome's first director. The $400,000 track, the twelfth in the country, was called the most complete track facility in the United States. Constructed to Union Cycliste Internationale (UCI) specifications, the 23-foot-wide track was 333⅓ meters long with 27-degree banks. The track used a new form of concrete called Chem-Comp that reduced the number of seams required in track construction. Instead of seams every 4 meters, the new material allowed the builder to install

track sections 7 meters wide and 21 meters long before a seam was required.

Allen Bell, a forty-two-year-old professional rider and a board member of the United States Cycling Federation (the new name for the Amateur Bicycle League of America), won the first senior sprint held at the Trexlertown track.

David Chauner and Jack Simes became partners in Omni-Sports, a company formed to operate the Trexlertown Velodrome and promote cycling events. In July 1976 Rodale Press and Omni-Sports hosted the three-day North American championships at Trexlertown Velodrome. The promoters rented a bus and recruited track racers who were attending the 1976 Montreal Olympics. Riders from Turkey, Australia, Chile, Czechoslovakia, Great Britain, and Trinidad endured an eleven-hour bus ride from Canada to Lehigh Valley in Pennsylvania.

A capacity crowd of 4,200 purchased $2.50 tickets to watch the races on the first day. One of the event highlights was the team pursuit. Promoted as the United States versus the world, the American team of John Vande Velde, Mike Walters, Paul Deem, and Ron Skarin beat a hastily assembled team of riders from Great Britain, Australia, and Trinidad. The 50-kilometer North American Madison championship was the final event. Ron Skarin and Gerry Ash finished 2nd and John Vande Velde and Paul Deem 3rd. The international riders returned by bus to Montreal the next day.

The track-building boom continued, and on September 15, 1977, the nation's fifteenth track opened in Shakopee, Minnesota, on the outskirts of the Twin Cities. Former six-day racer Cecil Behringer and his partner Bill Laurn purchased the portable track used in the unsuccessful 1973 Detroit six-day race and spent $500,000 to install it as a permanent facility.

The first event, a 20-lap scratch race, provided a premonition for the future of the Shakopee track. Butch Stinton lost his lead when his front wheel slipped out from under him. Slick green epoxy paint applied to the boards the day before the opening was credited with causing the accident. The steep 58-degree banks on the turns of the 200-meter course were unpopular with track racers.

Back at Trexlertown, the 1977 season ended with the international Madison championship on September 10 and 11. Seven foreign riders and twenty-one American riders competed in two-man teams. An Italian team won and American riders finished on the 2nd- and 3rd-place teams.

Rodale continued to provide financial support for events, but revenue from other sources was tenuous. In 1976, when the Olympic team made an appearance, twenty-one billboards surrounding the track were sold to advertisers. A year later none were sold, and increased ticket prices cut attendance. Though hampered by a lack of consistent income, the Trexlertown Velodrome was still the center of track racing.

In a bridge from one era to the next, Trexlertown awarded the Goullet Trophy to the velodrome's most successful rider. Alf Goullet, a champion six-day and track racer from 1900 to 1930, sponsored the award. In 1977 thirty-year-old Jerry Ash, nicknamed the "Gentle Giant," received the trophy and a $500 gift certificate.

In 1978 Robert Rodale negotiated a sponsorship package with the Shaklee Corporation. Shaklee donated $50,000 in cash and $20,000 in goods and services to become the primary sponsor of the

1978 junior world championships. Shaklee also provided $10,000 for souvenir items that the USCF sold for profit. The event was the first world cycling championship held in the United States since 1912. Shaklee also hired Omni-Sports as its agent to operate the event. The Shaklee contract was the first major source of income for Omni-Sports.

Simes and Chauner left Trexlertown at the end of 1978 to focus their full attention on their Omni-Sports promotion business, which had secured a $15,000 sponsorship for a team of four track riders: Jerry Ash, Leigh Barczewski, Dave Grylls, and Bruce Donaghy. In 1979 the team raced for the Panasonic-Shimano Cup, awarded to the top individual and team based on points earned in three domestic events.

Honoring Major Taylor

One of the last major track facilities opened in 1982 in Indianapolis. The city's first track, called the Newby Oval, was closed when the track's owners shifted their business interests to automobile racing at the Indianapolis Motor Speedway. The 333-meter Major Taylor Velodrome opened on July 15, 1982. Mrs. Sydney Taylor, Major Taylor's daughter, received a key to the city from Mayor William Hudnut III.

Roger Young, a former 7-Eleven rider, was named track director of the new track. The velodrome opened with the best riders in the country competing in the National Sports Festival. Steve Hegg, Leonard Nitz, Mark Gorski, Davis Phinney, and Rebecca Twigg came to Indianapolis. In the next twenty years, all five riders would go on to become great track and road racers of their generation.

The first gold medal was awarded to eighteen-year-old Steve Hegg. The future

Olympic medalist recorded his personal best—and the fastest time in the nation—finishing the kilometer time trial in 1:09.38. Hegg defeated Leonard Nitz by just 0.01 seconds. A state-of-the-art Omega photo timing system measured the margin. The tables turned when Dave Grylls narrowly defeated Hegg in the pursuit.

Mark Gorski set an American record, winning the 200-meter in 11.08. Les Barczewski took the silver and Nelson Vails the bronze. Davis Phinney and Rebecca Twigg won the 100-kilometer road races held in Eagle Creek Park.

The Olympic Velodrome

Preparations for the 1984 Los Angeles Olympics played a role in sustaining velodrome racing in the early 1980s. At the July 8, 1982, opening ceremonies, Los Angeles mayor Tom Bradley called the $3 million facility "a Velodream." The Southland Corporation, owner of the 7-Eleven chain of convenience stores, covered the construction costs as part of a sponsorship agreement with the U.S. Olympic Committee.

The 7-Eleven/Bicycling Grand Prix opened the Olympic velodrome's competitive history on July 8 and 9, 1982. Eric Heiden and Sheila Young-Ochowicz rode the first official laps. Cosponsored by SunTour, the Grand Prix was the culmination of a six-event qualifying series. Elite racers from Canada and Japan were invited to race against the American team and vie for $1,000 1st-place prizes for each of four events. Mark Gorski, Leonard Nitz, Brent Emery, and Dave Grylls were gold medal winners.

The 7-Eleven/Bicycling Grand Prix continued for two more years. 7-Eleven and Murray Bicycles sponsored two major teams of track riders to train and gain racing experience. The ultimate goal was Olympic gold.

In 1984, with the Soviet Union and other Eastern Bloc countries boycotting the Los Angeles Games, American track racers excelled in individual and team disciplines. Finishing 1st and 2nd, Mark Gorski and Nelson Vails, an ex-bicycle messenger from New York City, won the first American medals in the match sprint event.* In the individual pursuit Steve Hegg and Leonard Nitz brought home another pair of gold and silver medals. Hegg, Nitz, Brent Emery, and Pat McDonough won the silver medal in the team pursuit. Davis Phinney, Ron Kiefel, Andy Weaver, and Roy Knickman finished 3rd in the four-man team time trial.

Despite the success, 7-Eleven canceled the track series and shifted its financial support to road racing.

The Sundance Grand Prix

Although 7-Eleven ended its support, other companies were drawn to the patriotic zeal generated by the cycling team's Olympic performance. In the glow of Olympic success, gold medal winners Connie Paraskevin-Young and Mark Gorski signed with ProServ, a Washington, D.C. sports marketing firm. In 1988 the Sundance Juice Sparkler Grand Prix of Cycling debuted, organized by Gorski, Paraskevin-Young, and ProServ agent Steve Disson. The six-event series provided a competitive venue for track racers to compete for $75,000 in prize money. Disson produced six one-hour racing programs for ESPN, and four were broadcast.

The first year of the series included match sprints, points races, and pursuit events for men and women. At the series final in Los Angeles, Connie Paraskevin-Young won all six events. Mark Gorski

*Both Gorski and Vails were beaten on a regular basis by the dominant sprinter of the time, East German Lutz Hesslich.

faced fellow American and Pan American gold medalist Ken Carpenter and Canadian Olympian Curt Hartnett. Like Paraskevin-Young, Gorski won the first series.

In 1988 Adweek gave the Sundance Grand Prix promotion its "Best Event Marketing" award. The series made heroes of track riders and attracted interest from corporate sponsors like DuPont Lycra, Sundance, and Wheaties.

One year later the series was canceled. Stroh's, the parent company of Sundance, faced financial difficulties and sold the division to Texas-based Guinness. The new cost-cutting owners canceled all marketing programs including the Juice Sparkler Grand Prix. After losing the title sponsor, ProServ could not deliver the television coverage promised to the other supporting sponsors. DuPont withdrew support for Team Lycra, a top track development team.

Facing the Soviets

Without an ongoing series, track promoters focused on special events. In late 1988 the American team faced the Soviet Union for the first time in face-to-face competition. Promoted by ProServ, the USA/USSR Michelob Challenge was held on October 3 and 4 at the Olympic Velodrome in Carson, California. With boycotts in the 1980 and 1984 Olympics keeping the teams apart, the Challenge was filled with anticipation. Two earthquakes—one on the morning of the event—and 108-degree heat added more drama.

Guintaustus Umaras and Erika Salumiaee, the reigning world sprint champions, led the Soviet team. The three women and eleven men held six world championship titles. Eddie Borysewicz, the coach of the American team, called the

Soviets "the best track team in the world."

The American team included Pan Am Games sprint gold medalist Ken Carpenter and the gold medal pursuit team of Nitz, Carl Sundquist, David Brinton, Dave Lettieri, and Mike McCarthy. National sprint champion Scott Berryman, pursuit champion Rebecca Twigg-Whitehead, Nelson Vails, and two-time junior world champion Janie Eickhoff also competed. Mark Gorski and Connie Paraskevin-Young were too ill to compete.

More than 8,000 fans attended the two-day, three-session event. Facing some of the best track racers in the world, the American team held their own. Ken Carpenter and Scott Berryman defeated their Soviet opponents in the match sprint. In the all-American final, Carpenter beat Berryman in two of three heats. In the kilometer Rebecca Twigg-Whitehead set a new world record and upset Erica Salumiaee, the reigning world record holder. She beat her longtime rival by 1.89 seconds. Twigg-Whitehead finished 12 seconds ahead of Ludmilla Kutova to defend her world champion pursuit jersey. Her efforts kept the score close, but when the USA/USSR Michelob Challenge ended on Sunday afternoon, the American team trailed the Soviets by 14 points. The Soviets took the title 74-60.

1989 NEC World Cycling Invitational

A year later, at the $100,000 1989 NEC World Cycling Invitation, the American team raced its way to win the richest prize purse in track history to date. Teams from the Soviet Union, Italy, Australia, Canada, Denmark, France, and Japan competed at the 7-Eleven Olympic Velodrome in Carson, California. Points were awarded in twenty-six events over three racing sessions. Officials from NEC, the Japanese title sponsor, paid Greg LeMond, the 1989 Tour de France winner, an appearance fee and flew him and his wife to California in a chartered plane.

Nineteen-year-old Janie Eickhoff finished 1st in four events to lead the Americans to an upset victory. Six teammates split a $25,000 1st-place check. But as lucrative as the event was for the riders, the sponsors failed to achieve the expected attendance numbers and the event lost money.

Another "New" Beginning

In 1993 the USCF signed a four-year multimillion-dollar sponsorship agreement with Electronic Data Systems, a division of General Motors. The contribution from EDS made a significant difference in the USCF's ability to support new programs to develop riders and racers.

A renewed commitment to creating an elite-level track program was one of the immediate benefits of the EDS deal. Roger Young, a member of the 1972 Olympic track team and six-time national track champion, was named director of the track program. Young, national team director Mark Gorski, and athlete/coaching programs director Chris Carmichael developed formal standards for the track program.

Small companies also did their part to support track racing. The Air Products Development Program introduced new riders to track racing at the Lehigh County Velodrome (the new name for the Trexlertown Velodrome) in Pennsylvania. Graduates of the program captured 125 national championship medals. Nicole Reinhart won nine junior national titles and two golds at the Pan Am Games.

In August 1993 the Lehigh Velodrome racing season ended with an award presentation. Marty Nothstein received a certificate for outstanding achievement from Air Products. The twenty-two-year-old sprinter won nine national championships and four senior world championships and became the first graduate of the Air Products program to win a world championship medal.

In 1996 there were twenty active velodromes across the United States. With a formal plan from racing's governing body, the track directors formed the American Track Racing Association in January 1996.

ACTIVE VELODROMES IN 1996

Brian Piccolo, Cooper City, Florida
Dick Lane, East Point, Georgia
Kissena, Lynbrook, New York
Lehigh County, Trexlertown,
    Pennsylvania
Alkek, Houston, Texas
Baton Rouge, Louisiana
Dorias, Royal Oak, Michigan
Edward Rudolph, Northbrook,
    Illinois
Major Taylor, Indianapolis, Indiana
National Sports Center, Blaine,
    Minnesota
St. Louis, St. Louis, Missouri
7-Eleven, Colorado Springs,
    Colorado
Washington Park Bowl, Kenosha,
    Wisconsin
Alpenrose, Gresham, Oregon
Encino, Northridge, California
Hellyer Park, San Jose, California
Marymoor, Seattle, Washington
Olympic Velodrome, Carson,
    California
San Diego Velodrome, San Diego,
    California
Vandedrome, portable

The American Team Cycling League

For the uninitiated, nothing could be simpler than watching racers fly around a velodrome track—the first one across the line wins. In reality, the number of events, disciplines, and race formats left most new spectators confused. In addition, the lack of media exposure was often an obstacle in negotiating sponsorship agreements with marketing executives.

In 1998 Pat McDonough, director of the Lehigh County Velodrome, launched the American Team Cycling League to address both concerns. The four-team league debuted on June 5, 1998. The racing format combined keirin, a form of racing popular in Japan, and a points race. The keirin started with a motorcycle pacing the riders around the track. When the motorcycle moved to the infield, the riders jockeyed for position and points. Think of roller derby or NASCAR with track bicycles.

McDonough recruited experienced and well-known track racers to manage four teams: the Express, Speed Demons, Cyclones, and Thunder. Jack Simes, three-time Olympian and the first director of the Lehigh County Velodrome, managed the Express. Leigh Barczewski, medalist at the 1978 world championships, led the Speed Demons. Bruce Donaghy and Jeff Rutter managed the Cyclones and Thunder. McDonough required at least three Americans on each five- to seven-person team. Only four riders were on the track during the race.

The first championship finals of the American Team Cycling League were held in August 1998. Marty Nothstein, recruited to ride for the Express, scored a league record 62 points to lead his team to a 148–132 victory over the Speed Demons. The Express swept all three events leading up to the championship final. Gil Hatton, John Walrod, Ryan Oelkers, and Joe Masser were other members of the Express.

Track officials estimated that 2,000 spectators attended the championship event. McDonough negotiated broadcast rights with the Outdoor Life Network and the championship event was broadcast on September 3. Former racer Jessie Grieco and 7-Eleven team member Alex Stieda provided commentary and race reports for the network.

The EDS Track Cup

By 1997 the partnership between Electronic Data Systems and USA Cycling was flourishing. The best track riders in the United States and the world had venues, events, and financial support to justify their commitment to the sport. Track-specific teams like Cox Atlanta, Mrs. T's-Lexus, and Team EDS were founded to compete for team and individual honors. EDS hired Marty Nothstein, the top track sprinter in the United States, to work in the company's sports marketing division and race with Team EDS.

In addition to funding a national track series and sponsoring national track championships, EDS also financed the construction of the Superdrome velodrome in Frisco, Texas, a suburb of Dallas. Constructed in less than a year, the 250-meter track was built with marine-grade plywood attached to a stiff steel frame. A state-of-the art Advanced Techdrome time and scoring system tracked racers' progress using radio transponders. The National Sports Center velodrome in Blaine, Minnesota, was the only other 250-meter track in the United States. Existing American velodromes were built to 333-meter specifications, but international riders preferred the shorter 250-meter length.

In March 1999 EDS, one of the largest and most influential corporate sponsors of American track racing, announced major cutbacks in its sports marketing budget. EDS honored its commitment to the EDS Track Cup velodrome race series and three-year-old EDS Track Cup through 2000.

Honored by USA Cycling as the 1998 Track Program Development Club of the Year, Team EDS had a far-reaching impact on American track racing. Elite riders had a world-class facility for training and a high level of international competition to hone their skills before world championship and Olympic events. When Team EDS ended, its riders had tallied sixty-one national championships, twenty-one world championships, and two Olympic medals.

A New Commitment . . . Again

Creating a competitive American track racing team required consistent financial support, new track facilities, organizational commitment, and experienced coaches and trainers. The last fifty years have seen numerous proclamations from governing body officials and entrepreneurial promoters whose grand plans to revive track racing fell far short of success.

In 2004 USA Cycling launched another new track program initiative, this time focusing on coaching and administrative talents. On April 1 Pat McDonough left a fifteen-year tenure as director of the Lehigh County Velodrome to become the national track programs director for USA Cycling.

Shortly after McDonough assumed his new position, the U.S. team competed in the 2004 UCI Track Cycling World Championships in Melbourne, Australia. The American squad returned with a single medal, Jennie Reed's bronze in the keirin. Creating a team that could compete at a world-class level would not happen overnight.

Another piece of the puzzle was added in June 2004 when the first indoor velodrome in the United States opened on the campus of Cal State-Dominguez Hills. Constructed of Siberian pine, the 250-meter wooden track became the centerpiece for world-class competitions and training. The ADT Event Center is part of a 125-acre, $150 million Home Depot–sponsored sports facilities complex. In the first year the ADT Event Center hosted the junior national championships, 2005 UCI World Cup, and the UCI Elite World Championships.

On March 24 to 27, 2005, the United States hosted the UCI Track Cycling World Championships for the first time in nineteen years, at the new ADT Event Center. At the end of the four-day event, Australia led all teams with nine medals. In the competition's final event, Jennie Reed finished 6th in the women's keirin—no American would finish higher in any race discipline.

The 2005 competition was one of Marty Nothstein's last international cycling events. Over his career Nothstein captured Olympic gold and silver medals, seventeen world cup victories, and three world titles. Domestically, Nothstein held thirty-five United States national championships. With his partner, Colby Pearce, Nothstein could only manage a 10th-place finish in the Madison at Dominguez Hills.

Members of the team, frustrated with the lack of resources provided for their discipline, questioned USA Cycling's commitment to the track program. In response, USA Cycling added two experienced coaches. In late March Gary West joined McDonough's staff as head track coach. West had spent ten years with the Australian team and four more with the Japanese Cycling Federation. In November Colby Pearce became USA Cycling's first endurance track coach in five years. Over seventeen years Pearce accumulated nine national championships and held the American 10-kilometer track record.

Los Angeles World Cup

One year after leaving the world cup without a single medal, the track program's initiatives showed dividends. At the UCI track world cup at the same ADT Event Center, the riders for three American teams captured five medals against 200 athletes from thirty-six countries.

Becky Quinn, a member of the U.S. national team, finished 2nd in the women's 20-kilometer points race on the first day of the competition. The next day her teammate Sarah Hammer set a track record in her morning qualifying ride for the pursuit. Hammer faced Colombia's Marie Calle Williams, the 2004 Olympic bronze medal winner, and defeated her by almost 5 seconds. In the men's sprint Michael Blatchford of the U.S. national team finished 3rd, capturing his first world cup medal. Hammer won her second gold and Quinn her second silver when the pair finished 1-2 in the women's scratch race.

Shut out in 2005, riders from the U.S. national team, Team Spike, and TIAA-CREF performed well. After winning five medals, the Americans came very close to bringing home two more. Jennie Reed missed a bronze medal when the

women's keirin ended in a six-rider photo finish. Reed finished 4th. In the team sprint Team Spike riders Stephen Alfred, Ben Barczewski, and Giddeon Massie qualified for the bronze medal race against Australia. The Spike riders fell just short, losing by less than half a second.

Beijing 2008

All eyes are focused on the future. Officials at USA Cycling, directors of professional racing teams, corporate sponsors, and individual riders have marshaled their resources in an attempt to return the United States to Olympic glory on the track.

In September 2005 Biotest Laboratories announced its sponsorship of the Spike Professional Cycling Team. The sponsorship was the first of its kind in modern American track cycling. Two months later team director Bill Ramsey reported Raleigh America had signed a sponsorship contract. Spike team riders Stephen Alfred, Benjamin Barczewski, Michael Blatchford, Andrew Lakatosh, Ryan Luttrell, Giddeon Massie, Becky Quinn, Jennie Reed, and Kevin Suhr used Raleigh Team road bikes and track framesets.

In 2005 the Spike Pro Cycling Team was one of just seven international teams that met UCI regulations. Under the UCI's plan to reform track racing around the world, teams were required to provide health insurance and meet mandatory minimum rider salaries.

The drive to build competitive teams continued in 2006. In April Sarah Hammer captured the women's 3,000-meter individual pursuit title at the 2006 UCI Track Cycling World Championships in Bordeaux, France. Hammer's rainbow jersey represented the first American title since Rebecca Twigg's victory in 1995. Hammer followed her achievement by launching the American Women's Cycling Fund. The OUCH Sports Medical Center of Temecula, California, signed on as the title sponsor of the fund, created to support female riders in their quest for the 2008 Olympics.

In the first decade of the new century, track racing has secured new sources of corporate funding and recruited new riders to the discipline. Whether this is a long-term trend or another in a series of optimistic beginnings and quiet endings will be evident on the final day of the 2008 Beijing Olympics.

The 1970s Bring Changes

Categories and Coaches

The ABLA created a new performance-based ranking system in 1974. Men eighteen to thirty-nine were divided into Category I (national caliber), Category II (those who place in regional races), and Category III (first-year seniors and other riders who have not placed consistently in races). The ranking system was initiated to reduce the size of fields and make them more competitive.

In 1975, after decades of naming coaches based on political connections and cronyism, the ABLA named Oliver Martin, a two-time Olympian and Pan Am team member, as the road coach for the upcoming world championship. Jack Disney, a three-time national champion, was named as track coach. For the first time the coaches were involved in the selection and training of the teams.

Racing against the Clock

The first national 25-mile time trial championship was held in Port Washington, Wisconsin, on July 24, 1975. On the day of the race, high temperatures and gusty winds affected the riders. Wayne Stetina, riding for the Pasadena Follis team, selected a slightly smaller gear ratio than his competitors and finished 1st with a 0.46-second margin. Race officials had to recheck the chronometers to confirm the result. It was Stetina's first national championship jersey. John Howard was 2nd. Jacques Boyer, who returned from France to compete, finished 7th. Ninety-eight seniors competed in the men's event and nineteen finished the time trial in under an hour.

Two months later Raleigh's John Howard captured his fourth national road title.★ The 123-mile, 28-lap race was held on Milwaukee's

*Howard also won the first Red Zinger Classic in 1975.

ROBERT F. GEORGE

In 1975 the top racers came to compete in Milwaukee's Superweek National Championships. Wayne Stetina narrowly defeated John Howard for the national time trial championship.

Lake Michigan Parkway and residential areas. Before the race a debate concerning who was America's best racer pitted Howard against Jacques Boyer, Tom Officer, and Mike Neel, who were riding in Europe. Boyer had compared his own potential with Eddy Merckx.

The first half of the race was marked by solo attacks that the pack reeled in. On the 14th lap a lead group established a 45-second lead when Wayne and Dale Stetina led the pack up a steep climb. At the top of the hill, Alan Kingsbury joined the Stetinas and the trio pushed hard, splitting the pack. The chase group included Jacques Boyer, Tom Schuler, and John Eustice.

By the 18th lap the leaders fell back into the pack and a new attack was launched by George Mount, Tom Officer, and defending national champion John Allis. The thirty-five-rider pack split into several lead and chase groups. With 9 laps to go, Wayne Stetina and George Mount were in the lead. Stetina suffered a flat tire, losing 45 seconds before his support vehicle arrived with a new wheel. Five miles later Stetina's aggressive riding put him back in touch with the pack. At the front John Howard pushed the pace. With 7 laps to go, Howard made his first move of the day. Tom Officer and Marc Thompson responded but Stetina, spent after chasing the pack, fell behind.

On the bell lap Howard claimed his place as the best American racer. When Officer reached down to grab his water bottle on a twisting descent, Howard raced ahead. At the end of the descent, Howard had a 60-meter lead. At the top of the last hill, Howard had a 30-second lead, and he rode the last 500 meters unchallenged.

Internationally, American riders continued to perform at higher levels. John Howard became the first American to win the 1,643-kilometer Tour of Baja California. At the Milk Race in Britain, the American team finished 5th and Dave Chauner captured America's first stage win.

The ABLA Becomes the USCF

At the 1975 annual general meeting of the Amateur Bicycle League of America, officials voted to change the organization's name to the United States Cycling Federation. The August 8, 1975, edition of *Velonews* reported that the name was changed "because the word 'Amateur' was too negative, the word 'League' too archaic and the word 'America' incorrect."

Olympic Dreams on America's Bicentennial

Carl Schutte won the bronze medal at the 1912 Stockholm Olympics. In every Olympic Games between 1912 and 1976, America's best racers failed to win medals. Many of the teams were not even in serious contention. When the performances of American riders improved in the 1970s, hopes were raised for a medal breakthrough.

At the 1976 Olympics in Montreal, Dave Boll, Mike Neel, John Howard, and George Mount competed in the road race competition. All four raced aggressively near the front of the pack. Boll, Neel, and Howard fell out of contention after crashing on wet roads. Twenty-year-old George Mount stayed with the leaders until the final sprint. His 6th place was the finest American performance in sixty-four years. Mount's race received extensive newspaper coverage, and the frustration of past Olympic finishes was replaced with enthusiastic optimism for the future.

In the last half of the '70s, the national road championship became the signature event for American domestic racing. George Mount, enjoying the limelight after his 6th-place finish in the Olympics, joined the field in 1976 and raced against four other Olympians—Wayne

ROBERT F. GEORGE

In 1976 Wayne Stetina outsprinted Dave Boll and Tom Schuler to win the first of his two consecutive national road race championships.

Stetina, Tom Schuler, Dave Boll, and Jim Ochowicz. When he was eighteen, Stetina narrowly lost the 1972 national championship to John Howard. One of the top riders in the country, Stetina faced challenges with flat tires, crashes, and mechanical problems that kept him out of contention for the next three years. In 1976 his time had come. Stetina, Schuler, and Boll led a break the pack couldn't catch. With Boll and Schuler on each side, Stetina made an aggressive, all-or-nothing move and crossed the line just ahead of Boll. Mount finished 18th.

In the second national time trial competition, John Howard, who finished 2nd by less than a half second in the inaugural 25-mile time trial in 1975, captured the 1976 title, beating the 2nd-place rider by more than 1 minute.

John Howard won the 1976 25-mile national time trial championship, setting a new record and beating the 2nd-place rider by more than 1 minute.

The Rising Stars of the Late '70s

In the bicentennial year the USCF had more than 8,000 members, but just 500 were women. Despite the low numbers, American women were making their mark. The 1976 women's national championships marked the start of the career of one of the best female racers in American history, when Connie Carpenter defeated Mary Jane "Miji" Reoch (defending pursuit champion and world championship silver medalist) to win the 3,000-meter pursuit. In her first year of competition, Carpenter moved to a 25-meter lead over Reoch, but the defending champion responded and quickly narrowed the gap. Both riders pushed hard to the line, where officials armed with stopwatches gave Carpenter the victory. The winning margin was measured

ROBERT F. GEORGE

One of the rising stars of the late 1970's, Wayne Stetina (front right) rode with the Cool Gear/Exxon team from 1976 to 1978. In 1977 Stetina won his second national road championship with a 3-minute margin of victory.

in hundredths of seconds. In the road race Carpenter defeated Reoch, the 1971 road champion, to win her second stars-and-stripes jersey of the 1976 competition.

After the 1976 Olympics Mike Neel joined the Italian Magniflex team as a professional rider and finished 10th in the world road championship. Jacques Boyer became the second American rider to compete professionally in Europe when he signed a contract with the French Lejeune-BP team. However, by the end of the decade, there were no professional Americans racing in Europe. European riders and race directors questioned the ability of American riders to compete in European events, and Americans who did want to race in Europe found very little financial support.

The Coming of Eddie B.

In 1977 the USCF hired Eddie Borysewicz to replace Oliver Martin as the national coach. As a member of the Polish national road and track teams, Borysewicz won four national titles. He coached the Polish national team for a decade before moving to the United States.

Borysewicz, known as "Eddie B.," started quickly as the USCF's first paid full-time coach. The first-ever USCF rider clinic was held in Miami in January 1978. Thirty-two riders attended, and Borysewicz gave each rider on-the-bike critiques and individual instruction on riding positions. Eddie B. moved across the country, meeting riders and introducing them to his approach to racing.

Over the next twelve years, Eddie B. led a renaissance in American bicycle racing. Under his leadership, American racers captured fifteen Pan American medals, thirty world championship medals, and nine Olympic medals. When he left the USCF in 1988, Borysewicz moved to professional racing and managed the Subaru-Montgomery team that evolved into the U.S. Postal Service team.

ROBERT F. GEORGE

In 1977 Polish emigrant Eddie Borysewicz became the United States Cycling Federation's first paid full-time coach. When he resigned twelve years later, American racers had captured fifteen Pan American medals, thirty world championship medals, and nine Olympic medals.

American Women Take on the Best

For three days in early April 1978, the best women racers from ten countries were in Tucson, Arizona, to compete. The time trial that opened the Schlitz Light Women's International featured 102 women, including 6 past and present world champions. Top racers from Holland, Sweden, France, Canada, Italy, Switzerland, Belgium, Mexico, and Norway came to race against two American national teams and four club teams. Sponsored by Schlitz, the American team of Connie Carpenter, Miji Reoch, Jane Buyny, and Hannah North showed the world that American women could compete at the highest level.

Tracy Lea, a solo rider with PBC/Hill/Peugeot, was the first rider on the 10-kilometer time trial course. Her time of 13:09 put her in 14th place overall, the best finish for a rider competing without a team.

Connie Carpenter won the time trial in 12:23, 10 seconds faster then Holland's Keetie van Oosten-Hage.

The next stage was a criterium. Promoter K. K. Hall and the Tucson Wheelmen created a 50-kilometer course that challenged the riders. Keetie van Oosten-Hage, winner of twenty national championships in Holland, used her teammates to control the pace and the race. At the instruction of Eddie Borysewicz, coach of the American team, Connie Carpenter, Miji Reoch, Jane Buyny, and Carey Peterson kept pace with the lead pack. With 4 laps remaining, a brief

The 1978 Schlitz Light International race started with 102 women from ten countries, the largest field in the history of women's racing.

rain shower cooled the riders and created slippery road conditions. Reoch was leading Carpenter and a lead pack of thirty riders through a corner when, an instant later, half the pack was sliding across the road.

Between 1971 and 1980, Mary Jane "Miji" Reoch won nine national road and track championships.

Carpenter, back on her bike, was more than a half lap behind the leaders. Urged on by the cheering spectators, Carpenter moved back into contention but could not reach the leaders before the finish line. She finished 3rd behind teammate Betsy King.

The final stage was an 80-kilometer road race. Carpenter and leader van Oosten-Hage started the third stage 2 seconds apart in the general classification. Once again a crash affected the outcome. Van

Oosten–Hage attacked on the last corner of the course; Carpenter countered and entered the corner in an aggressive sprint. Crossing a seam in the road, she went down hard. She recovered and finished the road race in 8th place, losing an opportunity to pass van Oosten–Hage for the overall victory.

Carpenter finished the event in 2nd place, 10 seconds behind van Oosten–Hage. Although disappointed by the individual silver, Carpenter led her teammates to a decisive 10-minute victory in the team competition. American women had defeated the best in the world.

A New American Champion on the Horizon

By 1977 John Howard was moving away from full-time racing to concentrate on business opportunities. Picking and choosing which events to enter, Howard raced in the Tour of San Joaquin on April 9 and 10.

The father-and-son team of Bob and Greg LeMond were also in the field. Sixteen-year-old Greg needed special permission from race director Harry Morton to compete against seventy-five senior riders.

Twenty-two miles into the first day's race, twenty-five riders broke away from the pack. Greg LeMond and Dan Nall attacked the lead group and broke away. Howard matched the break, and when Nall faded, LeMond and Howard continued on, increasing their lead to 1:30. At the finish Howard beat LeMond by 6 seconds. The pair finished the second-stage 10-mile time trial in the same order. On Sunday Howard won the 68-mile road stage and finished 1st in the tour.

ROBERT F. GEORGE

Greg LeMond captured the attention of bicycle racing fans as early as 1977 when he won the first of two national junior road championships.

Greg LeMond finished 2nd in his first major senior-class race. This young rider with a bright future had pressed Howard, winner of three national road championships.

One year later LeMond took another step in the transition from one generation to the next. On May 21, 1978, senior road champion Wayne Stetina and LeMond, the reigning junior champion, broke away from the pack in the Cat's Hill Criterium in Los Gatos, California. From the halfway point to the finish, America's past and future rode side by side. At the time Stetina was the reigning Red Zinger Classic champion and the 1976 and 1977 U.S. national road champion. On the last lap twenty-four-year-old Stetina forged ahead of LeMond, but the race didn't finish in that order. LeMond crossed the finish line a bike length ahead. At the 1978 junior world championships, LeMond finished 9th in the road race and won the bronze medal in the 70-kilometer team time trial with Greg Demgen, Jeff Bradley, and Ron Kiefel.

It's Miller Time

During the 1973-74 racing season, Miller Brewing sponsored a race series called the Miller High Life Classics. Four years later Miller became one of American cycling's biggest supporters.

In a December 13, 1978, news conference, the Miller Brewing Company announced the largest corporate sponsorship in the history of U.S. amateur or professional bicycle racing. Managed under the company's Lowenbrau brand, the $100,000 sponsorship agreement supported the men's and women's national teams, the national championships, and a series of international grand prix events.

The additional funds allowed the USCF to send American teams to events in Mexico and Europe, including the world cycling championships in the Netherlands. The USCF had previously sent teams but often could not afford to pay travel expenses for coaches and support staff. A small but important benefit of the sponsorship improved American riders' chances in international events: With a budget expanded by the Lowenbrau sponsorship, American riders competing at the Pan American Games and other Central American events could bring along their own supply of bottled water and avoid the intestinal challenges that hampered previous teams. Individual racers did not receive salaries or bonus payments. The Lowenbrau International Grand

Prix races, launched to give domestic riders experience against elite international racers, were held in New York's Central Park, Washington, D.C., Milwaukee, and Philadelphia.

CHAPTER FOUR

The Rise of Sponsorship

The Decade of Firsts

IN 1979 THE USCF MOVED its headquarters from New York City to a four-room office suite at the United States Olympic complex in Colorado Springs, and hired Mary Cappy as the Federation's first full-time paid employee. The USCF received an $80,000 grant from the U.S. Olympic Committee (USOC) and dedicated $14,000 for the track program. In 1980 the USCF had an annual budget approaching $250,000. Fewer than ten full-time employees were needed to manage the organization's affairs. By the end of the decade, the USCF had 33,155 members, twenty-five full-time staffers, and a budget of more than $3 million.

The 1980s could be called the decade of "firsts" for American bicycle racing. In the ten-year span, American men and women collected their first Olympic gold medals, their first world road race championship, their first Giro d'Italia victory, and their first and second Tour de France victories. Year by year, across international and domestic events, American racers added their names to the record books. For the first time since the turn of the century, American racers stood shoulder to shoulder with the best riders and teams in the world. Greg LeMond, Davis Phinney, Andy Hampsten, and the 7-Eleven and Coors Light professional teams captured the attention of hard-core enthusiasts and introduced racing to casual fans.

A series of new races raised the competitive standing of American racers. Eddie Borysewicz launched the Tour of Texas as a spring training camp to prepare the U.S. national team for international competition. Races like the Redlands Classic and Tour of the Americas attracted the best professional racers in the world. American teams like 7-Eleven and Coors Light tested their abilities against the Russian national team and the best teams from across Europe.

After the resurgence of bicycle racing in America in the 1970s, other landmark events shaped the future of domestic, professional, and international racing in the following decade. A long fight for control over professional racing dominated the attention of the USCF throughout the 1980s.

Domestically, the USCF's formal steps to build a team capable of winning Olympic gold achieved its objective in 1984. By winning nine medals on home turf, American cyclists became the media darlings of the sports pages. The discovery that some members of the team had participated in blood doping caused a scandal, but the euphoria was scarcely dampened by the controversy.

The thrill of the Olympic victories was tempered by the challenge of staying at the top of international competition. In 1986 the world championships were held in the United States for the first time since 1912. At the 1986 worlds and at the Olympics two years later, American racers failed to match the historic levels set in Los Angeles.

 ## The Tour of Texas

 In 1981 Eddie Borysewicz, the national coaching director of the USCF, asked Richard DeGarmo to create a spring training camp event for the thirty-eight riders on the national team. At the time DeGarmo also served as USCF's president. In 1982 Puma offered financial support for Eddie B.'s camp, which was officially called the Spring Texas Tour. A separate women's race started the following year.

As the race became more popular and expensive to manage, national sponsors stepped in: first Frito-Lay in 1983, followed by Beatrice Foods from 1985 to 1986. Branders Jeans of Fort Worth, Texas became the title sponsor after Beatrice walked away in 1986. Branders signed the contract two months before the event was scheduled to start.

Throughout its history, the Tour of Texas marked the traditional start of the international racing season and attracted teams from Holland, Norway, Great Britain, the Soviet Union, Canada, West Germany, and Australia.

The 7-Eleven team captured both the men's and women's individual honors in 1987. Jeff Pierce took the leader's jersey on the prologue and defended it to the end of the race. Bunki Bankaitis-Davis also won the opening prologue. She lost the leader's jersey on the second stage but recaptured it by winning the third-stage time trial and the road race.

In 1989 a new stage race format was introduced that attracted eighty women and 125 men from sixteen countries. The tour drew America's best teams. On the men's side 7-Eleven, Coors Light, Celestial Seasonings, Wheaties-Schwinn,

ROBERT F. GEORGE

Andy Hampsten and Leonard Nitz lead a training ride at the 1982 Tour of Texas training camp.

Montgomery-Avenir, and Crest each fielded two five-man teams. Reebok, Shaklee, Team Carey, and IME also fielded teams. Six women's teams competed: Lowrey's, 7-Eleven, Team Lycra, Campagnolo-Michelin, Weight Watchers, and Subaru. The top ten women represented seven different teams.

The tightly contested ten-day event ended with a 75-minute timed criterium in Austin's Zilker Park, where Alex Stieda (7-Eleven) overtook the leader, Alexi Grewal (Coors Light), to win his second consecutive Branders Tour of Texas. It was the fifth straight year that a rider from 7-Eleven had finished 1st. Catherine Marshal, an eighteen-year-old French junior world champion, took the lead on the second day and kept it to the end. Americans Susan Elias and Jeanne Golay finished 2nd and 3rd.

The 1990 race centered on an intense competition between Coors Light and 7-Eleven. Chris Huber of Coors Light won the Tour's prologue by a narrow 2-second margin. Supported by his teammates and a race format that did not include time bonuses, Huber kept the leader's jersey until the end of the race, nine days later. The final general classification was so close that the top eleven riders were within 12 seconds of the leader. The highly anticipated fight between Coors Light and 7-Eleven ended with a surprise—the starting field of 156 included 121 amateurs who contributed to pack sprint finishes on every stage. In the end the AC Pinarello team finished 1st.

The Tour of Texas was canceled in 1991 after Branders Jeans asked to be released from its three-year contract. A falling economy hampered efforts to find a new sponsor. At one time the Tour of Texas was considered one of the top three men's events on the racing calendar. Only the Tour DuPont and Tour of the Americas ranked higher. The Tour was also considered a top international-caliber women's race.

The Sponsorship Game

Throughout the 1980s corporate sponsorships played a significant role in amateur and professional racing. From Fortune 500 companies that wanted to associate their brands with winning cyclists to small component suppliers looking for ways to introduce their products, riders' jerseys, support vehicles, and event banners were festooned with corporate logos.

The list of sponsors changed year to year as budgets shifted and marketing priorities changed. In some cases teams and events simply changed the name of the title sponsor and continued. In others, the events ended abruptly when promoters failed to find new sponsors.

In February 1982 Schwinn announced that it was dropping its sponsorship of the pro-am 7-Eleven team, after just one season. The previous season Schwinn had split the expenses with the Southland Corporation. The partners also shared the costs of a team manager, mechanic, and transportation. Schwinn's bill for the February to October period exceeded $100,000. The company remained a strong supporter of bicycle racing but decided to spread its financial backing to six cycling teams across the country.

Southland Corporation's sponsorship of the 7-Eleven team remained the largest in racing. During the same period AMF, Panasonic, and Austro-Daimler discontinued their support of racing teams.

The 7-Eleven Bicycle Racing Team

Peter Ueberroth and the Los Angeles Olympic Organizing Committee brought a different approach to preparing for the 1984 Games. For the first time corporate sponsorships were used to defray the costs of building facilities and supporting America's athletes.

In 1981 the Southland Corporation, parent company of the 7-Eleven convenience store chain, signed a sponsorship agreement and became one of the largest supporters of amateur and professional cycling in the history of the sport. In the early 1980s Southland financed construction of two world-class velodromes. The first, built on the campus of Cal State-Dominguez Hills in Carson, California, was the venue for the 1984 Olympic track events. The second was located near the U.S. Olympic training center in Colorado Springs.

In addition to funding the construction of track facilities, Southland formed the 7-Eleven amateur cycling team in 1981. Jim Ochowicz, a former racer and two-time Olympian, was named coach/manager. Eric Heiden, a former speed skater turned cyclist, was the team's first captain.

Heiden and Ochowicz formed their partnership when Ochowicz was hired to manage the U.S. national speed skating team. When Eric Heiden turned his competitive focus from skating to cycling, Ochowicz negotiated sponsorship agreements with Schwinn bicycles and Descente clothing. Looking for a larger sponsor, Ochowicz approached George Taylor, a New York–based sports agent. After learning more about Ochowicz and Heiden's plan to form a European-style bicycle team, Taylor approached Southland's John Thompson, Jere Thompson, and Joe Thompson. The brothers liked the connection between 7-Eleven, the Olympics, and a cycling team and agreed to fund it.

The 7-Eleven team made its first appearance in the Coors Classic in 1981, with a team that included Tom Schuler, Jeff Bradley, Greg Demgen, Eric Heiden, and Ron Hayman. The team finished without a stage win, 11th of 13 teams in the general classification.

In 1982 the company also sponsored Jacque Bradley, Sarah Docter, and Rebecca Twigg as the 7-Eleven women's team. The same year, Southland launched the 7-Eleven/*Bicycling* Grand Prix series to provide American cyclists with velodrome racing experience against international competition. Racers competed for a $100,000 prize purse. Southland and Murray Bicycles supported two major track teams in their preparations for the Los Angeles Olympics. Over the next two years, the 7-Eleven team, comprising the best American road and track racers, won almost half the races it entered.

The Los Angeles Olympics was a watershed event for American cycling. Winning nine medals—including the gold and silver in the women's first Olympic road race—attracted the attention of the national media and turned recreational bicyclists into racing fans. Southland's contribution played a major role in that success. Seven of the nine U.S. medalists had connections to the 7-Eleven racing team.

After the Olympics Southland canceled the track racing series and shifted its attention to road racing. In 1985 Jim Ochowicz changed the 7-Eleven team's status from amateur to professional, and Southland partnered with *Winning* magazine to create the 7-Eleven Cup, a national circuit of criterium and road races.

In May 1985 the 7-Eleven team made its European debut at the Etoile de Bessèges in France. Although Southland provided substantial financial support, racing in Europe was a new experience. Compared to the European teams with their large support crews and fleets of vehicles, 7-Eleven arrived with one red Murray bike per rider and a small equipment van loaded with a limited supply of spare parts. Ochowicz and the team's directeur sportif, Richard Dejonckheere, borrowed a chase car from the race director. The members of the first European 7-Eleven team were Jeff Bradley, Chris Carmichael, Matt Eaton, Ron Hayman, Eric Heiden, Ron Kiefel, Davis Phinney, Tom Schuler, and Richard Scibird. Later that season 7-Eleven became the first American team to compete in the Giro d'Italia.

Featured in Southland's extensive advertising and promotion campaigns, the 7-Eleven team was the most visible professional racing team in the United States. Winning major races brought more attention. In 1985 Eric Heiden won the first CoreStates USPRO championship. Teammates Tom Schuler and Ron Kiefel followed with victories in 1987 and 1988.

Motivated by the positive publicity, the Southland Corporation signed an agreement with the USCF to become the title sponsor of the 1986 world cycling championships in Colorado Springs.

In 1986 7-Eleven became the first American team to compete in the Tour de France. At the end of the first day's road race, Alex Stieda, a Canadian, became the first North American to wear the yellow jersey. The strong start continued when Davis Phinney won the third stage. The team's performance faded over the remaining stages, and Bob Roll, in 62nd place, was the team's highest finisher.

Jim Ochowicz continued to manage the team. The roster changed in following seasons as Ochowicz worked to create a team that could compete on the international level. In 1986 and 1987 Andy Hampsten won the Tour of Switzerland, and 7-Eleven riders won three stages. The next year Hampsten, wearing a 7-Eleven jersey, became the first American to win the Giro d'Italia.

While the professional team was achieving success, the 7-Eleven Cup was not drawing enough spectators to satisfy Southland's marketing executives. The Cup series was cancelled in 1987, and Southland reallocated its cycling support to teams rather than events. In 1988 the familiar red, green, and white 7-Eleven jerseys could be found on the shoulders of amateur and professional American men and women. The men's amateur team included U.S. national team members Norm Alvis, Frankie Andreu, and Tommy Matush. Jim Ochowicz and Tom Schuler managed. American riders on the professional team included Chris

Carmichael, Andy Hampsten, Ron Kiefel, Roy Knickman, Davis Phinney, Jeff Pierce, Bob Roll, and Doug Shapiro. Tom Schuler raced through June before taking on some of the management responsibilities. Eric Heiden, enrolled in medical school, planned to race with the team when his schedule permitted. Bunki Bankaitis-Davis, Susan Ehlers, Kathi Riggert, Inga Thompson-Benedict, and Tricia Walters formed the women's team.

By the end of the decade, eight years after its debut, 7-Eleven was the only American-sponsored team racing in Europe. The team, ranked 10th in the world, was the only American team invited to the 1989 Tour de France.

The Corporate World Supports American Racing

Patriotic frenzy over the 1984 Olympics brought new sponsorship opportunities to cycling, as Southland's record-setting financial contributions were followed up by other companies. Levi's, the official clothing supplier of the 1984 Olympics, sponsored a road team. Huffy, a bicycle manufacturer, paid $610,000 in cash and equipment to sponsor the U.S. cycling team. Corporate sponsorships ranged from financial contributions to the USCF for general use to the creation of racing teams and special events.

Race promoters and officials at the USCF had to become far more fluent in understanding marketing objectives and strategies, over and above the racing issues that already consumed the majority of their occupations. In many ways corporate sponsorships were difficult to manage. Thousands of man-hours were needed to create race schedules, negotiate secondary sponsorship packages, design courses, negotiate with city officials, and secure media coverage.

In February 1981 *Self* magazine announced a four-year contract to provide substantial sponsorship for women's racing. Connie Carpenter captured the first annual *Self* Cycling Circuit and won a Datsun B210 pickup truck, the largest prize to date for women.

In an example of the uncertainty of long-term corporate support, the top American women found limited sponsorship opportunities just four years later. Levi's was one of the top women's teams in 1983 and 1984, but the company decided to focus on men's racing only in 1985. Top riders like Inga Thompson were left unsponsored with little time to secure new backing before the racing season started. The Centurion and Winning Club/Peugeot teams were launched, but many women raced unsupported.

In 1985 corporate support for the USCF reached $1 million, almost double the year before. Nabisco was one of the new companies to approach the USCF that year to discuss sponsorship opportunities. Shortly after the initial meetings, the USCF hired promoter Dave Pelletier, who connected a series of criterium events across the country to create the Wheat Thins Mayor's Cup. He created a scoring system that accumulated points for every dollar won. Riders competed for a $200,000 total series purse.

The Wheat Thins series started in Jacksonville, Florida, and ended nineteen races and three months later in Boston. Each race featured a festival atmosphere and attracted large crowds, a response Nabisco's marketing officials were happy to see. At the final event in Boston, Davis Phinney covered the 35-mile course with an average speed of 31 mph to win the race. Tom Schuler, Phinney's 7-Eleven teammate, raced in most of the nineteen events and had the series championship wrapped up before the riders left the start line in Boston. By the halfway point in the series, Schuler had won enough race primes (sprint competitions held at various stages within the overall race) to take the overall lead. The $18,000 Alfa Romeo awarded to the winner of the Mayor's Cup provided him enough incentive to maintain the lead.

For women, the prize list didn't include a car. Betsy Davis, riding for Winning Club/Peugeot, won $1,000 and a set of Bose speakers for winning the women's series. Davis entered fourteen of the eighteen women's events and placed in eleven.

In its third year the Mayor's Cup was the richest stage race in the country, offering $225,000 in prize money over the fourteen-race series.

Races supported by corporate sponsorships often ended suddenly. In 1988 Nabisco announced it was ending its sponsorship of the Mayor's Cup, despite the series' success, and shifted its marketing dollars to promotions focused on the 1988 Olympics in Seoul. Del Monte, another Cup sponsor, decided to end its relationship at the same time. After three years and more than fifty races, Dave Pelletier was unable to attract a new sponsor to replace Nabisco.

★ Redlands Classic ★

 Since 1985 the Redlands Classic stage race has hosted the world's best professional teams and riders. From Levi's-Raleigh in 1985 to Toyota-United in 2006, the twenty-two-year-old Classic has documented the changing fortunes of America's top-ranked professional teams.

Less than a year after the 1984 Olympics, officials in Redlands, California, launched a plan to host a professional bike race to encourage Memorial Day weekend tourism in the small town. Their three-day, four-stage race offered a purse of $13,650. Still enjoying the post-Olympic spotlight, Alexi Grewal, Steve Hegg, Roy Knickman, and Thurlow Rogers came to Redlands to race for the $13,650 purse. Rogers won individual honors and his Levi's-Raleigh team—including Greg Demgen, Ron Hayman, and Steve Hegg—also finished 1st.

For the next two years, 7-Eleven dominated the Classic. In 1986 teammates Raul Alcala, Doug Shapiro, Bob Roll, Ron Kiefel, Chris Carmichael, and Eric Heiden escorted Davis Phinney to victory in the individual and team honors. The team won its second consecutive victory in 1987, when Dag-Otto Lauritzen took the general classification.

The winning teams were not always American. Despite appearances by strong 7-Eleven and Coors Light teams, the Russian national team swept the individual and team standings in 1990.

Three years later organizers moved the race date up from Memorial Day to March to avoid the conflicts that had prevented the best riders from entering in the past. In 1993 top teams Chevrolet-L.A. Sheriff, Subaru-Montgomery, and Coors Light clipped in at the start line. Malcolm Elliott, a British racer on the Chevrolet-L.A. Sheriff team, finished 1st, followed by Bart Bowen of Subaru-Montgomery and Ron Kiefel of Coors Light.

The first women's event, offering a $4,000 purse, was added in 1993. Linda Brenneman and Team Kahlua faced little challenge from the Chevrolet, TGI Friday's, Shaklee, or Bodywise teams. The field included Rebecca Twigg, Eve Stephenson, Sally Zack, and Inga Thompson.

By 1996 the Redlands Classic had become the annual season-opening event for American professional road racing. The racing schedule expanded from the inaugural three-day event to a six-day stage race for men and women. Redlands, California—population 65,000—drew 15,000 fans each day.

At the end of the 1990s, U.S. Postal replaced Saturn as the top team at Redlands. From 1996 to 1999, a member of the Postal squad finished 1st.

At the turn of the twenty-first century, new names and new teams stood on the winner's podium. In 2000 the UCI, the international governing body of racing, awarded the Classic a UCI Category 2.5 ranking. The opportunity to earn points in the world rankings and race for a $52,000 prize list reinforced the Classic's reputation. The UCI's rules also played a part in the 2000 edition's finish. Team Mercury's Chris Horner was awarded the victory over David Zabriskie of Colorado/7-UP, even though both racers finished with the same official time. Officials followed the UCI's rule and awarded the win based on hundredths-of-a-second differences in the street sprint prologue and individual time trial.

Horner went on to win again in 2002, riding for Prime Alliance. He won again in 2003 for Saturn, and again in 2004 with Webcor Builders. After winning the men's and women's team titles in 2003, Saturn canceled its sponsorship, leaving top riders like Horner to look for new teams.

When Horner did not return to race for a fourth consecutive win in 2005, Chris Wherry (Health Net) took the individual title. In 2006 Nathan O'Neill of Health Net took the individual honors and Toyota-United was the 1st-place team.

1990 - Dmitri Zhadanov
1991 - Randy Whicker
1992 - Scott Fortner
1993 - Malcolm Elliott
1994 - Malcolm Elliott
1995 - Scott Moninger
1996 - Tomasz Brozyna
1997 - Dariuz Baranowski
1998 - Jonathan Vaughters
1999 - Christian Vande Velde
2000 - Chris Horner
2001 - Trent Klasna
2002 - Chris Horner
2003 - Chris Horner
2004 - Chris Horner
2005 - Chris Wherry
2006 - Nathan O'Neill

WINNERS OF THE REDLANDS CLASSIC

WOMEN

1985 - Cindy Whitehead
1986 - Suzanne Sonye
1987 - Cindy Whitehead
1988 - Mo Manley
1992 - Linda Brenneman
1993 - Linda Brenneman
1994 - Jeanne Golay
1995 - Linda Brenneman
1996 - Alison Dunlap
1997 - Susy Pryde
1998 - Mari Holden
1999 - Lyne Bessette
2000 - Alison Dunlap
2001 - Genevieve Jeanson
2002 - Judith Arndt
2003 - Genevieve Jeanson
2004 - Lyne Bessette
2005 - Christine Thornburn
2006 - Amber Neben

MEN

1985 - Thurlow Rogers
1986 - Davis Phinney
1987 - Dag-Otto Lauritzen
1988 - Alexi Grewal
1989 - Scott Moninger

2006 REDLANDS CLASSIC TEAM LIST

Toyota-United
Team Monex
Priority Health
Jittery Joe's
Target Training
AEG-Toshiba-JetNetwork
Jelly Belly
Navigators Insurance
Team TIAA-CREF
Team Health Net
Colavita-Sutter Home Winery
VMG Racing
Kodak Gallery-Sierra Nevada
BMC
Fiordifrutta
CRCA/Sakonnet Technology
Kahala-LaGrange
Broadmark/Hagens Berman
California Giant/Village Peddler
Sienna Development/
   Goble Knee Clinic
Team Spine

Schwinn, Wheaties, and Del Monte

Throughout its history Schwinn was a major supporter of amateur and professional racing. In the 1970s its sponsorship of the Wolverine Cycling Club in Detroit supported the racing careers of Roger and Sheila Young, Connie Paraskevin, Sue Novara, and Tom Schuler. Their names can be found among lists of Olympians, world champions, and U.S. national champions.

One of the original sponsors of the 7-Eleven team, Schwinn returned to the professional racing circuit in 1986. Thomas Prehn, a member of the Schwinn-Icy Hot team, won the 1986 CoreStates USPRO championship. In 1988 Wheaties replaced Icy Hot as cosponsor. The two-year agreement allowed the team to compete in Europe for the first time. The nine-rider team included five Americans: Tom Broznowski, Steve Tilford, Steve Speaks, Mike Engleman, and Doug Smith. The Schwinn team performed well domestically, winning the 1987 Tour of Texas and the 1987 Mayor's Cup title.

PETER NYE, JEFF GROMAN, MIKE TYSON/WWW.SIXDAYBICYCLERACE.COM

Schwinn's support of racing goes all the way back to the velodrome days. Here the company's logo is shown on turn three at the New York Armory in 1948.

The annual chase for corporate sponsorships continued through the end of the decade. Men's teams were relatively stable, but it was feast or famine for top American women.

Del Monte was introduced to cycling through its partial sponsorship of the Wheat Thins Mayor's Cup series that began in 1985. A year later the sixteen-race series included two events at the world championships in Colorado Springs that energized racing fans.

On February 6, 1987, Jerry Lace, the USCF's executive director, introduced Del Monte Fresh Fruit as the newest major sponsor of amateur racing. Del Monte's vice president Don Chmiel committed $250,000 to the women's national team in 1987 and announced plans to double that amount by the 1988 Olympic Games. Sue Novara-Reber, the national women's coach, used the funding to recruit new women, fund training camps, and send the twenty-three-member team to more races.

The same year, Sundance, a subsidiary of Stroh's Brewery, was looking for a way to promote its fruit juice and mineral water combination. Their twenty-member team was called Sundance-Fuji America and focused on women's events. SunTour, Vittoria, Mavic, Bell, Alita, and Ray-Ban were cosponsors.

 Tour of the Americas

 The 1988 racing season started with the first running of the Pepsi Tour of the Americas. At that time the Coors Classic was the only other major stage race in the United States.

The 795.3-mile Pepsi Tour of the Americas was held February 19 to 28, 1988. Ninety-six professional riders from fifteen countries raced for the $150,000 prize purse. At the time it was largest purse offered in the Western Hemisphere. Twelve professional teams—seven from Europe, three from Colombia, and two from the United States—competed in the inaugural event. The 7-Eleven and Wheaties-Schwinn team represented the United States. Olympic teams from Brazil, Mexico, and Venezuela arrived, ready to take their place in international racing.

Race promoters German Blanco and Dr. Erwin Vasquez, new to cycling, hired Oliver "Butch" Martin to be race director. The event was originally planned as one tour, with seven stages in the United States and three in Venezuela, but the promoters changed the format after Fédération Internationale de Cyclisme Professionnel (FICP) rules prevented the Tour schedule from covering two weekends. The Tour was split into the three-stage Tour of Venezuela, with a $30,000 purse, and the seven-stage Tour of the Americas, offering $60,000. Combined overall results of the two races offered another $60,000 in prize money.

In Venezuela 500,000 enthusiastic spectators lined the race route. In Florida the crowds were small and the race received limited media coverage. The promoters were reported to have lost $300,000 the first year, partly due to the low turnout.

Riding for the PDM team, Greg LeMond finished 6th in Venezuela and 4th in the United States. It was LeMond's best finish in eighteen months after missing the 1987 racing season recovering from a broken wrist, a shotgun blast, and appendicitis.

At the end of the first Florida stage, in Jacksonville, LeMond and Davis Phinney broke away from the pack on the last lap. Phinney crossed the finish line less than a half second ahead of LeMond. Phinney captured three of four stages in Florida and finished 1st in the Florida Tour's general classification. The 7-Eleven team won more than $25,000 in the competition.

Limited sponsorship shortened the 1989 Tour of the Americas to five days of racing in Venezuela and a two-day, three-race event in Florida. The field included 1988 Giro winner Andy Hampsten and three Tour de France winners: LeMond, Pedro Delgado, and Stephen Roche. The second Tour of the Americas was the first competitive test for LeMond and his newly formed Coors Light-ADR team. Returning to his previous top-level form, LeMond finished 3rd in the combined classification.

The 1990 Tour of the Americas started in Florida, then shifted to Puerto Rico and finished in Venezuela. The ten-stage race attracted teams from Spain, Italy, Belgium, Austria, Great Britain, Colombia, Puerto Rico, and Venezuela. The American representatives included Coors Light, 7-Eleven, and the smaller American Commerce Bank and AC Pinarello teams.

Riders from the less well-known teams had the highest finishes. Mike Carter, who moved from Coors Light to AC Pinarello, finished 4th in the combined Tour of Florida and Tour of Venezuela events. Andy Bishop, riding for American Commerce Bank, captured the mountain competition, beating riders like Pedro Delgado. In the final team standings, 7-Eleven and Coors Light were 10th and 14th, several positions below American Commerce and AC Pinarello.

The Official Car

The goal of cycling's corporate sponsors was to get their brands and products in front of as many of their customers as possible. Logos on team jerseys drew attention at racing events, but companies were looking for new ways to align themselves with the then positive image of bicycle racers.

In 1988 Subaru signed a four-year contract for the right to be called "The Official Car" of the USCF. To promote the new title, the company created the Subaru Cycling Series, which linked seven major races, from the U.S. national championship in New York to the series championship in Beverly Hills. The series used a criterium racing format to make the racing exciting for spectators. Men raced 40 miles over 80 laps, and women 20 miles and 40 laps. A new Subaru station wagon and $100,000 prize purse made the Subaru Cycling Series the richest in the United States. Davis Phinney of 7-Eleven captured the final race in Beverly Hills and Rebecca Twigg finished the women's race in 1st place. 7–Eleven added a new Subaru to its growing list of prizes.

The list of professional racing teams shifted again in 1988. On October 19, 1988, the Adolph Coors Company ended its nine-year sponsorship of the Coors Classic. Coors shifted its financial support from a single event to the Coors Silver Bullet men's professional racing team. Greg LeMond, who signed a contract to race with the European ADR team, helped arrange a partnership between ADR and Coors that allowed him to race in the United States and Europe.

Prompted by its sixteen victories in 1987, Pepsi renewed the sponsorship of the Pepsi-Fanini team. The team's roster included three Americans—John Eustice, Dan Fox, and Robert Nichols—and Italian sprinter Roberto Gaggioli. DuPont, after sponsoring a women's team in the 1987 Ore-Ida Women's Challenge and Coors Classic, formed full men's and women's teams for the 1988 season.

On the women's side, the Lowrey's team included national road champion Janelle Parks and world team time trial silver medalists Jane Marshall and Leslee Schenk. Katrin Tobin and Judy Caunter were also members. Their rival Celestial Seasonings included Rebecca Twigg, Janie Eickhoff, Madonna Harris, Genny Brunet, Ruthie Matthes, and Henny Top. Weight Watchers, another competitive team, began its third racing season in 1988.

The list of "official" sponsors included Campagnolo in 1989. The company became the exclusive component supplier of the men's road and 100-kilometer team trial squads through 1992. Team USA, the USCF's Olympic development team, used bikes equipped with the latest Campagnolo products, including SGR clipless pedals and Ghidi fluid-dynamic disc wheels.

Huffy, which bought the rights to become the official bicycle of the USCF before the 1984 Olympics, ended its five-year sponsorship with a $25,000 donation to Team USA.

The Fight for Control of Professional Racing

Under the presidency of Otto Wenz (1975–1979), the USCF had invested in the development of professional racing. In one step the USCF received permission from the UCI to classify all American races as pro-am, to give professional riders more opportunities to compete. But further work to create a professional racing class was not completed, and in 1979 the total number of professional riders dropped from ten to four, and there were no professional races on the 1980 calendar.

Behind the scenes a major battle was brewing between the USCF and the Professional Racing Organization over which organization had the authority to govern professional racing. The USCF considered itself to be the official governing body for amateur and professional racing and issued licenses to pros John Bartle, Ken Woods, William Guazzo, and Wally Summers.

Conflicts and Negotiations, Part 1

Former racer Chris Van Gent formed the Professional Racing Organization (PRO) in 1970. Gent affiliated his organization with the Fédération Internationale de Cyclisme Professionnel (FICP), the international governing body of professional racing. The affiliation granted PRO the role as the sole rule-making and sanctioning organization in the United States.

Van Gent incorporated PRO in 1972, began issuing professional licenses, and sanctioned the six-day races held in Los Angeles and Detroit. He continued to pay the FICP $1,000 annual dues for five more years. In 1977 Van Gent offered to transfer his organization's affiliation to the United States Cycling Federation if the American governing body assumed responsibility for the annual payments. Executives at the USCF accepted the offer, but Gent soon became disenchanted with the USCF's lack of attention to professional racing.

In 1978 Jack Simes and Dave Chauner, former top-level racers, formed Omni-Sports, a cycling promotion firm. Plans to expand their race offerings included approaching the USCF. In their background work Simes and Chauner discovered that Van Gent, not the USCF, held the original PRO affiliation. Through Arthur Greenberg, a UCI commissar from Pennsylvania, Simes and Chauner confirmed that the FICP still recognized Van Gent and PRO as the American governing body.

Van Gent, Greenberg, Simes, and Chauner formed a board of commissioners to manage PRO activities. When Van Gent received the FICP's 1980 dues statement, the new group paid the bill and the past due fee from 1979. Despite USCF's assuming financial responsibility for the 1977 and 1978 dues, Van Gent believed he still held the rights to the original FICP affiliation.

Simes, Chauner, Van Gent, and Greenberg approached Mike Fraysee, the USCF's president, to discuss how the two organizations could work together to promote separate amateur and professional racing calendars. Under their plan PRO would create a new professional racing constitution complete with bylaws, racing rules, and competition standards, and the USCF would oversee only amateur racing.

The USCF responded in a strongly worded statement from Fraysee. In an interview published in the April 20, 1980, issue of *Velonews,* Fraysee said, "I believe that PRO is going about it the wrong way. They're doing it as promoters; they aren't doing it for the love of anything. The federation looks at it with a different view. We're in charge of cycling altogether and we want to see cycling become big, not for professional gain or money gain or anything else." Fraysee believed the UCI saw PRO as under the control of the USCF and called into question PRO's position as the holder of the FICP affiliation. When George Mount turned professional in May 1980, he registered with both organizations to protect his right to race.

Negotiations between the rival bodies were contentious, confusing, and politically charged. In May 1980, after a stalemate within the USCF board of directors failed to produce a settlement, representatives of PRO met with officials of the Union Cycliste Internationale. The FICP fell under the UCI's umbrella.

For Michel Jekiel, general secretary of the Union Cycliste Internationale, the first task was to clarify ownership of the official affiliation between the two opposing organizations. Affiliation papers on file were not clear. Documents at the UCI listed PRO as the U.S. professional organization, but listed the address as the USCF in Colorado Springs. Jekiel offered both parties a compromise agreement intended to end the impasse and its stifling effect on American professional racing. In late August Fraysee met with Greenberg and Simes at a women's world championship race in Sallanches, France, to sign an agreement designating PRO as the official governing body of U.S. professional cycling.

Representing their organizations, Fraysee, Greenberg, and Simes signed the document. Michel Jekiel also signed. After months of rancor the agreement recognized PRO as the U.S. federation for professional cycling and the USCF as the governing body for amateur cycling. The headline "It's official. PRO is U.S. pro federation" appeared in the September 12 edition of *Velonews.*

At the USCF's October 18 board of directors meeting, a series of resolutions undermined the agreement. First, members of the board rejected the terms of the agreement already approved and signed by its president. Second, Fraysee complained that UCI officials had pressured him to sign the document. Chaos returned when, in secret session, the USCF's PRO committee recommended that the full board reject the agreement and seek a restraining order to protect USCF interests.

The press release distributed after the meeting announced: "As the national governing body for cycling recognized by the U.S. Olympic Committee, the USCF must be able to demonstrate that it is autonomous in the governance of the sport, in that it independently determines and controls all matters central to such governance." In relation to PRO the release continued, "The directors realized that the proposed USCF-PRO committee to oversee licensing and issuing of sanctions would violate these requirements for autonomy and independence in governing amateur cycling."

On November 27, 1980, the UCI's executive committee met in Geneva to address the American situation. Instead of clarifying its position, the UCI's actions created more uncertainty. In a letter dated November 20 to promoter Richard Nader of Madison Square Garden, UCI officials had written: "the PRO is competent to present professional competitions to the international calendar of the UCI."

Seven days later the executive committee announced that the USCF was the recognized governing body of American professional cycling. Michel Jekiel, who signed the disputed agreement, said he did not agree with the decision and could not comment on the deliberations. PRO announced that it would appeal the committee's decision.

Cycling magazines were filled with official claims and counterclaims. Each side presented pieces of documentation they felt proved their position. Angry editorials and defensive follow-up letters fueled the debate.

After months of tense negotiations, fierce internal debates, and personal attacks, the USCF board voted 22-1 to allow the promoters a pro-am racing option at their January 23, 1981, board meeting. In return, PRO dismissed its $300,000 lawsuit against the USCF. *Cycling USA,* the official publication of the USCF, announced, "USCF and PRO Bury the Hatchet."

With the governing body debate settled, the first professional championship in eight years was launched on June 6, 1982. Produced by

Simes and Chauner's Omni-Sports company and Baltimore's WMAR-TV, it featured 72 professionals from twelve countries racing for $25,000 in prizes. Australia's Shane Sutton won the race. The top American, John Eustice, in 6th place, was awarded the first national professional champion's jersey since Jack Simes won the title in 1974.

In 1985 the race for the professional championship moved to Philadelphia. Over the next twenty-two years, the USPRO championships would become the premier single-day professional race in the United States.

CHAPTER FIVE

Olympic Dreams
Lost and Found

ACTING IN RESPONSE to the Soviet Union's invasion of Afghanistan, President Carter announced an American boycott of the 1980 Olympic Games. Riders like the Stetina brothers and Greg LeMond lost their opportunity to compete for gold. Dale and Wayne Stetina were the top riders of their generation, and young LeMond's performances had observers speculating about America's first gold medal. Unable to compete in the Olympics, LeMond turned his attention abroad and signed a $50,000 contract to join the French Renault-Gitane professional racing team.

America's Golden Olympics

The 1984 Olympic Games were held in the United States, for the first time in fifty years. Matching the United States in political gamesmanship, the Soviet Union announced that it would boycott the Los Angeles Games. The Soviet Union's Eastern Bloc satellite countries followed suit.

Eddie Borysewicz, the USCF's national coaching director, reacted favorably to the news. His team's chances to win the first Olympic medals since 1912 increased significantly with the absence of the Soviet team.

Fueled by extensive television and newspaper coverage, excitement surrounding the Olympics moved Americans to the edge of their living room couches on the

ROBERT F. GEORGE

Connie Carpenter was one of the most dominant women in American racing history. Her list of accomplishments includes world championship medals, national championships, and a gold medal in the first women's road race at the 1984 Los Angeles Olympics.

first day of the Games. On July 29, 1984, Borysewicz' prediction came true. In front of a reported fourteen million viewers, Connie Carpenter and Rebecca Twigg captured gold and silver medals in the first Olympic women's road race. Alexi Grewal, riding after receiving a last-second reprieve from a suspicious drug test, captured the men's road race gold. On the track Steve Hegg, Leonard Nitz, Mark Gorski, and Nelson Vails added to the collection of gold and silver. By the end of the cycling competition, America's cyclists had captured nine medals and created a standard that has been unmatched for twenty-two years. Later it was revealed that at least some of the team had used controversial methods to achieve their results.

Blood Doping Scandal

On Thursday, November 8, 1984, Dave Prouty, executive director of the USCF, received a telephone call from Dr. Thomas Dickson. Dickson was an orthopedic surgeon who often worked with the national team. During the call Dr. Dickson reported that members of the U.S. cycling team had received blood transfusions days before and again during the Los Angeles Olympics.

Even more damaging, Dickson said Olympic coach Eddie Borysewicz and team manager and USCF board member Mike Fraysee had supervised the procedures. Ed Burke, director of the USCF's Elite Athlete Program, had recruited a doctor to perform the transfusions. A number of medal-winning cyclists were also implicated. Prouty, concerned about the implications on many fronts, moved into crisis-management mode.

Blood doping wasn't new in 1984. The idea of improving a rider's performance by increasing the oxygen-carrying capacity of the red blood cells had been debated for more than a decade. The questions surrounding the transfusions covered moral, ethical, legal, and medical grounds. More frustrating was the lack of scientific documentation that validated the process and its risks. At the time, sports organizations like the USCF were trying to create policies governing the controversial tool.

Ed Burke was a strong supporter of the technique. In a memo dated September 30, 1983, Burke outlined his professional opinions and asked the USCF's board of directors, management, staff, and athletes to explore the possibility of using blood transfusions. Prouty's response called for cautious study and evaluation before any formal decision was made. As time passed, Burke continued to press for approval for a blood transfusion research project. In December 1983 he asked Dr. Casey Clarke, director of the USOC's own Elite Athlete Program, to write a formal letter to USOC executive director F. Don Miller asking for permission to proceed with blood doping from a research perspective. Miller rejected the request outright. Prouty believed the subject was closed until he took the call from Dr. Dickson.

Uncomfortable with what he witnessed at the Ramada Inn in Los Angeles, where the team had been allowed to stay at the special request of Borysewicz, Dr. Dickson wrote a letter to USOC officials describing the transfusions. The USCF and USOC opened investigations into his claims.

Through interviews with team members and officials, Dr. Irving Dardik, chairman of the USOC Sports Medicine Council, learned that five medal-winning members of the Olympic cycling team had received blood transfusions and Dr. Herman Falsetti, a cardiologist who taught at the University of Iowa, had administered them. Medal winners Steve Hegg, Leonard Nitz, Brent Emery, Rebecca Twigg, and Pat McDonough received transfusions four days before the start of the Games. Mark Whitehead, John Beckman, and Danny Van Haute also received transfusions.

On January 19, 1985, the USCF officially banned blood doping and announced penalties and sanctions against staff members involved in the scandal. Repercussions affected the highest levels of the organization. Rob Lee, president of the USCF, resigned over the controversy. Eddie Borysewicz and Ed Burke received thirty-day suspensions without pay and formal letters of reprimand. Mike Fraysee was demoted from first vice president to third vice president.

After the glory of winning nine medals, the blood doping scandal tempered the celebration. Interest in sports science waned following the official blood doping ban. Corporate sponsors who gave generously to support American athletes on home soil were less motivated to continue that level of financial contribution when the Games left the country.

Back to Reality

Eddie Borysewicz resigned on January 16, 1988. Hired in 1977 to improve American racers' international competitiveness, Borysewicz led his first Olympic team to nine medals.

In 1986 the USCF split coaching responsibilities by gender. Borysewicz' title changed from national coaching director to national men's coach. Over the next two years, Borysewicz became increasingly uncomfortable with the USCF's politics and coaching philosophies. After announcing his retirement, he remained an advisor through the 1988 Olympics before turning his attention to managing the Korean-sponsored Sunkyong-SKC team. To replace Borysewicz, the USCF created a new position, national team director, and hired Mark Hodges to fill the role.

At the 1988 Olympics in Seoul, the United States and the Soviet Union and its Eastern Bloc partners competed against each other for the first time in eight years. After winning nine medals in 1984 against an incomplete field, American cyclists faced the best in the world and claimed just one medal. Connie Paraskevin-Young captured the bronze in the match sprint.

Disappointment from riders, sponsors, the cycling press, and the general public led to a major reorganization of the USCF's approach to Olympic competition. Team USA, an Olympic development team, was formed to focus the organization's energies on the next Games in Barcelona.

★ The Pursuit of Olympic Gold ★

 Every four years athletes from around the world hone their skills to peak at the Olympic Games. Knowledgeable fans and newcomers alike turn their attention to sports not seen on regular network schedules. Swimming and track and field draw much of the media attention, but American cyclists, both men and women, have created lasting legends of Olympic performance.

The first modern Olympics were held in Athens, Greece, in 1896. Bicycle racing was already popular around the world, and riders in Athens competed in five track events—the 1-lap time trial, 6-lap sprint, 10-kilometer scratch race, 100-kilometer motor-paced race, and twelve-

hour marathon. The first road race gold medal went to Greek rider Aristidis Konstantinides, who covered the 87-kilometer course 20 minutes faster than August Godrich of Germany.

In Paris four years later, John Henry Lake won the United States' first Olympic cycling medal, finishing 3rd in the sprint.

Olympic teams of that era were small and national support was limited. In 1904 the Olympics were held in St. Louis, in conjunction with the national championships. Racers from other countries did not attend. Although the fledgling international Olympic governing body did not recognize the standings, records show Marcus Hurley took 1st place in four of the seven contested events.

America's next medal-winning performances came at the Stockholm Olympics in 1912. Carl Schutte won the bronze medal in the 320-kilometer time trial. Contested as an individual and team event, his performance led the U.S. team to the bronze medal.

Seventy-two years passed before Americans once again stood on an Olympic podium and lowered their heads to receive a medal.

Welcome to the Olympic Team

Russell Allen's selection to the team pursuit squad for the 1932 Los Angeles Olympics was announced in a letter dated July 25, 1932:

Dear Mr. Russell (sic):

Please accept my congratulations on your selection as a member of the Olympic Team of the United States for the Tenth Olympiad. You have the best wishes of the American Olympic Committee for success in your competition and I hope you will be able to come forth from the contests with the highest home honor in amateur sport, an Olympic Championship.

As a member of the American Olympic Team you have accepted the responsibility of upholding the American tradition for clean, honest, sportsmanlike competition—"a fair field for all and may the best man win."

Everyone with whom you will come in contact will unconsciously judge our entire athletic system by your personal conduct both on and off the field of competition. The champion athlete today is the hero of the public. His actions are watched by many pairs of eyes and his influence in setting standards, especially for growing boys and girls, is incalculable. Your demeanor, skill of performance, observance of training rules, and sportsmanship will be closely observed by all those who see you. It is important that you leave the most favorable impression.

May I point out to you that in these Games we have the added obligation of host. All foreigners in attendance are guests of our country and should be

Russell Allen received this letter from the United States Olympic Committee.

treated as would be a guest in your own home. You will come in contact with representatives of fifty different nations, each speaking a different language, each with different ideas of life and living, each with different customs, many of which may seem peculiar to you. I trust you will extend to them all, athletes and officials alike, every courtesy that you would expect if you were in a

Russell Allen's 1932 Olympic team photo.

continued

RUSSELL ALLEN COLLECTION

foreign land, handicapped by not knowing the language or customs of the people. When coming into contact with foreign officials please remember that they have been delegated to their responsible positions by the International Federation in control of the sport and respect their authority.

To those that live in the Olympic Village, may I point out that our team is the largest and that foreign athletes will take their queue (sic) from you. The Organizing Committee has provided the best accommodations that have ever been enjoyed by any Olympic athlete. It is strictly up to the athletes themselves to determine whether this splendid idea, carrying out the finest Olympic ideals, will be successful or unsuccessful. Americans, generally, with their free and independent ideas, have the reputation of being less amenable to discipline than foreigners. Please respect the rights of others and

observe the rules and regulations that have been set down to insure the comfort and happiness of all. We have here the greatest opportunity ever presented to build up international goodwill for the United States.

Any questions of any kind must be taken up with your manager or coach of your team. While a member of the team you are under the direction of your manager and coach who have the authority to dismiss you from the team and send home anyone whose conduct is unsatisfactory.

With confidence in your ability to demonstrate to the world that American athletes are sportsmen and women and ladies and gentleman, I am

Sincerely yours,

Avery Brundage
President
American Olympic Committee

The Rose Bowl in Pasadena, California, was the site of post-1932 Olympic racing events.

Although the 1932 Olympics coincided with the Great Depression, interest in cycling and racing was strong. Thirty thousand people paid a few dollars for tickets to attend the cycling events in the Rose Bowl. John Sinibaldi Jr., who held the national 100-kilometer individual time trial record that stood for fifty years, competed at the 1932 Games in Los Angeles and the 1936 Games in Berlin. Cycling was a much more important sport then in Europe and the Soviet Union, and riders from those countries dominated the Games. American riders had little cause for Olympic celebration until the Games returned to Los Angeles in 1984.

The Schwinn Paramount

Beginning in 1948 Schwinn, the dominant bicycle manufacturer in the United States at the time, donated bicycles and equipment to support American riders. Top Schwinn dealers and corporate executives took on team management and coaching responsibilities.

In preparation for the Munich Games in 1972, Schwinn dealers Jerry Rimoldi and Al Toefield were selected to coach and manage the U.S. Olympic cycling team in Munich, West Germany. Rimoldi was also the coach of the 1968 U.S. Olympic team and 1971 Pan American team. At the time Toefield was acting as vice president of the Amateur Bicycle League of America, the national governing body for competitive racing (which later became the United States Cycling Federation).

The team competed on the best bikes the country had to offer. Outfitting the racers was part of the Schwinn bicycle company's heritage. Schwinn donated high-performance Paramount racing bikes, painted opaque blue and decorated with Olympic decals. The team received twelve road bikes, fourteen track bikes, and two modified tandems. The frames were custom-fit for each team member, and riders could select component options from Schwinn's accessory catalog. Schwinn's fingertip handlebar controls were a popular choice.

ROBERT F. GEORGE

George Mount's 6th-place road race finish at the 1976 Montreal Olympics marked the highest American finish in decades.

1976: America's First Top-Ten Finish in Sixty-four Years

In the 1968 and 1972 Games, the best American racers, like John Howard, Ron Skarin, and John Allis, were buried in the pack. The team did show steady improvement in those years, which was all that could be reasonably hoped for. At the 1976 Olympics in Montreal, twenty-year-old George Mount from Lafayette, California, secured his place in American cycling history by finishing 6th in the road race.

Racing on a road slick from intermittent rain, 134 riders covered fourteen 12.5-kilometer circuits around Mount Royal near Montreal. A group escaped on the 7th lap up the Mount Royal climb. Mount stayed with the final ten-man break, increasing the American coaches' hopes that a cycling medal was in reach. In the final sprint Mount lost momentum, fading to 6th place. (Mount's teammates David Boll, Mike Neel, and John Howard were competitive as well, but all three crashed on the rain-slicked roads; Boll and Howard got back on their bikes and finished 50th and 42nd.) Major newspapers covered Mount's performance, and his story dominated American cycling publications for several months.

ROBERT F. GEORGE

The 1976 Olympic time trial team of John Howard, Wayne Stetina, Alan Kingsbury, and Marc Thompson (front to back) represented the best American riders of the time.

Boycott

In 1980 President Carter announced that the U.S. Olympic team would boycott the Summer Olympics in Moscow to protest the Soviet Union's invasion of Afghanistan. The Olympic trials were still held, and fourteen cyclists earned the honor of being named to the 1980 Olympic team. The track team included Les Barczewski, Mark Gorski, Leonard Nitz, Dave Grylls,

Bruce Donaghy, Danny Van Haute, and Brent Emery. Eric Heiden was one of three alternates. The road team included Tom Doughty, Andy Weaver, Greg LeMond, Dale Stetina, Wayne Stetina, Bob Cook, Tom Schuler, and Doug Shapiro. The makeup of the team represented the best of two generations. Wayne and Dale Stetina represented a generation at its zenith. Their credentials

COR VOS

In the early 1980s Greg LeMond (front) and Bernard Hinault (to LeMond's left) rode as mentor/student, teammates, and competitors.

included national road championships and victories at the Coors Classic.

In November 1980 France's Bernard Hinault visited Greg LeMond's home in Nevada and left with LeMond's signature on a contract to race for the Renault/Gitane team. Many of the track riders named to the 1980 team would go on to win gold, silver, and bronze medals in future Olympics.

The political gamesmanship continued four years later. On May 7, 1984, the USSR announced that it would not send an Olympic team to Los Angeles. Eastern Bloc countries like East Germany and Czechoslovakia followed the boycott. At the time, riders from the Soviet Union and East Germany held five of the eight current world championships in Olympic events. Their absence improved the chances the American team would compete for medals.

Los Angeles 1984

After fifty years on foreign soil, the Olympics returned to Los Angeles in 1984. Peter Ueberroth's vision and masterful planning turned a national event that often ended in long-term debt into a profitable marketing campaign for the United States and its athletes.

In July 1983 Peter Siracusa, the commissioner for cycling for the 1984 Olympics, invited the officials from the USCF, the UCI, and the Los Angeles Olympic Committee to California to review plans for the cycling competition. At the urging of Siracusa and his staff, the delegates agreed to change the order of Olympic cycling events. According to tradition, the team time trial was scheduled to be the first cycling event receiving broadcast coverage following the opening ceremonies, and the road race last. The media-savvy Los Angeles team wanted to switch the team time trial and road races to give the television audience a better experience. If the delegates agreed to the switch, ABC-TV would broadcast the men's road race to a worldwide audience estimated at 2.5 billion people. Reluctant at first, the delegates finally succumbed to Siracusa's request.

Eddie Borysewicz, the national coaching director, believed that the Soviet Union's boycott of the 1984 Games dramatically improved the medal opportunities for American riders. Claiming to be nervous about local media reports forecasting freeway gridlock, Eddie B. lobbied David Prouty, the first executive director of the USCF, to move the team from the Olympic Village—two hours away from the competition venues—to a Radisson Inn a mile from the Olympic velodrome. Despite the USOC's preference for athletes to stay at the Olympic Village, Prouty approved the request. The decision would have major implications for the American team's performance and reputation.

As the start of the Games drew near, anticipation and excitement spread through the team. But controversy threatened to change the makeup of the team at the very last moment. On Thursday, July 19, ten days before the Olympic road race, Alexi Grewal failed a drug test at the Coors Classic. By policy, Coors officials tested the top three finishers at the end of each day's stage. Grewal had been tested the three previous days and the results were negative. He said an herbal capsule given to him by his massage therapist fifteen minutes before the start of the race contaminated the results.

At the time of Grewal's test, the USOC listed 3,700 banned substances. An American rider had been disqualified and suspended for thirty days for inadvertently using Visine eyewash. Athletes were confused and nervous about how ingredients in the products they used in everyday life would impact drug testing.

A decision over jurisdiction was the first obstacle Grewal had to address in order to appeal the test. If the rules of the international governing body were used, Grewal could not compete in the Olympics until his appeal was heard. Under USCF rules, Grewal could compete while the appeal process was under way.

Prouty did his best to convince the international official at the Coors event to see the situation from the USCF's perspective. Looking for any way to save Grewal's starting position in the road race, Prouty contacted two doctors, Casey Clarke and Robert Voy, to assist him in Grewal's defense and verify the herbal ingredients claim.

After reviewing the medical files, Clarke felt the testing procedures were unreliable. Grewal, in addition to taking the herbal supplement, also took albuterol to control exercise-induced asthma. Fortunately, Grewal had followed all international and USCF requirements and had received formal permission to use the medication in competition.

Grewal's albuterol use clouded the results of the test. The lab technicians acknowledged that they could not determine whether the negative test result was due to the approved medicine or the banned herbal ingredient. An intense deliberation between USCF and UCI officials ended with a decision to judge Grewal under USCF rules.

The jury of five convened and listened to almost eight hours of testimony from Grewal's lawyer, representatives from the laboratory, and Robert Voy. The jury met from 6 p.m. Sunday to 4:30 a.m. Monday before reaching a decision that was

announced at a morning press conference. The jury foreman informed the assembled crowd that Grewal had been found not guilty due to a defective test. He was back in the Olympics.

American Women Enter Olympic History

At 9 a.m. on July 29, 1984, the Olympic cycling tradition welcomed women to the competition field for the first time. The women's 79-kilometer road race was the inaugural event. Forty-five women started and all but one finished. Two American women, Connie Carpenter and Rebecca Twigg, found their names inscribed in Olympic cycling history. Less than 200 meters from the finish line, Carpenter and Twigg were part of an eight-woman pack sprinting for the first cycling gold medal. The other six riders did not intend to let the American women pass them. Motivated by the high-pitched cheers of 50,000 hometown fans, Carpenter and Twigg split to each side of the pack. The move slowed their momentum for an instant and increased the apprehension of American cycling officials watching the finish.

Carpenter, already a legend in American cycling, had postponed her retirement after learning the women's road race would be added in Los Angeles. Twigg represented a bright future for American women on the international level. Driving hard past the six riders, who failed to block their break, Carpenter and Twigg were side by side with meters to go. Twigg appeared to have the slightest edge, but Carpenter threw her bike forward, crossing the line with her arm raised in celebration. With her arm around Twigg, the two competitors shared the sweet glory of winning gold and silver in the first women's road race.

Carpenter's performance had larger historical significance: Her gold was the first Olympic medal awarded to an American rider in seventy-two years.

According to a network television executive, fourteen million viewers watched Connie Carpenter outsprint Rebecca Twigg for the women's road race title.

Later that day Grewal vindicated the intense support he received from USCF officials by winning the men's road race gold medal. Riding in front of 200,000 enthusiastic spectators, Grewal broke away early and withstood a late challenge from Steve Bauer. The Canadian rider passed Grewal on the last lap, but in the final sprint to the line, Grewal beat Bauer by two bike lengths. Three of his teammates finished in the top ten—Davis Phinney, Thurlow Rogers, and Ron Kiefel.

The American team would not stop with three medals on the first day. U.S. cyclists won four gold and a total of nine medals before the Games ended. Steve Hegg and Leonard Nitz won gold and bronze in the individual pursuit. Teammates Mark Gorski and Nelson Vails won gold and silver in the match sprint. They were the first American medals in the event. The team pursuit squad of Hegg, Nitz, Brent Emery, and Pat McDonough captured silver. Finally, the four-man team time trial team of Davis Phinney, Ron Kiefel, Andy Weaver, and Roy Knickman proudly wore the bronze medal.

At the end of the Games, gold medal winner Alexi Grewal signed a contract with Holland's Panasonic-Raleigh for the 1985 season. His $40,000 salary made him the second-highest-paid American cyclist behind Greg LeMond.

The glory surrounding the team's performance was only slightly diminished by the revelation that many of the American medal winners had received illicit blood transfusions at their Ramada hideaway and that the procedure had been supervised by some of the big names in U.S. cycling.

Seoul 1988: Momentum Stalls

The 1984 Olympic team, Greg LeMond, and CBS network coverage of LeMond's victory at the 1986 Tour de France fueled interest in cycling and competitive racing. In 1983 network television broadcast less than three hours of bicycle racing. Five years later the schedule expanded to almost twenty-five hours of coverage. In 1983 the USCF had 15,315 licensed riders. By 1988 that number had almost doubled.

Bicycle racers were also making names for themselves in advertising and promotions. Olympic sprint champion Mark Gorski signed a marketing agreement with ProServ after the 1984 Olympics. In 1987 Steve Disson, an agent at ProServ, had Connie Carpenter, Davis Phinney, Nelson Vails, and Connie Paraskevin-Young as clients. ProServ's cycling division was a $4 million business and the firm's fastest-growing segment.

The Twenty-fourth Olympic Games in Seoul, Korea, were the first non-boycotted Games in eight years. New U.S. national team director Mark Hodges predicted medal performances in the men's and women's match sprint and the women's road race. But four years after the American cycling team dominated the 1984 Olympics, winning nine medals, the team returned from Seoul with just a single medal. Connie Paraskevin-Young won the bronze in the match sprint. Bob Mionske's 4th place in the road race was the only other significant story of the

Seoul Games for the U.S. cyclists.

The four-man pursuit team exemplified the struggles faced by U.S. cycling. Team members were not selected until September 10, just thirteen days before the first race in Seoul. One week before the squad was scheduled to leave for Korea, Steve Hegg failed a drug test due to excessive caffeine. Hegg's appeal was denied. Alternate Carl Sundquist joined Dave Lettieri, Mike McCarthy, and Leonard Nitz on the team. They missed the quarterfinal round, finishing less than a half second behind the 8th-place Italians.

Less than sixty days after the closing ceremonies of the Seoul Olympics, the USCF announced a major reorganization. Reacting to complaints from the riders, the USCF shifted coaching assignments. The USCF board also created the U.S. Olympic Development cycling team program. Called Team USA, the program was designed to prepare and train a select group of amateurs for the 1992 and 1996 Olympics. Team USA riders received equipment, clothing, and limited financial support from the Federation. The team trained year-round and competed in international events.

Bronze in Barcelona

In the four-year period between Seoul and Barcelona, the USOC awarded the USCF $1.7 million in financial support. In terms of amount received, cycling ranked thirteenth among all sports contested at Summer Olympic events.

The team returned from Barcelona with two bronze medals. Rebecca Twigg finished 3rd in the women's individual pursuit. Erin Hartwell captured 3rd place in the men's kilometer time trial.

After the success of the road team in 1984, hopes for consecutive gold medals

fell on the shoulders of Lance Armstrong. Armstrong, who won more than a dozen races leading up to the Olympics, finished 14th, far out of medal contention. The Barcelona race ended Armstrong's amateur career. When the closing ceremonies ended, Armstrong became a member of the Motorola professional cycling team.

The USCF sent teams to each Olympics with a set of expectations— some realistic, some based on hopes of once-in-a-lifetime performances. The cyclists often failed to meet the medal objectives set when the team was selected. In the aftermath, programs were changed, training tactics were modified, and organizational charts were shifted. In late 1992 the USCF promoted Chris Carmichael to director of athletes and programs. Carmichael championed new approaches to training, technology, and development of athletes.

Another change at the end of 1992 would have a far-reaching impact on Olympic cycling. In December the UCI formally announced a new set of eligibility rules. For the first time, professional cyclists would be allowed to race in Olympic events. After the change American riders like Lance Armstrong and Andy Hampsten could ride for professional teams and the U.S. Olympic team.

Olympic organizers also added three new events for the 1996 cycle racing schedule. Mountain biking racing, the individual time trial, and the women's points race would make their debut in Atlanta.

Project '96: Atlanta

In 1984 American cyclists arrived at the Los Angeles Games with bikes that stretched the traditional definition of a racing bicycle. Under the direction of the USCF's Cycling's Ed Burke and Chester

Kyle, a new generation of track bikes was introduced. Nicknamed "funny bikes," the new frames and components reduced aerodynamic drag and gave American riders a technological edge. One of the most visible changes was the solid disc wheel. The UCI approved the use of this type of wheel early in 1984, and the riders quickly adopted the technology. Engineers reported that at 30 mph, the new bikes produced 25 percent less drag than a standard racing bike. The U.S. team went on to dominate the 1984 Games, winning the first American cycling medals since 1912.

After disappointing results at the 1988 and 1992 Olympic Games, the USOC and USCF launched an aggressive initiative designed to bring home more gold medals at the 1996 Olympic Games in Atlanta. In 1993 the USCF opened discussions with Electronic Data Systems (EDS), General Motors, and other corporate supporters to find ways to improve rider performance. With the difference between 1st and 4th place measured in milliseconds, technological advantages provided a competitive edge. The effort, called Project '96, was inspired and led by national coaching director Chris Carmichael. Project '96 called for analysis, from the ground up, of every aspect of the U.S. team's cycling technology and rider training.

Corporate support was crucial to the effort. Companies like EDS, GT Bicycles, Korbel Champagne, Mavic, Pearl Izumi, Powerade, and Sportspep funded research. Through its sponsorship relationship with EDS, USA Cycling (formerly the USCF) received access to a General Motors wind tunnel facility to test bicycle designs and the impact of rider position on performance.

After almost six months of testing and revising prototypes, the USCF introduced the SuperBike at the 1994 world championships in Italy. Called the SB-I, the new bike design was credited with helping the team pursuit team win a silver medal. The SB-I design was also ridden to a gold medal at the 1995 Pan Am Games and a bronze medal at the 1995 world championships.

While testing of frame materials and components continued, the performance characteristics of the rider's helmet and clothing were also improved. Troxel created an aerodynamic helmet that had the lowest drag of any helmet tested in the wind tunnel. Special dimples on the surface reduced aerodynamic drag when the riders reached 30 to 35 mph.

At the time, most riders wore one-piece nylon or spandex racing suits. For Project '96, Pearl Izumi used the latest fabric technologies from around the world to create racing suits with incredible attention to detail. The suits were constructed after taking detailed measurements of each racer in the riding position. Seams were not used in areas where they could cause air turbulence. Minute ceramic particles embedded in the stars-and-stripes graphic helped reduce heat buildup.

New training and testing regimes were also used to prepare cyclists. Using a measurement tool called the Wingate test, team physiologist David Morris measured peak power output and fatigue ratios. All eight riders at the team pursuit camp at the Olympic Training Center in Colorado Springs were tested, and the data was used to seed the starting positions for the team pursuit competitions.

Testing was an integral part of the riders' training programs. EDS contributed data management software to measure physiologic functions for each rider. The

SRM power meter used a special crank with strain meters to measure the amount of power the rider applied to the pedals. In one test using the SRM system, Lance Armstrong sustained a 31 mph speed for 1 lap on his time trial bike. When variables like the position of his seat and handlebars were adjusted, Armstrong was able to increase his speed to 32 mph with the same power output.

Team officials also changed training procedures. In 1988 the pursuit team riders had very little opportunity to get used to one another's strengths and riding personalities. The 1996 team worked and raced together for almost a year before the Games.

As the Atlanta Games drew closer, engineers and designers used advanced CADD 5 modeling software, contributed by Computervision Corporation, to create the second-generation SuperBike II. In January 1996 another round of wind tunnel testing revealed that the new design was even faster than the original. Moving from design to prototype for the SB-I design took five and a half months. The redesigned and reengineered SB-II was built in two and a half weeks.

Tests indicated that the aerodynamic design of SuperBike II improved its performance by 15 percent over competitive bikes. The frame formed a symmetrical airfoil that conformed to engineering standards used in aircraft construction. Every component on the SB-II reflected Project '96's commitment to the finest details. The wheels, bottom bracket, and crank arms were constructed as integrated systems. Recessed Allen bolts replaced traditional locknuts on the front fork. The back of the seat tube was cut away and closed off to fit around the wheel. The stem and fork crown had a similar airfoil shape and incorporated the headset to reduce wind resistance.

From a side view, the seventeen-pound track bike was the evolution of early so-called funny bikes. The rear wheel was bigger than the front, and there were no crossbars or handlebars—just an aerodynamic grip. Head-on, it seemed to disappear. There wasn't a single nut, screw, or bolt protruding. Even the shoes of the rider were integrated with the pedal cranks.

At an estimated cost of $15,000 each, twelve SB-IIs were custom-tailored to the USA Cycling team riders. They were delivered in April, and the riders had three and a half months to familiarize themselves with the bike's performance characteristics.

Project '96 invested more than three years of work and a $1 million budget to field a cycling team that could match or exceed the medal total from the breakthrough 1984 Games in Los Angeles. Facing stiff competition and internal challenges, the U.S. track cycling team finished the Twenty-sixth Olympiad in Atlanta with only two silver medals. The team also found some solace in a bronze medal in the mountain bike competition and eight other top ten finishes.

The men's kilometer event was expected to show the world America's technological prowess. Erin Hartwell, riding the state-of-the-art SuperBike II, set an Olympic record riding against Japan's Takanobu Jumonji. Hartwell covered the last lap more than six-tenths of a second faster than Jumonji could manage on his traditional steel bike. Hartwell was in 1st place with two riders remaining. The next rider to face Hartwell, France's Florian Rousseau, started his ride aggressively, building a half-second lead at the halfway point. Although his last 2 lap times were slower than Hartwell's,

Rousseau finished ahead by two-tenths of a second. The final rider, Australian Shane Kelly, never had a chance to compete for the gold medal. As the electronic starter signaled the beginning of his race, Kelly's left foot came off the pedal. The judges did not permit Kelly to start again. America's SuperBike II captured silver, not gold.

After losing to Germany's Jens Fiedler, American Marty Nothstein rode against Canadian Curt Hartnett for the men's match sprint silver medal. Nothstein won the first sprint by two bike lengths and secured the silver, sweeping high off the bank to take the second ride.

At the Olympic cycling trials, eight riders were named to the team pursuit squad. Dirk Copeland, Matt Hamon, Mike McCarthy, and Carl Sundquist had previous Olympic experience. Zach Conrad, Mariano Friedick, Adam Laurent, and Christian Vande Velde joined them. All eight riders signed a contract to split the $60,000 gold medal bonus prize equally. All four members of the final pursuit team rode the SuperBike II. Enthusiastic fans cheered for McCarthy, Laurent, Friedick, and Copeland. Starting out strong, the American team was a tenth of a second faster than the 1st-place French team at 3 kilometers. But the team faltered for just an instant, moving them from medal contention to a 6th-place finish. It was the team's best performance at sea level, but that wasn't the outcome USA Cycling had hoped for.

Shortly after the 1996 Olympics, the International Cycling Federation called a stop to the development of such technological marvels as the SuperBike II. The decision was made to maintain a competitive relationship among all countries, regardless of financial resources.

On the Road

On April 27, 1996, Lance Armstrong became the first American professional to qualify for the Olympic team. USA Cycling Olympic team selection procedures allowed Armstrong to qualify for the team based on his top-15 position in the world cup standings. With his place on the team secured, Armstrong did not attend the U.S. Olympic cycling team trials.

The Atlanta Olympic Games marked the first time the road race was open to professionals. The peloton started 183 riders; only 116 finished. The average speed was a professional-quality 45.285 kph (28.139 mph). The fastest lap speed was recorded at 49.193 kph. Swiss rider Pascal Richard won the gold medal, covering the 137.8-mile race in 4:53:56. Lance Armstrong attacked on the 14th lap of 17 through Atlanta's Buckhead neighborhood, but was not able to sustain the break. His teammate Frankie Andreu, who spent much of the race supporting Armstrong, pushed the leaders on the final 2 laps and finished 4th. Armstrong finished 12th, Greg Randolph 74th, George Hincapie 76th, and Steve Hegg 93rd. Later in the Olympic cycling schedule, Armstrong finished the individual time trial in 6th place, 2:26 behind gold medalist Miguel Indurain.

France's Jeanne Longo dominated the women's road race, winning by 25 seconds over Italy's Imelda Chiappa. Jeanne Golay was the top American finisher, in 29th place.

First Mountain Bike Race

On October 30, 1996, more than 30,000 fans gathered on a grassy area the locals called Holy Hill to watch the first Olympic mountain bike cross-country race. Looking for their place in Olympic history, riders faced 90-degree heat and high humidity

—even though the race was being held in October to avoid the prohibitively intense heat of August.

Under Olympic rules, two-person teams were entered in the event. Juli Furtado, Susan DeMattei, Tinker Juarez, and Don Myrah were named to the first U.S. Olympic mountain bike team.

Once again, the selection process played a cruel joke. Ned Overend needed to finish in the top 4 at the National Off-Road Bicycle Association (NORBA) national mountain bike championships to secure his place on the team beside undisputed team leader Tinker Juarez. One and a half miles from the finish of the 22.5-mile Olympic qualifier, Overend suffered a flat tire and finished 8th.

The course on Stone Mountain did not include any large climbs, taking away a competitive advantage for American riders. Italy's Paola Pezzo won the 10.63-kilometer inaugural women's cross-country race. Riding a Diamondback, Susan DeMattei finished behind Canada's Alison Sydor to win the bronze medal. Juli Furtado finished 10th, her performance affected by heat.

Despite competing on U.S. soil in the only cycling discipline created here, American men did not win a medal. Juarez and Myrah finished together in 19th and 20th.

Sydney 2000

In Atlanta the highly anticipated SuperBikes of Project '96 were expected to dominate the Games. Instead, the U.S. team came away with three medals: two silvers and a bronze. To increase its medal chances in Sydney, USA Cycling sent its largest team in Olympic history. Antonio Cruz and Nicole Freedman, who won the men's and women's road race trials, were the only racers who received automatic

berths to the twenty-seven-member team. Other members were selected by a committee of coaches who evaluated racing performances in the months leading up to the Sydney Olympics. Basing decisions on a single race, as had been done in the past, had sometimes skewed the team, since some of the best riders picked the wrong day for a poor race effort.

Behind the scenes, financial issues caused friction between USA Cycling officials and the riders. In addition to a $200,000 deficit and the $100,000 price tag of sending the team to Australia, the governing body had to address a significant decrease in corporate sponsorships. USA Cycling's annual budget of $1.9 million had to cover all the training camps, competition expenses, and stipends for elite athletes at all levels. In contrast, the U.S. Postal team budgeted at least $6 million to fund sixteen members. The budget crisis required USA Cycling to cut the riders' stipends. Instead of the $2,500 they expected, elite riders received $1,440 augmented by a one-time $2,500 grant from the USOC.

Nothstein's Gold

At the Atlanta Olympics in 1996, Marty Nothstein went to the starting line of the sprint finals convinced that he was the man to beat. The painful memory of settling for silver in Atlanta fueled his ambitions in Sydney.

Nothstein won all eight heats to win the men's match sprint gold medal. Facing Germany's Jens Fiedler in the semifinals, Nothstein reveled in defeating the man who beat him four years earlier in the final round. Riding at his peak, Nothstein blew past French rider Florian Rousseau and raised his fist in victory before the pair crossed the finish line.

Marty Nothstein had won the first gold medal in a track event since the 1984 Olympics, and the only track gold in a non-boycotted Olympics since 1904.

Armstrong's Bronze

In August 2000, just one month before the start of the Sydney Olympics, Lance Armstrong crashed on a training ride in Nice. The defending Tour de France champion was attempting to make a left turn when he was struck by a car coming the other direction. Armstrong broke his neck. The fracture of the C-7 vertebra healed quickly but limited his training time for the Olympics.

Conditioning played a role in the 239.4-kilometer road race in Australia, where Armstrong finished 13th, trailing gold medal winner Jan Ullrich by 1:39. Armstrong also competed in the 46.8-kilometer individual time trial, finishing 3rd behind U.S. Postal teammate Viatcheslav Ekimov and Jan Ullrich. By winning the bronze medal, Armstrong became the first cyclist to win the Tour de France and an Olympic medal in the same year.

America's largest cycling team returned from Sydney with a medal of every color—Marty Nothstein's gold in the sprint, Mari Holden's silver in the time trial, and Lance Armstrong's bronze in the time trial.

Athens 2004

The Olympics returned to Athens 108 years after the city hosted the first modern Games. USA Cycling sent eighteen riders to Athens. Overall, the team was smaller and younger than the Sydney team, and expectations were modest. Team USA was looking ahead to Beijing in 2008.

Lance Armstrong, initially a member of the Olympic road team, sent USA Cycling officials a letter informing them of his decision to skip the Athens Olympics to spend more time with his family. USA Cycling selected Levi Leipheimer to replace Armstrong. Leipheimer, George Hincapie, Bobby Julich, and Tyler Hamilton rode in the 2004 Tour de France before joining the full American team in Greece. Julich, Leipheimer, and teammate Jason McCartney made their first Olympic appearances.

Gold for the Road

American riders claimed gold, silver, and bronze in the road race to mark the U.S. cycling team's best performance in Olympic history.

Dede Barry's silver medal in the women's time trial started the celebration. She finished 24.09 seconds behind defending gold medal winner Leontien Zijlaard-van Moorsel of the Netherlands. Christine Thorburn finished 4th, missing the bronze medal by less than 20 seconds. Following the accomplishments of Connie Carpenter, Rebecca Twigg, and Mari Holden, Barry became the fourth American woman to win an Olympic road medal.

The performance of Tyler Hamilton and Bobby Julich in the individual time trial added to the celebration. Hamilton finished 1st in the time trial, covering the 48-kilometer course in 57:31.74. During his gold medal ride, Hamilton averaged over 50 kph and beat the defending gold medalist, Viatcheslav Ekimov of Russia, by almost 19 seconds. The last time an American cyclist had won a gold medal in the road race was 1984, when the feat was accomplished by Alexi Grewal and Connie Carpenter. Bobby Julich won the bronze medal despite riding with a broken right wrist suffered on the thirteenth stage of the Tour de France.

Kristin Armstrong's 8th-place ride in the women's road race was the first top-10 finish since Carpenter and Twigg finished 1st and 2nd in 1984.

The American track team could not match the success of their teammates. Marty Nothstein's goal to win medals in three consecutive Olympiads failed when he did not qualify for the keirin. Erin Mirabella's 4th-place finish in the points race was the best by an American on the track at the Athens Games. When Colombia's Maria-Luisa Calle Williams's drug test returned with a positive result, the International Olympic Committee (IOC) awarded Mirabella the bronze medal. After a lengthy appeal, the Court of Arbitration for Sport found the disqualification of the Colombian racer was unwarranted, and Mirabella returned her medal. No other racer on the track squad finished higher than 10th in any event, and the United States failed to medal on an Olympic velodrome for the first time in six Olympiads.

USA Cycling sent three mountain bikers to Athens. Jeremy Horgan-Kobelski and Todd Wells won spots on the men's team and Mary McConneloug was the sole American woman in the field. USA Cycling originally named Sue Haywood to the team based on USA Cycling's point system rankings. Based on her understanding of the rules, McConneloug, ranked 2nd in the world, appealed the decision, calling into question the way race points were tallied at the end of the season. An arbiter reviewed the process and overturned the decision. The report questioned USA Cycling's decision to add 15 points to Haywood's international total, which moved her ahead of McConneloug by a single point. McConneloug's place on the team was secured when a federal judge denied Haywood's second appeal. In Athens McConneloug finished in 9th place.

The men's mountain bike race was the final event of the Athens Olympics. First-time Olympians Todd Wells and Jeremy Horgan-Kobelski finished 19th and 21st. Since mountain bike racing was introduced to the Olympics in 1996, no American male has finished higher than 19th position.

The American team won three medals on the road but trailed other countries in total medals. Australian riders took ten cycling medals and Germany finished 2nd with six.

Hamilton Fails Blood Doping Test

Olympic athletes are subject to extensive drug-testing protocols. On August 19, 2004, the day after his gold medal ride, Tyler Hamilton took the routine drug test, administered by the IOC. The tests were standard and routine; the results, however, surprised Hamilton and USA Cycling officials. One month after the test Hamilton was told that he had failed a blood doping test. The lab reported that Hamilton's sample showed a "mixed blood cell population" that was illegal under IOC regulations.

On September 11 Hamilton was competing in the Tour of Spain when he received a request from the IOC for a second test. The second test, under the oversight of the UCI, also showed a positive result. Hamilton aggressively maintained his innocence and questioned the reliability of the tests and laboratory procedures.

Controversial blood transfusions have plagued international cycling events for decades. In 1984 the procedure was formally banned after a number of American riders confessed to using blood doping to improve their performances. Until the Athens Olympics, oversight bodies like the IOC and UCI could not accurately evaluate an individual sample for blood doping. The new test, developed by an Australian research firm funded by the World Anti-Doping Agency and the U.S. Anti-Doping Agency, is able to detect blood from another person in the sample.

The IOC's investigations into the allegations against Hamilton were hampered by a laboratory mistake. Instead of refrigerating the sample taken at the Tour of Spain, a lab technician placed the materials in a freezer, effectively destroying the blood cells and preventing further analysis and investigation. Although Hamilton was allowed to keep his Olympic gold medal, repercussions of the failed test followed. Hamilton was fired by his Phonak cycling team and banned from professional racing. This ended his six-figure Phonak salary and put at risk endorsement contracts with a list of top sponsors, including Nike and Oakley.

In April 2005 he received a two-year suspension from the U.S. Anti-Doping Agency. Hamilton battled to restore his reputation, filing appeals first with the American Arbitration Association and then with the Court of Arbitration for Sport in Switzerland. Both organizations upheld the original suspension. Under the suspension timetable, Hamilton was eligible to return to competitive racing in April 2007.

2008 Beijing: BMX

In June 2005 the UCI announced that the men's kilometer and the women's 500-meter races would not be contested at the 2008 Olympics in Beijing. The UCI made the change to accommodate the addition of men's and women's BMX (bicycle moto-cross) events. Erin Hartwell was the only American ever to medal in the men's kilometer event, winning bronze in Barcelona and silver in Atlanta. American riders have never reached the medal podium in the 500-meter time trial.

Administration and Insurance

Conflicts and Negotiations, Part 2

Five years after reaching an agreement on the management of professional racing in the United States, the USCF and USPRO continued to hold differing opinions. Concerned with the way USPRO was issuing racing licenses, the USCF filed a formal complaint with the UCI. In April 1986 Michel Jekiel, general secretary of the UCI, asked officials from the USCF and USPRO to meet to discuss unresolved issues. Typically strained, the meeting ended without reaching any agreements.

In November 1986 the USCF's board of directors announced plans to charge a limited professional license fee of $500, effective January 1,

1987. The new rule required any professional racer entering a USCF event to pay the fee.

In the November 14, 1986 issue of *Velonews,* Phil Voxland, the USCF's president, explained the fees: "the USCF puts money into the developments of athletes, riders like Greg LeMond, Roy Knickman and Davis Phinney. Over the years the federation spends money on coaching, room and board. Then those riders turn professional and the federation doesn't get any money back. There are about 100 pros, at $500 that brings $50,000 to the federation." In the same issue, USPRO's executive Jack Simes responded, "We're not going to sit around and let it happen. The licensing of professional cyclists in the U.S. is only done by the United States Professional Cycling Federation. Period. And nobody is going to come into this country and issue professional licenses."

Despite the harsh rhetoric, another working agreement was hammered out. Nine more years would pass before the two organizations fully resolved their differences.

Insurance Crisis

In 1986 bicycle sales continued to soar, with mountain bikes driving much of the growth. Halfway through 1986 bicycle sales reached 6.6 million—almost one million more than at the same point in 1985. Membership in the USCF grew from 7,500 in 1979 to over 22,000 in 1986. The number of races jumped from 692 to 1,131 in 1985.

Behind the positive sales reports a crisis was brewing. Early in 1986 the USCF and thirty other amateur sports organizations did not have current liability insurance. The USCF had held both accident and liability insurance policies. The accident insurance covered medical costs for a rider injured at a sanctioned race event. That portion of the policy was renewed for 1986. The liability policies were under fire by all insurance companies. The USCF's $5 million policy expired December 31, 1985, and the insurance carrier, National Union Fire of Pittsburgh, said it would not offer the policy in 1986.

In a memo to districts, David Prouty, executive director of the USCF, wrote, "Competitive cycling has the worst insurance record over the past 3-5 years of all amateur sports." Prouty reported that settlement payments for insurance claims were exceeding premiums by a two-to-one ratio. And the numbers were rising so fast that the underwriter canceled the USCF's liability policy.

The USCF hired a consulting firm to help it find coverage. Even then, the premium for the policy was expected to rise from the $21,000 paid in 1985 to over $150,000 for 1986. In response, the USCF initiated an insurance surcharge fee to recoup some of the increase.

The USOC stepped in to support amateur sports under its umbrella and created a self-insurance program. The USCF paid $193,000 for one year of coverage. The fee, based on the number of licensed riders, amounted to $10 per rider. In 1985 the USCF listed 19,290 licenses.

The increase in accidents, lawsuits, and settlements led to the USCF's formal decision to require mandatory use of hard-shell helmets at all sanctioned races. On September 21, 1985, the USCF passed a rule that made approved hard-shell helmets compulsory in all USCF-sanctioned events beginning on January 1, 1986. Rider complaints about extra weight and heat did little to sway the decision.

PART THREE

Bicycle Racing in the Modern Era

The 7-Eleven team competing at the Coors Classic. For more than a decade, the Coors Classic was one of the world's most popular races.

CHAPTER SIX

America's Growing Competitiveness

The World Takes Notice

ELEVEN YEARS AFTER Audrey McElmury became the first American to win the world championship professional road race, Beth Heiden captured America's second world road title at the 1980 race in Sallanches, France. Just two years later Rebecca Twigg became the first American to win a pursuit gold medal on the track.

In 1982 six Americans traveled to Goodwood, England to race in the world championship professional road race. Jacques Boyer, Greg LeMond, George Mount, John Eustice, David Mayer-Oakes, and Eric Heiden joined 130 other riders at the start of the single-day 275-kilometer race. On the 18th and final lap, LeMond and Boyer were still in contention. One kilometer from the finish, Boyer attacked and moved into the lead. LeMond and Italy's Giuseppe Saronni answered Boyer's attack and passed him in the last 500 meters. LeMond trailed Saronni in the final sprint. LeMond's silver was the first world championship road race medal awarded to an American male.

One year later, in Altenrhein, Switzerland, LeMond captured the rainbow jersey awarded to the winner of the world championship road race. Uninterested in leaving the final results to be decided in the sprint, LeMond rode aggressively off the

ROBERT F. GEORGE

In 1980 Beth Heiden finished 1st in the Coors Classic women's stage race. At the women's world championship road race in Sallanches, France, she became the second American to win a world championship road race.

front and finished more than 1 minute ahead of the 2nd-place rider. LeMond's success in Europe would continue until the end of the decade.

American women contributed record-setting victories to the growing list of accomplishments achieved at European events. At the 1986 Tour of Norway, also known as the PostGiro, Inga Thompson, Janelle Parks, Judy Caunter, Rebecca Twigg, and Katrin Tobin captured the team title, defeating seventy-six riders from eleven countries. Thompson finished the eleven-stage, nine-day race in 2nd place. Twigg, still one of America's best racers, won the climbing competition.

American women returned to the PostGiro in 1988 and improved on their 1986 performance. Labeled as one of the most important women's stage races in the world, the PostGiro was dominated by the American team of Bunki Bankaitis-Davis, Inga Benedict, Katrin Tobin, Mindee Gurtis, and Sally Zack. At the end of the eleven-stage race, Bankaitis-Davis finished 44 seconds ahead of Norway's Uni Larsen. Benedict was 7th, Tobin 8th, and Zack 22nd; Gurtis, riding in her first PostGiro, finished 34th and won the sprint competition. In the team competition the American squad captured three of eleven stages and finished more than 7 minutes ahead of the 2nd-place team.

Andy Hampsten and 7-Eleven

Although LeMond's 1986 Tour de France victory captured the interest of novice bicycle racing fans in America, serious enthusiasts knew there was much more to celebrate. Andy Hampsten's victories in classic European races proved that the United States had more than just Greg LeMond to compete for the 1st-place jerseys.

At the Tour of Switzerland in 1986, Andy Hampsten and his 7-Eleven teammates dominated. The yellow jersey remained on Hampsten's shoulders for all but one stage. He finished 1st, unchallenged, almost a minute in front of his closest competitor.

Returning to Switzerland in 1987, Hampsten found a much closer race. Over ten days the lead changed seven times, and Hampsten didn't move into 1st place until the end of the second-to-last stage. On the final day Hampsten held a 1-second lead over Dutch rider Peter Winnen. The 145-kilometer final stage featured a 10-second bonus sprint at the 60-kilometer mark. Only the winner of the sprint would receive the time bonus. The 7-Eleven team of Raul Alcala, Jeff Bradley,

Jonathan Boyer (who had changed his name to Jacques Boyer when he moved to Europe), Dag-Otto Lauritzen, Davis Phinney, Jeff Pierce, Bob Roll, Doug Shapiro, and Ron Kiefel kept the pace fast to protect Hampsten's tenuous lead. Winnen attacked in an attempt to win the bonus, but 7-Eleven rider Kiefel edged him in a photo finish to secure Hampsten's second Tour of Switzerland victory.

In 1988 twenty teams of nine riders started the Tour of Italy. Better known as the Giro d'Italia, the Tour of Italy was the second-biggest stage race in the world behind the Tour de France. In one of the most dramatic stage race performances in European history, Hampsten, captain of the 7-Eleven team, raced up and over the windswept, snow-covered Gavia Pass to capture the Giro.

 ## Hampsten il Conquistatore

 Andy Hampsten started his professional racing career in 1985 as a member of the Levi's-Raleigh team. Based on his growing reputation as a strong climber, 7-Eleven hired Hampsten to ride with the team in the 1985 Giro d'Italia. Entering the Giro for the first time, 7-Eleven gave notice that American riders were capable of racing with Europe's best—Ron Kiefel and Hampsten each won a stage.

Hampsten spent the 1986 season riding on the La Vie Claire team with Bernard Hinault and Greg LeMond. In his second year as a professional, Hampsten was already racing at the highest level. He won the Tour of Switzerland and finished 4th in the Tour de France, earning the maillot blanc as the best new rider in the Tour. Hampsten rejoined the 7-Eleven team in 1987 and added more honors to his resume, winning two stages of the Coors Classic and the Tour of Switzerland for the second time.

In 1988 the Giro d'Italia was the second-largest stage race in the world.

The field started with 180 riders divided into twenty teams of 9. The 7-Eleven team arrived at the '88 Giro full of high hopes. Raul Alcala, Ron Kiefel, Roy Knickman, Dag-Otto Lauritzen, Davis Phinney, Jeff Pierce, Bob Roll, and Jens Veggerby joined Hampsten at the start line.

Hampsten's quest for the Giro's distinctive leader's pink jersey began on June 3, when he won the 205-kilometer twelfth stage in the mountains of northern Italy. The stage included three major climbs and an uphill finish. Hampsten made his move 3 kilometers from the finish and crossed the line 11 seconds ahead of Pedro Delgado.

The fourteenth stage was a wicked climb up a mountain pass called Gavia. Rising 2,621 meters above sea level, the route had not been used in twenty-eight years. The peloton started the stage in dismal, cold, and rainy conditions. A steady rain turned to snow above 6,000 feet, just as the riders faced the steep climb and 8,600-foot descent of Gavia Pass. The first nine riders in general classification were within 3 minutes of the lead.

COR VOS

During the fourteenth stage of the 1988 Giro d'Italia, the riders encountered snow, ice, and high winds on the Gavia Pass. Andy Hampsten endured the brutal conditions and finished the stage in 2nd place but took the overall lead.

At 6 a.m. snow was falling at the top of the Gavia climb. Race organizer Vincenzo Torriani was told that snowplows had cleared the course ahead of the riders. Still, the road conditions were far from ideal. The riders were ill-prepared to handle unseasonable mud, snow, ice, and dropping temperatures. Even in perfect weather the Gavia would be tough enough.

Mike Neel, director of 7-Eleven, suggested Hampsten cover his exposed skin with Vaseline to protect him from the elements. Doing the best he could to stay warm, Hampsten added a long-sleeved polypropylene shirt, wool jersey, and rain jacket. Neoprene gloves offered limited protection for his hands. Thinking ahead, the 7-Eleven team manager positioned support cars at regular intervals through the climb. As the riders neared the summit, Jim Ochowicz rewarded their efforts with dry clothing. Ochowicz gave Hampsten a balaclava, wool hat, and new plastic rain jacket.

Low clouds over the mountains prevented helicopters from providing television coverage. Radios crackled with the announcement that Johan van der Velde

was leading at the top of the climb, with Hampsten and Holland's Erik Breukink following close behind. When the hypothermic van der Velde stopped at his team car, only Hampsten and Breukink remained to fight for the stage.

Wind-driven snow blasted Hampsten on the icy descent. A pair of goggles did little to improve visibility—constantly fogged by the warm air rising from under his balaclava, the lenses were smeared with a greasy film of Vaseline that transferred from his legs to gloves to lenses when he tried to clear the snow.

Hampsten finished the stage 7 seconds behind Breukink but 15 seconds ahead of him in the general classification. He earned the right to wear the pink jersey of the race leader. At the end of the day, the riders with any realistic chance of competing for the lead had fallen far behind Breukink and Hampsten, and the race for the pink jersey became a two-man competition.

Most of the riders arrived at the finish of stage fourteen suffering from the cold, frostbitten and deeply fatigued. Bob Roll, Hampsten's 7-Eleven teammate, suffered from hypothermia and was one of many riders who required medical attention after the ride over Gavia.

Hampsten extended his lead in the snow-shortened fifteenth stage, gaining another 27 seconds on Breukink. The eighteenth stage, a challenging uphill time trial, was the last opportunity for the top riders to change their positions in the standings. Hampsten listened to the advice of his teammates and changed the setup of his time trial bike. Instead of standard chainrings of 53 and 39, Hampsten used an eight-speed freewheel and chainrings of 53 and 42. Massimo Testa, the 7-Eleven team doctor, equipped Hampsten with a heart rate monitor and advised him to maintain his pulse in a narrow range of 180 to 185 beats per minute. Armed with the team's expertise, Hampsten finished the time trial in 1st place. More important, he added 1:04 to his lead over Breukink.

The final stage was a 43-kilometer individual time trial. Rain and slick roads led to a number of crashes. Alerted about a dangerous curve by 7-Eleven coach Mike Neel, Hampsten survived the wet conditions and finished the time trial in 7th place. Erik Breukink finished two spots ahead of Hampsten and cut his margin by 23 seconds, but it wasn't enough. Hampsten, who won two stages and the King of the Mountains award, finished the twenty-one-stage race in

On June 12, 1988, Andy Hampsten wore the *maglia rosa*, the pink jersey awarded to the winner of the Giro d'Italia. The Italian press called him "Hampsten il conquistatore."

97:18:15. On June 12, 1988, after twenty-two days of racing, twenty-six-year-old Andy Hampsten wore the *maglia rosa*, the pink jersey awarded to the winner of the Giro d'Italia. Italian newspapers proclaimed, "Hampsten il conquistatore." He was the nineteenth foreigner and first American to win the Giro since the race began in 1909.

Americans in Paris

At the end of the 1981 Tour de France, a rider far from the winner's podium changed history. Jonathan Boyer became the first American to enter and race in the Tour, finishing in 32nd place. A year later he finished nine positions higher. Boyer made Europeans notice when he finished the twelfth stage in 13th place.

USCF officials received and declined an invitation to send an American team to compete in the 1984 Tour. Boyer and Greg LeMond would race as Americans on foreign teams. In his first year in the Tour, LeMond received the white jersey (maillot blanc) awarded to the best young rider.

A women's version of the Tour de France debuted in 1984. American Marianne Martin surprised the European women by winning two stages, capturing 1st place, and leading her five American teammates to the top of the team rankings.

In late 1984 the French La Vie Claire team signed LeMond to a three-year, $1 million contract. The contract changed the economic foundation of professional racing. Before LeMond, top riders may have earned $150,000 per year. After LeMond's contract was announced, the salaries of top riders like Pedro Delgado and Stephen Roche rose to $750,000.

LeMond's First Victory

The 1986 Tour de France was a landmark event for American racers. For the first time, the starting field included a professional team from the United States. By the end of the first road stage, Alex Stieda, a Canadian rider for 7-Eleven, wore the yellow jersey. Teammate Davis Phinney won the third stage. The team performed well, but LeMond captured the headlines and hearts of America. For the first time since the Tour started in 1903, an American stood at the center of the winner's podium.

Following LeMond's victory, interest in the Tour de France and its American entrants exploded. But after he was wounded in a hunting accident in April 1987, LeMond's recovery would keep him away from Paris for two years. He returned in 1989 to defeat Laurent Fignon in the closest finish in the history of the Tour.

Sports Illustrated Athlete of the Year

The 1989 Tour de France ended with high drama. Greg LeMond returned from career-threatening gunshot wounds to win the yellow jersey in the closest finish in the history of the race. France's Laurent Fignon started the final day's time trial with a 50-second lead that many observers felt was large enough to protect his 1st-place position.

Using a state-of-the-art helmet, handlebars, and position, LeMond flew over the road from start ramp to finish line. Physically and mentally spent, he could only watch and wait as Fignon, the last man on the course, tried to match his pace. With each passing kilometer, Fignon's lead melted away. LeMond won his second Tour de France by just 8 seconds.

He followed that performance by defeating 190 riders at the world championship professional road race in Chambery, France. Only four other riders had won the Tour de France and world championship in the same calendar year, and only a handful had won the world championship twice.

His performance placed him at the center of a bidding war. In September 1989 LeMond signed a three-year, $5.7 million contract to race for the French Z team. A record-setting year was capped with a cover photo on *Sports Illustrated*. The magazine named LeMond 1989's athlete of the year.

The Pan American Games Come to Indianapolis

European bicycle racing has a long, storied history. But the countries of Latin America have their own racing heritage. First held in Buenos Aires in 1951, the Pan American Games offered American racers their first taste of victory on an international stage.

The Pan Am Games are awarded to a different city every four years. Chicago hosted the first Games in the United States in 1959. Twenty-nine years later, in 1987, the Games returned to the United States. One year after a disappointing world championships in Colorado Springs, the U.S. team had eleven reasons to celebrate at the Major Taylor Velodrome in Indianapolis. With six golds, four silvers, and a bronze, the American team captured more medals than any other country.

 The Pan American Games

 The Pan American Games have provided an opportunity, relatively close to home, for American riders to gauge their progress against international competition. In the beginning, success for Americans at the Pan Am Games was measured in small increments. By the 1990s, though, American men and women dominated the Games, sweeping the podiums and tallying double-digit medal counts. Along the way, the American teams were beaten by bad water, scandalous officiating, and at times, better riders.

There have been fourteen Pan American Games since the competition was founded. Held every four years, the

Games were scheduled to take place in years without Olympic Summer Games. The Games were originally planned to start in 1940, but World War II put a hold on all plans. The first official Pan American Games were held in Buenos Aires in February 1951.

In 1955 riders from different nations won each of the four cycling events. The American pursuit team was fighting for a bronze medal when Al Stiller became ill and the team was forced to ride one man short. They finished 4th, 10 seconds behind the bronze medal winners.

Chicago hosted the 1959 Pan American Games. More than 2,000 athletes came to compete, making it the largest international sports event ever held at the time. Dr. Milton Eisenhower opened the Games on August 27 on behalf of his brother, President Dwight D. Eisenhower. Forty thousand people gathered at Soldier Field in 90-degree heat to watch the opening ceremonies.

On the road as well as in a new velodrome in Gately Stadium on the south side of Chicago, Argentina dominated, winning three of five events. The American team's excitement about Allen Bell's gold medal on the track was abruptly cut short when Brazil filed a successful protest, claiming Bell's starter gave him a push. It would not be the last time a questionable protest affected the Americans' medal hopes.

America's First Gold Medal

Competition has been intense between North and South American cities vying to host the Pan American Games. Of the fourteen Games held thus far, the United States has hosted only two. In 1971 Champ, Missouri, lost the honor of hosting the sixth Games to Cali, Colombia.

John Howard, a twenty-three-year-old

In 1971 at the Pan American Games in Cali, Colombia, John Howard defeated Brazil's Luis Carlos Florez in the 198-kilometer road race. Florez was the 2nd-ranked amateur in the world. Howard's gold was the first for the United States in Pan American Games competition.

Army soldier from Springfield, Missouri, battled Brazil's Luis Carlos Florez in the 198-kilometer road race in Cali. At the time Florez was the second-ranked amateur cyclist in the world. Two hundred fifty thousand spectators cheered the riders as they rode through Cali's city streets. Near the 100-kilometer mark, Florez and Mexico's Austin Alcantara attacked and moved ahead of the pack. Howard covered their move. Alcantara faltered, and Howard and Florez raced on just inches apart. Fifty meters from the finish, Howard burst forward with an aggressive sprint. The cover photo of *Competitive Cycling* shows Howard with head thrown back and arms thrust in the air, crossing the line to win the first gold medal for the United States in the history of the Pan American Games. He had been scheduled to compete in the team time trial but became sick—fortunately, he recovered in time for the road race.

Howard's dramatic victory drew nationwide media coverage to cycling for the first time in decades. An Associated Press story appeared in newspapers around the country. The *New York Times* placed the story and the photo of Howard crossing the finish line on their front page.

In the track events in Cali, sprinters Skip Cutting and Carl Leusenkamp failed to reach the event finals. John Vande Velde finished 4th in the pursuit. Clif Halsey was the only individual track rider to bring home a medal, finishing 3rd in the kilometer.

Mexico City 1975

In Mexico City the opening ceremonies set the tone for the American team. As the athletes paraded through Azteca Stadium on October 12, 1975, 110,000 spectators lustily booed the American contingent, the crowd unhappy with America's treatment of Cuba. Boos turned to cheers when the Cuban team made their entrance. The opening address of Mexico's pro-American president Luis Echeverria was met with more jeers than cheers.

Before leaving for Mexico, members of the cycling team received a complete Montgomery Ward's wardrobe and suitcases to help them make the appropriate fashion statements at the Games. While they were dressed for success, the athletes' accommodations could be called spartan at best. Ron Skarin, a member of the team and a building inspector in Los Angeles, said the team's accommodations in the Pan Am Village were not up to U.S. building and sanitation standards. Several members of the team suffered bouts of vomiting, diarrhea, and bronchitis.

Battling illness, riders were also distracted by the reception at the opening ceremonies and comments heard around the athlete village. Rumors reached the

road racers that some residents of Mexico City were planning to drop bricks on them from bridge overpasses.

John Howard, Alan Kingsbury, Marc Thompson, and Wayne and Dale Stetina were named to the team time trial team. Before the Games started, Wayne broke his wrist and Dale suffered knee problems. The Stetina brothers were recovering from their injuries but fell ill in Mexico City. The final squad consisted of John Howard, Alan Kingsbury, Marc Thompson, and Rich Hammen. The American team was expected to win a medal but ended up 4th behind Mexico, Colombia, and Cuba. The team complained about getting spit on as they raced through the streets.

Chaos on the Track

The match sprints were held on October 20, the last day of the competition. American sprinter Steve Woznick easily won his first-round rides, and teammate Carl Leusenkamp's 11-second 200 meters was the fastest in the first round. Riders from Cuba and Argentina joined the two Americans in the semifinal round.

In the first semifinal Leusenkamp led Argentina's Octavio Dazzan at the 200-meter mark of the 1,000-meter race, coming down to the pole and shutting off Dazzan just before the third turn. Falling behind the American, Dazzan rode into the infield and raised his arms to place a protest. Leusenkamp continued to the line. In the infield, American, Belgian, Colombian, and Uruguayan judges confirmed Leusenkamp's victory.

In the second heat Leusenkamp started in the following position and stayed there until the bell lap. At 280 meters he first dived low then swooped back up the banking. When Dazzan tried to pass underneath, Leusenkamp blocked him and won the second sprint. Race officials announced that Leusenkamp would move to the final.

Steve Woznick lost his first ride against his Cuban opponent, J. Lescay, in a photo finish and came back to win the second ride. In the third and deciding heat, as Woznick and Lescay raced through the last turn, the Cuban pushed inside and the two bumped elbows. Woznick crossed the line first, creating an all-American final.

When the race for 3rd and 4th place was set to begin, there was an unusual delay. The Argentine and Cuban team managers were aggressively complaining about Leusenkamp's first ride and Woznick's last ride. After thirty minutes of tense waiting, the judges reversed their decision and disqualified Leusenkamp's first heat, claiming he forced Dazzan into the infield. The judges declared that another ride was needed to determine the winner of the semifinal. No English-speaking judges were on the jury of review, and the American officials were denied access to the evidence that led to the reversal.

Leusenkamp had already competed in eight heats against the best in the world. Dazzan had an easier draw and had only raced in four heats. Once again, Leusenkamp and Dazzan raced to determine the semifinal winner. Dazzan led out the last 300 meters. At 200 meters, Leusenkamp trailed by three bike lengths. He surged forward and fell just millimeters short in a photo finish.

Then the track announcer told the crowd that the judges were also reviewing Woznick's victory over the Cuban rider Lescay. Standing in the middle of the large infield with coach Jack Simes and Leusenkamp at his side, Woznick put his head in his hands, trying to shake off

ROBERT F. GEORGE

Frustrated by a series of controversial decisions by judges at the 1975 Mexico City Pan American match-sprint event, Steve Woznick surprised spectators with a dramatic protest. Woznick slashed his tires with a knife and threw his bike and clothes on the center of the track. Woznick ultimately won the gold medal in the event.

the events of the last few minutes. Suddenly, he picked up his track bike and walked to the banked track. Lifting the front wheel off the track, Woznick smashed his hand down, exploding the tire. Spinning the bike around, he repeated his gesture and punctured the rear tire. The crack of the explosions caught the attention of the other riders, judges, and spectators. Woznick laid the damaged bike on the track, placed his shoes, jacket, and warm-ups on top of the bike, and stormed off.

Watching from the stands, UCI commissar Signor Paccharelli approached Woznick and Leusenkamp and asked them to return and collect "the medals they deserved."

With the chaos finally under control, Leusenkamp faced the Cuban Lescay for the bronze medal. After a restart, Leusenkamp won the first ride. In the second, just after Leusenkamp made an aggressive jump to take the lead, the lights in the velodrome abruptly went dark. Bill Lambert, the starter, fired his pistol to signal a restart. With guards posted to prevent another accidental power outage, the riders prepared for a fourth ride. It was Leusenkamp's thirteenth start in the event. He won the bronze medal with a final ride of 10.9 seconds.

Woznick faced Dazzan for the gold medal and beat him easily in the first ride. In the second heat, a tactical error by Woznick allowed Dazzan to slip underneath with 175 meters to go. Unfazed, Woznick attacked in the final turn and defeated Dazzan in a photo finish. His 10.78-second time was the fastest in the entire sprint series. With gold medal in hand, Woznick also received a thirty-day suspension from the UCI commissars for his unusual protest.

The 4,000-meter pursuit finals were held after the chaotic sprint event. Motivated by the turmoil surrounding their teammates, Paul Deem, Roger Young, Ralph Therrio, and Ron Skarin rode hard right from the start. The American riders won the gold with a time of 4:29.03. Colombia finished 2nd in 4:31.59, after Balbino Jaramillo (individual pursuit gold medalist) was dropped off the back. The win was the United States' first Pan Am pursuit gold since Charlie Hewitt, Jim Rossi, Bob Pfarr, and Dick Cortright won the 1959 event in Chicago. The ecstatic team rode 5 victory laps.

In 1975 the U.S. team won a medal in every track event except the individual pursuit, in which Ron Skarin, hampered by a hacking cough, finished 6th.

San Juan 1979

Montgomery Ward provided the U.S. team with clothing in 1975. Four years later the cycling team received the support of some of the best equipment manufactur-

ROBERT F. GEORGE

In 1975 the U.S. 4,000-meter team of Paul Deem, Roger Young, Ralph Therrio, and Ron Skarin (front to back) won the gold medal at the Pan American Games in Mexico City.

ers in the world. Mavic sent the team 120 track and road rims. Avocet donated saddles, seat posts, and hubs for the time trial wheels. 3M donated hundreds of cans and tubes of cement for attaching tires to rims. The largest contribution—a $10,000 credit for parts purchases—came from Ultima/Campagnolo.

Instead of the oval tubing used on most time trial bikes at the time, the American team used new aerodynamic pear-shaped tubes made by Reynolds. Frame-builder Dave Moulton assembled the bikes with the help of Steve Aldridge, the U.S. team mechanic. Aldridge hand-built the wheels used by the time-trialists. The cost of each bike was estimated at $8,000.

When the track riders' one-piece skin suits were lost just before the competition, Roger Young's stepmother, Dorothy Young, came to the rescue. With short notice, she designed and stitched new suits with white tops and red and blue trim. Since the design was not registered with the UCI, the team had to pay a fine for wearing them.

ROBERT F. GEORGE

The American 100-kilometer team time trial squad of Wayne Stetina, Tom Doughty, Tom Sain, and George Mount captured the gold medal in 1979. It was the team's only medal.

The San Juan Games' cycling competition opened with the 100-kilometer team time trial. The American team time-trialists had finished 4th at the 1975 Pan Am Games and 19th at the 1976 Olympics. Committed to a better result, Andy Weaver, Tom Sain, Tom Doughty, Wayne Stetina, George Mount, and Dale Stetina frequently trained together in Europe and Colorado Springs.

Two days before the race, Weaver crashed hard. He woke up the morning of the event with a high temperature caused by an infected thigh wound. Coaches Mike Neel and Eddie Borysewicz woke up George Mount and asked him to get ready to race.

Seeded 4th, the team of Doughty, Mount, Sain, and Wayne Stetina won the gold medal, covering 100 kilometers in 2:15:42. The American squad had a 1-minute lead after the first 25 kilometers and gained steadily. The lead was up to 4 minutes when they crossed the finish line. Stetina credited the white fabric of Young's suits with reflecting the hot sun in Puerto Rico. The U.S. team would not win another cycling medal at the 1979 Games.

Ian Jones, George Mount, and Wayne and Dale Stetina rode for the United States in the road race. As the race unfolded, Mount, Jones, and Dale Stetina rode in support of Wayne Stetina. As the finish line approached, Dale gave Wayne a long leadout. At the finish Stetina and Colombia's Gonzalo Marin appeared to cross the line simultaneously. Careful analysis of the Omega photo sprint camera was needed to determine that Wayne Stetina came within millimeters of winning the bronze; his brother Dale placed 5th. Mount dropped out but was credited with blocking competitors for Wayne and Dale throughout the race. Jones suffered on an unfamiliar bike, after his race bike was damaged in shipping.

The track team that brought home medals in three of the four events held in 1975 was shut out in 1979. Mechanical problems, accidents, and inexperience hampered the squad. Coaches Mike Neel and Eddie Borysewicz expected better results.

ROBERT F. GEORGE

The 1983 Pan American team won seven medals (six gold) under the leadership of "Eddie B."

The Golden Years

Four years later the American squad replaced the disappointment of San Juan with a golden celebration. Of the seven medals captured at the 1983 Games in Caracas, six were gold. Dave Grylls won the individual pursuit and joined with Leonard Nitz, Brent Emery, and Steve Hegg to finish 1st in the team pursuit. Rory O'Reilly won the kilometer and Nelson Vails the match sprint. John Beckman won the points race. Davis Phinney, Thurlow Rogers, Andrew Weaver, and Jeff Bradley finished 3 seconds ahead of the Cuban team to capture the team time trial gold medal.

In 1987 the Games returned to U.S. soil for the first time since 1959. At the 1959 Chicago Games, Americans won two golds, a silver, and a bronze—the Americans' first significant international showing in a long time. In Indianapolis American cyclists again thrived on the home country advantage, winning eleven

medals in eight events. The team won more medals than any other nation and equaled the gold medal tally from 1983.

Women's events were added to the Pan Am Games for the first time in 1987, and American women celebrated by capturing medals in each event. Rebecca Twigg-Whitehead broke away from the pack early in the 57-kilometer road race and remained unchallenged at the finish line. Teammate Inga Thompson-Benedict finished 2nd and Katrin Tobin outsprinted Canada's Sara Neil for 3rd. Pan American rules allowed only two medals per country in any single event. Although Tobin crossed the line ahead of Neil, the Canadian rider received the bronze medal.

Competition in the women's track events was limited to five competitors. Twigg-Whitehead took her second gold, winning the pursuit. Connie Paraskevin-Young, the reigning national sprint champion, beat teammate Renee Duprel in the final.

PAN AM GOLD MEDAL WINNERS

MEN

Jeremiah Bishop (mountain bike cross-country 2003)
Kent Bostick (4,000-meter individual pursuit 1995; 100-kilometer team time trial 1987)
Andy Paulin (100-kilometer team time trial 1987)
John Frey (100-kilometer team time trial 1987)
Leonard Nitz (4,000-meter pursuit 1987)
Steve Hegg (100-kilometer team time trial 1987)
Christian Vande Velde (road race 1999)
Marty Nothstein (1,000-meter sprint 1995 and 1999; keirin 1999)
Ken Carpenter (1,000-meter sprint 1987)
Rory O'Reilly (track time trial 1983)
Dave Grylls (4,000-meter individual pursuit 1983)
Carl Sundquist (men's 100-kilometer team time trial 1987)
Dave Brinton (men's 100-kilometer team time trial 1987)
Dave Lettieri (men's 100-kilometer team time trial 1987)
Steve Woznick (1,000-meter sprint 1975)
Nelson Vails (1,000-meter sprint 1983)
Tinker Juarez (mountain bike cross-country 1995)
Steve Larsen (mountain bike cross-country 1999)
John Howard (road race 1971)
Wayne Stetina (1,000-kilometer team time trial 1979)
Tom Doughty (1,000-kilometer team time trial 1979)
George Mount (1,000-kilometer team time trial 1979)
Tom Sain (1,000-kilometer team time trial 1979)
Davis Phinney (100-kilometer time trial 1983)
Dylan Casey (4,000-meter individual pursuit 1999; points race 1999)
Clay Moseley (road time trial 1995)

WOMEN

Rebecca Twigg (3,000-meter individual pursuit and road race 1987)
Janie Eickhoff (3,000-meter individual pursuit 1995; points race 1999)
Dede Demet (road time trial 1995)
Connie Paraskevin-Young (1,000-meter sprint 1987)
Tanya Lindenmuth (1,000-meter sprint and keirin 2003)
Kendra Kneeland (3,000-meter individual pursuit 1992)
Alison Dunlap (mountain bike cross-country 1999)
Jeanne Golay (road race 1991 and 1995)
Erin Veenstra (3,000-meter individual pursuit and points race 1999)
Karen Dunne (road race 1999)
Elizabeth Emery (road time trial 1999)
Kimberly Bruckner (road time trial 2003)

PAN AMERICAN GAMES HOST CITIES

1951	Buenos Aires, Argentina	1983	Caracas, Venezuela
1955	Mexico City, Mexico	1987	Indianapolis, Indiana
1959	Chicago, Illinois	1991	Havana, Cuba
1963	Sao Paulo, Brazil	1995	Mar del Plata, Argentina
1967	Winnipeg, Manitoba, Canada	1999	Winnipeg, Manitoba, Canada
1971	Cali, Colombia	2003	Santo Domingo,
1975	Mexico City, Mexico		Dominican Republic
1979	San Juan, Puerto Rico	2007	Rio de Janeiro, Brazil

The men's 100-kilometer team time trial was held on the banked track of the Indianapolis Speedway. Challenged by temperatures in the high 90s and gusting winds, the American team of Kent Bostick, Andy Paulin, Steve Hegg, and John Frey finished 1st in 2:09:17. Their time was 6 minutes off the record set by the 1983 American team.

Hometown crowds filled the Major Taylor Velodrome to capacity to watch American riders Mark Gorski and Ken Carpenter compete head-to-head for the sprint final, with Carpenter winning in two rides. Track coach Eddie Borysewicz selected David Brinton, Leonard Nitz, Carl Sundquist, and Dave Lettieri to race in the final of the 4,000-meter team pursuit. The squad finished 1st in 4:26:18, more than a second faster than the 2nd-place Argentineans. Brinton won silver in the individual pursuit.

Havana 1991

Known for his long speeches, Cuban president Fidel Castro opened the Pan American Games with a brief statement: "Distinguished guests, athletes and compatriots, I declare open the 11th Pan American Games. Thank you." Many of North and South America's best riders did not compete at these Games, preferring to train for the world championships to be held later.

American women dominated their events and the full cycling team captured ten medals: three gold, four silver, and three bronze. In the women's road race, Americans took 4 of the top 6 places. Jeanne Golay won gold, Jan Bolland bronze. Golay, Dede Demet, Shari Rodgers, and Bolland won the 50-kilometer team time trial, beating the Cuban team by more than 2 minutes. Kendra Kneeland added another gold in the pursuit. In the match sprint Julie Gregg finished 2nd behind Canada's Tanya Dubnicoff, and Jessica Grieco took the bronze.

On the men's side, 2nd-place finishes were habit-forming. Dirk Copeland won the silver in the pursuit behind Cuba's Raul Dominguez. Erin Hartwell, the U.S. national pursuit champion, wore silver after the 1,000-meter time trial.

The Cubans won the team pursuit gold medal. Americans Jim Pollak, Tim Quigley, Matt Hamon, and Chris Colletta finished just 5 seconds behind, adding another silver medal. The U.S. time trial team of Steve Larsen, Rich McClung, John Loehner, and David Nicholson finished 3rd.

Mar del Plata 1995

At the 1995 Pan American Games in Mar del Plata, Argentina, American riders won an unprecedented fourteen medals.

Just shy of his forty-second birthday, Kent Bostick beat a rider half his age to take gold in the individual pursuit. Jeanne Golay won the 4-lap, 61-kilometer road race after breaking away midway through and leading the final 2 laps. The defending champion became the first female road cyclist to win back-to-back gold medals at the Pan American Games.

Golay's gold medal on the final day of cycling competition tied the Pan American Games record of eleven medals won in 1987 in Indianapolis. A 2nd and 3rd place by Mariano Friedick and Fred Rodriguez in the men's 169.4-kilometer road race broke the record. The United States won nine golds, four silvers, and a bronze medal, in mountain biking, track, and road events. American Alison Dunlap won mountain bike gold by attacking on the hills to escape Canada's Alison Sydor.

2003 Santo Domingo

The 2003 Games in Santo Domingo ended with an experienced and deep American team capturing thirteen medals across all events: two in the mountain bike cross-country race, three in the individual time trial, and eight in track competition. By the end of the Games, American men and women stood on the medals podium to collect two gold, seven silver, and four bronze medals.

The team included national time trial and road champions with international experience. Tanya Lindenmuth, Jame Carney, Giddeon Massie, and Stephen Alfred arrived in Santo Domingo shortly after competing in the 2003 world track championships in Stuttgart, Germany. Kimberly Bruckner, the two-time U.S.

national time trial champion, came to Santo Domingo after finishing 2nd in the final time trial in the Giro d'Italia. Bruckner won the time trial gold medal. Lindenmuth and Massie won four silver medals in Santo Domingo.

In the thirty-two years since John Howard won the first gold medal in Cali, Colombia, the performance of American teams at the Pan Am Games had evolved from tempered enthusiasm over a 5th-place finish to medal sweeps in track, road, and mountain disciplines.

Mountain Biking in the Pan Am Games

While it took decades for American riders to rise to dominance in road and track disciplines, medal-winning performances in mountain bike events came as soon as the discipline was added to the Games in 1995. In Argentina Tinker Juarez won the first men's cross-country and Juli Furtado finished 2nd in the women's event. Four years later Steve Larsen and Carl Swenson finished 1st and 2nd, and Alison Dunlap won the women's gold medal.

In 2003 Jeremiah Bishop and Mary McConneloug continued the American team's successful performances, on a cross-country course that twisted through villages in the mountains around Jarabacoa in the Dominican Republic. The men's event evolved into a two-man race between Bishop and Brazil's Edivandro Cruz. Just before a technical downhill section, Cruz attacked. Bishop responded, passed Cruz, and extended his lead with his own attack on the next climb. Bishop crossed the finish line unchallenged.

Mary McConneloug and Argentinean Jimena Florit were expected to contend for the women's gold medal. Another competitor's crash on the 1st of 8 laps gave the two riders an opportunity to break away. Florit attacked and extended her lead to 1 minute. McConneloug lost contact with Florit on the 4.4-kilometer loop but continued to ride aggressively until she crossed the finish line in 2nd place. After fourteen Pan American Game competitions, McConneloug's silver was the 141st medal Americans had collected against the best riders in North and South America.

America's First Homegrown Racing

In the early 1980s some bicycle riders in California spent their spare time modifying sturdy Schwinn bicycle frames and racing their creations down dirt mountain roads. On January 23, 1983, a group of these riders formed the National Off-Road Bicycle Association (NORBA) to organize and manage a new way to race bicycles. The founders included Joe Breeze, Jack Ingram, Charlie Kelly, Charlie Cunningham, Scot Nicol, and Jacquie Phelan.

Later that year Glenn Odell took over management of the fledgling organization and put together the first national championship. Steve Tilford, a professional road racer, holds the distinction of winning the first NORBA championship. At the end of its first year, NORBA had 112 members.

Odell and NORBA faced the same liability insurance crisis the USCF was dealing with. In 1985 the annual liability premium for the two-year-old organization skyrocketed from $4,000 to $40,000.

In 1985 Odell offered to sell NORBA to the USCF for $25,000. The offer was rejected without consideration. Odell then approached the American Bicycle Association, the BMX sanctioning body. The ABA purchased the National Off-Road Bicycle Association for $13,000, reported to be the amount of money in NORBA's bank accounts at the time of the sale. The USCF responded by warning its licensed riders that they would be suspended if they participated in NORBA events. Participation in NORBA events continued to grow at a fast pace, and USCF officials reconsidered their position on mountain bike racing.

As interest in mountain bike racing increased, amateur road racing continued to grow as well. By the end of 1987, the USCF had more than 30,000 licensed racers, 30 percent more than the year before. An increase in the number of sanctioned races matched the rise in membership.

On January 21, 1989, the USCF signed a letter of intent to purchase NORBA for $190,000. The organization moved to Colorado Springs. In March 1989 the UCI, recognizing an exploding racing discipline, announced that it would officially sanction a world championship for off-road racing in 1990.

After years of debate and negotiation, the USCF, USPRO, and NORBA had moved forward with a formal structure to promote American racing interests. Bicycle racing was poised for another leap forward.

The Coors Classic

The Red Zinger Classic made its debut in June 1975. Created by Mo Siegel, the founder of Boulder, Colorado's Celestial Seasonings Tea Company, the Classic would become one of the most important races in American history.

The first Red Zinger Classic included a 70-mile road race, a 10-mile time trial, and a 50-mile criterium. John Howard added victory in the first Red Zinger to a long list of racing accomplishments.

When running the race began to consume more resources and energy than he or his company had to spare, Siegel sold the event to race director Michael Aisner for $1.00 in 1979. Aisner quickly negotiated a new title sponsorship with the Adolph Coors Brewery. The 1980 Coors Classic began with just seventy-five riders, the fewest since 1975. One year later, due to Aisner's relentless promotion and commitment, the starting field included the Soviet national team, in their first appearance at an American race. Greg LeMond, his racing career on a steep upward curve at the time, stunned the field by winning the 1981 Classic. CBS Sports presented two weekends of race coverage and broadcast the final stage live. The Coors Classic had become the official American tour and one of the most popular races in the world.

The appearance of the Soviet national team just one year after the boycotted 1980 Olympics shows how important the Coors Classic had become in international competition. In 1984 racers from sixteen nations used the Classic as an Olympic training race. The best riders in the world also used the Coors Classic to prepare for the world championships in Colorado Springs two years later.

By 1987 financial challenges hampered the Classic. Aisner's attempt to expand the race with stages in Hawaii and California saddled the event in debt. Frustrated by the added travel, many internationals stayed home—only fifty-nine men started the 1987 race. Davis Phinney finished 1st in 1987 and repeated in 1988, when his 7-Eleven team won nine of sixteen stages, captured the team competition, and gave the BMW 325i they were awarded to coach Jim Ochowicz.

7-Eleven's lopsided victory would mark the end of the Coors Classic. After fourteen years, nine under the title sponsorship of Coors, the brewery ended the relationship.

America's largest stage race came to a close, but not before promoter Michael Aisner and the Coors Classic had created a new modern environment for bicycle racing. The corporate sponsorships, television coverage, and international fields of the Coors Classic set the standard for American races that followed. The Tour de Trump, which would become America's national tour in the post-Classic era, prospered due to the experience its staff had gained running the Coors Classic. Aisner was also the first promoter to give women the same status as their male counterparts. His introduction of a women's race pushed international promoters to add similar events to their races. His efforts were credited with motivating organizers of the Tour de France to create the Tour de France Feminin.

Even when the Coors Classic ended after its fourteen-year run, its legacy lived on.

 The "America's Tour"

 **The Red Zinger Classic**

In 1975 Mo Siegel, founder of the Celestial Seasonings Tea Company, was looking for an altruistic way to get more people to ride bicycles. His brainchild was the Red Zinger Classic, a three-stage race held in Boulder, Colorado. The first Red Zinger Classic, named after the company's most popular brand of tea, was held on June 21 and 22, 1975. Fifty-two men and thirteen women from around the country competed in a 70-mile road race, 10-mile time trial, and 50-mile criterium.

There were few spectators to witness the start of the road race at 7 a.m. on June 21. After 70 miles of racing, John Howard, Dave Boll, and Dale Stetina sprinted to the finish line. Howard finished 1st, then added 16 seconds to his lead when he won the 10-mile time trial held later that day. Ron Skarin won the third-stage criterium, however Howard won the race's overall title. Hannah North won the first women's Red Zinger Classic.

The reaction from the riders and spectators was so positive that Siegel planned to hold the race again in 1976. Advertising and promotion for the second

Red Zinger began in May and continued until the event in early August. Celestial Seasonings spent more than $50,000 organizing the race and offered $20,000 in prizes from Bose Speakers, Crisman Stereo Components, Campagnolo, and National State Bank. The men's field more than doubled, from 52 racers in 1975 to 114 in 1976. Competitors included two U.S. Olympic development squads, a team from Mexico, and a Commonwealth team composed of Olympic riders from Australia, Great Britain, and New Zealand.

For the second consecutive year, John Howard won the first stage, a 10.8-mile time trial. His time was 22:42.18, which was 20 seconds faster than 2nd-place finisher Tom Doughty. Clyde Sefton finished 1st in the 93-mile road race and Bill Nickson won the 50-mile criterium. Howard did not finish high in the second and third stages, but he maintained his lead. Fifteen thousand fans gathered to watch the 69-lap North Boulder Park criterium. A thirty-minute downpour soaked riders and spectators with 25 laps remaining, but it didn't have any effect on the outcome. Howard had calculated his lead over the other riders. Riding to an easy 28th-place finish in the criterium still gave him his second overall victory. Tom Doughty and Dudley Hayton finished 2nd and 3rd in the final standings.

The Red Zinger Classic did not include a women's event in 1976.

In 1977 Siegel met Michael Aisner and asked him to handle publicity for the Red Zinger. Siegel had been impressed with Aisner's work on a documentary covering seal-hunting controversies produced for the International Fund for Animal Welfare.

Armed with an $80,000 race budget and $40,000 prize list, the organizers

MICHAEL AISNER

In 1975 Mo Siegel (with hat), the founder of the Celestial Seasonings Tea Company, launched the Red Zinger Classic. The first event, won by John Howard, included a 70-mile road race, 10-mile time trial and 50-mile criterium.

added two more stages to the men's event for 1977 and brought back the women's three-stage race. The men's field held steady with 116 riders from twenty-nine teams. Thirty-nine women also entered.

As in the first two Red Zingers, the winner was never in doubt after the first stage. Wayne Stetina won the 80-mile first stage and kept the leader's jersey on his back the rest of the way. After the final stage Wayne's brother Dale was in 2nd, 9 seconds back. Connie Carpenter dominated the women's event, winning all three stages.

In 1978 the Red Zinger Classic continued to grow in every aspect. Michael Aisner became the race director and managed a $115,000 budget and 250 volunteers. The Red Seal Potato Chip Company and Shaklee joined Celestial Seasonings as cosponsors. With a prize list valued at over $30,000, the Red Zinger was billed as "the richest amateur bicycle competition in the world." The men's race grew to nine stages over eight days and the women's event expanded to seven stages. The Federation Internationale Amateur de Cyclisme (FIAC) rewarded the Red Zinger's growing reputation by classifying the event as a national tour, meaning that riders from around the world who competed in the event could accumulate points for international rankings.

In 1978, for the first time, the first day's winner did not finish 1st overall. When the riders started the seventh stage, George Mount was in 8th place and trailed leader Wayne Stetina by 3:12. The 92-mile Morgul-Bismark stage was the third and last road race of the '78 Zinger. On the second of seven 13.2-mile laps, George Mount and Alan Kingsbury made a decisive move. With 55 miles remaining they held a small lead over competitors like Bob Cook and Wayne and Dale Stetina. Riding together, Mount and Kingsbury extended the lead to 5 minutes on the last lap of the windy course through the rolling hills southeast of Boulder. Mount kept driving and finished 1:18 ahead of Kingsbury. In the ninth and final stage, Mount extended his lead to 5:38. Bob Cook finished 2nd and 1977 winner Wayne Stetina finished 3rd. Mount celebrated his victory by driving away in the 1st-place prize, a Volkswagen Rabbit.

Fifty-six women came to ride the seven-stage Red Zinger in 1978. Connie Carpenter crashed twice during the rain-soaked second-stage criterium to fall out of contention. Holland's Keetie van Oosten-Hage won the Zinger, finishing 3:27 ahead of Beth Heiden in 2nd. Top women received an all-expenses paid trip to Hawaii.

By 1979 Aisner's promotional skills

put the nine-day, 500-mile Red Zinger Classic on NBC's *Today Show* and in front of 60,000 local spectators. Five minutes into the Washington Park criterium, Bob Cook* crashed turning the second corner of the course. Instead of improving on his 2nd-place finish of 1978, Cook suffered a broken collarbone and left the race to the remaining seventy-nine riders.

When George Mount won the 1978 Red Zinger Classic, he received a Volkswagen Rabbit for the victory.

Jacques Boyer climbed past Wayne and Dale Stetina to win the fourth stage, a 100-mile road race from Manitou Springs to Hoosier Pass, but his celebration was short-lived. Boyer received a 5-minute penalty for crossing the double-yellow line. Instead of taking the lead over Wayne Stetina, Boyer found himself 3 minutes down.

*Bob Cook is a tragic figure of American cycling. One of the most naturally talented riders of his generation. Cook won the Mount Evans Hillclimb every year from 1975 to 1980, then died of cancer at a very young age.

BOTH PHOTOS: ROBERT F. GEORGE

Jacques Boyer, who raced in Europe and the United States, was a top competitor in early Red Zinger and Coors Classic races.

Davis Phinney, a twenty-year-old Boulder native, gave the hometown fans someone to cheer for in the fifth stage. Phinney beat sixty-five other riders and defeated Australian Phil Anderson in the final sprint. His victory ride was featured on the *Today Show*.

In the final stage Jacques Boyer moved into 2nd place when Wayne Stetina suffered a flat tire with 2 laps remaining. Dale Stetina won the 1979 Red Zinger and Jacques Boyer was 47 seconds back. Greg LeMond, competing as a junior, finished 4th. Keetie van Oosten-Hage won for the second consecutive year, finishing 2:14 in front of American Sarah Doctor. Beth Heiden was 3rd.

From Red Zinger to Coors

Increasing in popularity and reputation, the Red Zinger Classic was also straining the resources of Mo Siegel and Celestial Seasonings. Race expenditures were growing exponentially. Siegel was spending more than what Celestial Seasonings received from selling tea in Colorado. Leading up to the race, the company's staff was paralyzed with planning, logistics, and details.

Looking to concentrate on his tea business, Siegel sold the Red Zinger Classic to Aisner for $1.00 and promised continued support. Aisner made a pitch to marketing executives at Adolph Coors Brewery. Initial interest from Coors moved to telephone conversations between Mo Siegel and Pete Coors and a signed sponsorship agreement.

In 1980 the Adolph Coors Brewing Company took over sponsorship of the Red Zinger Classic. Under race director Michael Aisner's leadership, the Coors Classic became the most recognized race in the United States.

The eight-stage Coors Classic debuted in 1980. The field of seventy-five men and thirty-nine women was the smallest since 1975, but the racing was dramatic. ESPN broadcast daily reports documenting an incredible victory for Jacques Boyer. Boyer, who finished 2nd the year

Jacques Boyer and Beth Heiden captured victories at the 1980 Coors Classic. ESPN offered daily race reports.

before, trailed the leader, Colombia's Antonio Londono, by 4:11 at the start of the final stage. Working with committed teammates, Boyer lapped Londono three times during the 50-mile criterium. Boyer attacked with the crack of the starting pistol. By the 19th of 72 laps, Boyer had made up 90 seconds of the deficit. Continuing to push hard, Boyer passed the Colombian again on lap 32. Londono seemed to lose energy as Boyer gained strength. With two-thirds of the criterium completed, Boyer moved into 1st place overall. At the finish line Boyer had a 9-second lead and the winner's jersey.

Beth Heiden dominated the women's race in 1980. In the third-stage Maroon Bells road race to Snowmass Village,

steep climbs took a toll on all the riders. Heiden and Heidi Hopkins broke away and battled each other to the finish line. Like the previous day at the Estes Park road race, Hopkins led until Heiden's unbeatable finishing kick propelled her across the line first. Heiden also won the sixth-stage Morgul-Bismark road race.

Red Jerseys in the Rockies

Aisner intended to stay true to the "international" aspect of the event that he advertised in some promotional materials. At a ceremony promoting the Coors Classic on the steps of the capitol building in Denver, shortly after the sponsorship agreement was signed, Aisner gave the governor and Pete Coors just a moment's notice of the contents of his speech. In front of the assembled press corps, government officials, and bicycle racing enthusiasts, Aisner challenged the Russians to send their top riders to compete in the Coors Classic.

Complicated and time-consuming negotiations continued by cable and telex for almost two years. When the Russians finally agreed to send a team, Aisner had to ask Coors for additional funds to pay for nine transatlantic airfares.

In 1981 the number of stages in the men's event grew to eleven and the prize list reached $55,000. Coors reportedly spent more than $250,000 on race-related expenses. Staff salaries and travel pushed the total bill to approximately $400,000.

The Soviet Union responded to Aisner's challenge and entered a team led by 1980 Olympic road champion Sergei Soukhoroutchenkov (known to some simply as "Soukho"). One year after the controversial American boycott of the 1980 Olympics, local residents enthusiastically greeted the Soviet team when they were introduced at a Fourth of July event promoting the Classic.

The Soviet riders won the team title by over 30 minutes and all five riders finished in the top twenty, but they returned home without the winner's jersey. Twenty-year-old Greg LeMond won the race with a 4:47 margin. In the final stage, a criterium around North Boulder Park, LeMond experienced a mechanical problem and finished out of the top ten. His problems in North Boulder Park had little effect on the final standings.

The 7-Eleven team made its Coors Classic debut in 1981 with a squad that included Tom Schuler, Jeff Bradley, Greg Demgen, Eric Heiden, and Ron Hayman. Without a stage win and finishing 11th of 13 teams, the debut didn't accurately foreshadow the team's later dominance in the same event.

Connie Carpenter, who won the Red Zinger in 1977, won the first of eight stages and wore the leader's jersey from start to finish.

By 1982 the Coors Classic became known around the world as "America's Tour." The race budget exceeded $400,000 and Aisner managed a staff of more than 400 people, including 76 paid staffers. 7-Eleven signed on as a cosponsor.

More than 100,000 spectators watched the 1982 Classic unfold over eleven days.

Once again international riders made news. The Soviet team returned, and the Colombian team captured the team title. Jose Patrocinio Jiminez of Colombia became the first foreign rider to win the Coors Classic. His teammate Martin Ramires finished in 2nd. The highest-placed American, Alexi Grewal, finished in 4th behind the Soviet team's Victor Demidenko.

On the women's side, Aisner created

one of the premier stage races in the world in 1982. Only the world championships drew more competitors. The event began with a two-hour timed criterium at the Boulder Mall. Els Gottschal (7-Eleven) mastered the eight-cornered course to win the stage. Connie Carpenter finished 3rd. Carpenter won the Queen of the Mountain sprint but finished 2nd to Henny Top in the 35-mile Estes Park road race. The head-to-head battle between Carpenter and Top continued in the Vail criterium, but this time Carpenter won the stage and captured the overall lead. She won five of nine stages.

CBS Sports filmed the race and broadcast the coverage over two consecutive weekends. The second show finished with live coverage of the final stage, reportedly the second live national broadcast of cycling in U.S. history. Despite Carpenter's impressive performance, the coverage did not address the women's race.

In 1983 the Coors Classic sold more than 50,000 race-oriented souvenirs. A $448,000 race budget kept a staff of 500 buried in logistics and details.

The twelfth and final stage featured a fast and flat 114-mile road race. Starting in 3rd place, Dale Stetina used an aggressive 30 mph breakaway to move into 1st. Four years after winning in 1979, Stetina won his second Red Zinger/Coors Classic without winning a single stage.

Connie Carpenter, so dominant in previous Classics, did not finish the 1983 race. She was leading the first stage, a criterium in Boulder, when she crashed and broke her arm. Rebecca Twigg won in 1983, beating Italian Maria Canins by 2:23.

Behind-the-scenes drama dominated the story of the tenth Coors Classic in 1984. Held before the highly anticipated Los Angeles Olympics, the Classic's schedule conflicted with the wishes of Eddie Borysewicz, national coaching director of the United States Cycling Federation. Borysewicz felt the race was too long and would make it difficult for his riders to recover in time for the Olympics. At the direction of USCF road coach Tim Kelly, Connie Carpenter and Davis Phinney withdrew from the race. When they left, Phinney was in 5th place and Carpenter had won four of seven stages. She was leading Maria Canins by 57 seconds when she dropped out. Canins and Doug Shapiro, a rider for a composite 7-Eleven-USA team, went on to win the Classic.

"The Badger" Comes to America

The 1985 Classic started in San Francisco, outside of Colorado for the first time in its eleven-year history. Thirteen stages over fifteen days included hundreds of miles through California's wine country and the Sierra Nevada. The men's roster included at least one celebrity rider—Celestial Seasonings paid Bernard Hinault and his La Vie Claire team $100,000 to wear Red Zinger jerseys for the Classic. The Classic's race budget approached $1 million, with $100,000 in prize money.

The 1985 edition featured just one individual time trial. The world's best riders—Hinault, Hampsten, and LeMond—finished 1st, 2nd, and 3rd. During the fifth-stage road race between Tahoe and Reno, LeMond and Hampsten led the pack by more than 4 minutes. At the end of the stage, LeMond held the overall lead, 1:25 ahead of Hampsten.

Aisner arranged for the riders to be flown to Grand Junction, Colorado, to continue the race. Over the next few days, LeMond's lead increased to 1:55. The Boulder Mountain stage began at the Coors Brewery in Golden. Before the start

the organizers learned that the highway department's attempt to improve a dirt section of the course had spread rocks over a large section of road, making it treacherous for the riders. The route was shifted to Coal Creek Canyon.

Andy Hampsten made his move 13 miles in. As the road turned upward beside Coal Creek, he broke away, attempting to leave LeMond behind and narrow the time gap. Twenty-three miles later Hampsten's effort had resulted in a tenuous 1-minute lead over LeMond, Doug Shapiro, and four other chasers. Facing a stiff headwind and riding solo, Hampsten was caught at mile 48.

Anticipating the end of the stage after 88 miles of hard riding, the peloton encountered chaos at the finishing area. The police, struggling to clear the crowd of spectators, set up a roadblock more than 2 miles from the finish without informing Aisner or the riders. Each rider had to decide for himself how to proceed. Shapiro, a Boulder resident, maneuvered his way through the traffic and finished in front of LeMond and Hampsten's group by 2:05. Every stage of the Classic finished with stories to be told. This was one for the books, and LeMond was the overall winner.

At the 1986 Tour de France, Bernard Hinault ("the Badger") finished 2nd to Greg LeMond. Hinault then came to the 1986 Coors Classic to race the final stage race of his amazing career and switched places with LeMond in the final standings. The field was filled with eighty-four of the world's best male riders. In addition to LeMond and Hinault, it included future world champion Moreno Argentin, former world champion Giuseppe Saronni, and Tour of Switzerland winner Andy Hampsten. Eleven professional teams lined up: Red Zinger-La Vie Claire,

In 1985, the Coors Classic offered a $100,000 prize purse. Reflecting its stature on the international racing scene, Celestial Seasonings paid Bernard Hinault and his La Vie Claire team $100,000 to wear Red Zinger jerseys during the race.

7-Eleven, Levi's, Schwinn-Icy Hot, Colnago-Del Tongo, Bianchi, Peugeot, French Pro, Holland Pro, West German Pro, and Killian's Irish. Amateur teams from the Soviet Union, Holland, and the United States provided strong competition for the pros. American amateurs Todd Gogulski, Gary Mulder, and Mark Southard finished 18th, 21st, and 22nd, and the Lowenbrau-USA team beat four professional teams in the final standings.

American Ron Kiefel (7-Eleven) won his fourth straight Coors Classic prologue, covering the 1.05-mile course up San Francisco's Telegraph Hill in 3:13. LeMond pleased the hometown crowd by winning the 99-mile Squaw Valley-to-Reno road race, outsprinting Doug Shapiro and Jaanus Klum to the line. Kiefel finished the race the way he started, winning the final stage. Kiefel took the lead halfway through the 61-mile North Boulder Park stage and finished 2:13 ahead of his pursuers.

The general classification was sewn up by Hinault in the high-altitude Vail Pass time trial, which he won by 1 minute over his teammate LeMond. Hinault never gave up the leader's jersey. He won the 1,100-mile, two-week event

Greg LeMond and Andy Hampsten join Bernard Hinault at the start of a Coors Classic stage.

in 42:05:07. LeMond was 2nd in 42:06:33.

Defending women's champion Jeanne Longo won three of eleven stages and finished 2nd or 3rd in six more. She wore the leader's jersey from the first day to the last. Inga Thompson-Benedict and Susan Ehlers challenged Longo throughout the race. Thompson-Benedict gained a 3-second lead on Longo in the 2.8-mile hill climb prologue near Grand Junction. Longo recaptured the lead the next day and extended her margin over the next stages. But Thompson-Benedict made a strong charge in the 8.4-mile Niwot time trial and trailed by just 35 seconds with three stages left.

With the help of her Centurion-Texas Metro teammates, Sue Ehlers broke away on the 43-mile Morgul-Bismark road race and narrowed her time gap to Longo and Thompson-Benedict by almost 4 minutes. Ehlers also won the 20-lap, 33-mile North Boulder Park circuit race. At the end of the 400-mile Classic, Ehlers finished 1:37 behind Longo, with Thompson-Benedict at 1:58.

The 1987 Coors Classic was the longest stage race in U.S. cycling history—nineteen stages covering 1,376 miles. Michael Aisner moved the start to the Big Island of Hawaii. The prize list was not large enough to entice top foreign riders to compete just thirty days before the world championships. Only fifty-nine riders were present at the start. Four races were held in Hawaii, beginning with a flat 2.8-mile time trial. The first stage was 105 miles along the road circling the crater of the active Kilauea Volcano. Two months before the race, a lava flow cut off the circuit road; the course was rerouted as an out-and-back.

Aisner arranged to fly riders to San Francisco to continue the race in California, Nevada, and Colorado. The 107-mile thirteenth stage from Aspen to Copper Mountain crossed the Continental Divide, reaching the highest elevation in Coors Classic history as it went over 12,095-foot Independence Pass.

Andy Hampsten, back with 7-Eleven after a year with LeMond and Hinault on La Vie Claire, won two stages, and his teammate Raul Alcala won the individual title. After 1,385 miles Alcala finished 1st in 57:07:14. Jeff Pierce and Hampsten

finished 2nd and 3rd to complete the sweep for 7-Eleven.

The women's race was decided quickly. France's Jeanne Longo pulled away from the forty-rider field on the first climb of the first stage to build an insurmountable 3-minute lead. Nine days and 365 miles later, she finished more than 6 minutes ahead of American Inga Thompson-Benedict. It was her third consecutive win. Longo won four stages and the mountain and points competitions as well.

In 1988 the Coors Classic returned to San Francisco. Seventy-seven men—twenty-five pros and fifty-two amateurs—competed for a small prize list that featured a $35,000 BMW and $46,000 in cash. The field did not include any former Classic winners.

7-Eleven dominated the race. Seven years after the team's 11th-place debut, 7-Eleven won nine of sixteen stages and finished 1st in the team competition by over 30 minutes. Five 7-Eleven riders finished in the top ten, including the overall winner.

Davis Phinney, riding in his eleventh Classic, won the 0.8-mile hill climb prologue from North Beach to Coit Tower in San Francisco, finishing 2 seconds ahead of Ron Kiefel. Alex Stieda and Hampsten finished within 6 seconds of the lead.

The road race from Squaw Valley to Sparks presented a critical challenge for Phinney and his 7-Eleven teammates. Phinney and Kiefel fell off a nine-rider break at mile 65. A determined Phinney led an 8-mile chase on the climb through Virginia City to the Geiger Summit. Phinney and Kiefel rejoined the lead group near the top of the climb, and 2 miles from the finish, Phinney attacked again for the stage victory. After the win he trailed teammate Stieda by 1:04 in the overall standings. The gap was cut signifi-

Chris Carmichael, Alan McCormack, and Bob Roll stand on the podium after the difficult 1985 Coors Classic Morgul-Bismark stage.

cantly when Phinney won the Aspen circuit race. In addition to a 28-second finishing gap, he also received a 30-second victory bonus. Stieda's lead was narrowed to 6 seconds. Phinney took the lead the next day, winning a pair of 5-second midrace time bonuses and finishing 3rd. Now the 6-second gap was in Phinney's favor.

The 10-mile Vail time trial decided the overall winner. Hampsten won the trial (27:24), but Phinney and Stieda were only concerned with the competition between them. Phinney won their head-to-head battle by 12 seconds. The 7-Eleven riders supported Phinney over the last three stages to protect his lead. At the end, Phinney owned the winner's white jersey, with a 1:59 cushion over Stieda. Teammates Andy Hampsten finished 2nd, Stieda 3rd, Ron Kiefel 8th, and Jeff Pierce 10th.

When France's Jeanne Longo decided not to compete, it seemed the 1988 Coors Classic would be a two-woman race between Inga Thompson-Benedict and

New Zealander Madonna Harris. Arriving late to the start ramp, Harris gave 36 seconds to Thompson-Benedict before she had even begun riding her prologue. In the Aspen road race, Thompson-Benedict and Harris received conflicting directions from course officials at the Maroon Bells turnaround. The marshals pointed Thompson-Benedict to a loop that was shorter and lower in altitude, while Harris was sent on a longer and higher course. Thompson-Benedict realized the error and received a 5-second penalty for the inadvertent shortcut. Thompson-Benedict maintained her lead through the remaining stages to capture victory in the final Coors Classic.

In October 1988 Aisner heard from a reporter at the Denver airport that Coors was canceling its sponsorship contract. Coors marketing executives wanted to generate more interest at a national level, for a longer period of time, and so shifted their financial commitment from the two-week Classic to a Coors-branded cycling team.

CHAPTER SEVEN

Turning Pro

Racing for the Stars and Stripes

IN 1979 FEWER THAN FIVE American cyclists called themselves professional racers. Three years later the number reached twenty, and promoters began planning a showcase for the professionals.

On June 6, 1982, the inaugural U.S. professional criterium championship was held in Baltimore. Produced by Omni-Sports and Baltimore's WMAR-TV, the race offered $25,000 in cash prizes. It was the first U.S. professional championship since 1974.

Race director Jack Simes set up a 1.5-mile course that put spectators close to the action and challenged the racers' handling skills. A half-mile section of the course zigzagged through a parking lot, crossed 100 yards of running track, then moved through a dark 25-foot-long tunnel before running over a cobbled section of road. The cobbled section included a 90-degree turn and a small incline. After the practice laps the riders persuaded Simes to cover the first 20 yards of the cobblestones with a carpet.

The cobblestone road hammered the riders and caused frequent crashes. Seventy-two riders from twelve countries started the race. By the end of the 10th lap, only thirty-four riders remained, with 32 circuits still to ride before the finish.

With 10 laps to the finish, Roger Young and prerace favorite Jonathan Boyer were in the lead positions. When Young crashed 4 laps later, the crowd shifted their loyalties to Boyer. Since the lead riders were starting to lap the pack, the announcers whipped up the crowd and called for them to watch for Boyer's arched white cap. At the bell lap with 1.5 miles to the finish, Boyer faded and used his final energy to support John Eustice, his American teammate on the French SEM/France/Loire professional team. At the finish Shane Sutton of

Australia outsprinted teammate Danny Clark. Finishing 6th, Eustice captured the stars-and-stripes national champion's jersey as the highest-placed American pro. Boyer finished 9th. Everyone involved, from racers to Baltimore's mayor, called the race a success and looked forward to the next year.

Davis Phinney won the U.S. professional cycling championship in 1983, covering the 100-kilometer course in 2:24:56.8. Phinney beat Canada's Steve Bauer to the finish line by just five-hundredths of a second. Because he was riding as an amateur, Phinney's $25,000 1st-place award went to the USCF. Although he finished 15th, Eustice defended his title as the best pro racer in the United States.

The race's sponsor, Baltimore's WMAR-TV, put up $100,000 in prizes, calling it the richest one-day race in the world. The sponsors commissioned Eric Knight, principal conductor of the Baltimore Symphony Orchestra, to create "The Great Bicycle Race," a signature song for the race. William D. Schaefer, Baltimore's mayor, estimated that 80,000 spectators watched the action.

ROBERT F. GEORGE

On June 6, 1982, the first U.S. professional criterium championship was held in Baltimore. John Eustice, who finished 6th, captured the stars-and-stripes jersey awarded to the highest American professional finisher.

The CoreStates USPRO Cycling Championship

Inspired by the race in Baltimore, Philadelphia racing enthusiasts Jack Toland and Jerry Casale wanted to find a way to bring professional racing to their hometown. Toland mentioned the idea to Tom Bamford, a friend who worked at CoreStates Financial Corporation. Toland called Dave Chauner, who organized the race in Baltimore, and shortly afterward CoreStates' board of directors voted 4–3 to sponsor a professional championship race.

Race planning started in March, when most of the summer's dates were already taken. With little flexibility the race organizers selected June 23—the same day the European riders competed in their national pro championships. Top riders like Greg LeMond, Phil Anderson, Steve Bauer, and Sean Kelly declined to enter, citing preparations for the Tour de France.

At 8:33 a.m. on the morning of Sunday, June 23, 1985, the starter's pistol fired. Sixty-six riders—thirty-five Americans and a collection of racers from England, Australia, Canada, Switzerland, Ireland, Belgium, and Mexico—raced through downtown Philadelphia and the surrounding parkways. Eric Heiden won the first USPRO championship, riding for 7-Eleven.

Two years later the prize list reached $100,000. Tom Schuler, another 7-Eleven rider, captured 1st place and the winner's $20,000 check. A dominant team at the time, 7-Eleven captured the team championship in 1985, 1987, and 1988.

By 1989 the CoreStates USPRO championships attracted the best riders and teams in the world. American riders, who spent much of the racing season in Europe, were motivated to perform well in front of their home fans. Even as its title sponsor changed and changed again, the USPRO championship would remain an important date on the American calendar for years to come.

 ## The USPRO Championships

 Following the success at the 1984 Olympics, the general public's interest in bicycle racing was piqued. At the first CoreStates USPRO championships in 1985, thousands of fans lined the course in Philadelphia, trying to identity the American and European riders and keep track of the leaders. Connie Carpenter provided race commentary for a local radio station. In between reports she ran to the roadside to cheer her husband, Davis Phinney, as he climbed the Manayunk Wall, a 17 percent grade that would influence the outcomes of many future USPRO championships.

On the 7th of 10 laps up the steep climb, Eric Heiden, Tom Schuler, Tom Broznowski, Jesper Worre, and Jens Veggerby broke away. The pack cut their 2-minute lead to 23 seconds 30 miles from the finish. Heiden had expected his

Olympic bronze medal–winning 7-Eleven teammates Davis Phinney and Ron Kiefel to close the gap and take control of the front. With 7 miles of racing on Philadelphia's Benjamin Franklin Parkway left to go, Heiden changed his mindset from that of 7-Eleven team support rider to that of a 1st-place finisher. Heiden outsprinted Danish riders Jesper Worre and Jens Veggerby to win the inaugural CoreStates USPRO cycling championship. Nine of the first eleven finishers were Americans.

In 1987 the CoreStates' prize list reached $100,000. Thirty-year-old Tom Schuler had reduced his racing schedule and shifted to management support of the 7-Eleven team. With 50 miles left, Schuler followed teammate Roy Knickman's attack to take the lead. Schuler outsprinted four other riders to the finish line and collected a $20,000 check for 1st place. He finished in 6:04:43, breaking the record set by Thomas Prehn's 1986 6:22:15 finishing time.

By the fifth edition of the CoreStates event, the top international professional teams were competing for individual, team, and sponsor honors. Team rivalries between 7-Eleven, Coors Light-ADR, Wheaties-Schwinn, and others became part of the CoreStates lore. In 1989 Greg LeMond made his first appearance, flying from Paris on the supersonic Concorde to join eleven Coors Light-ADR teammates. The Soviet national team entered but was forced to withdraw after last-minute instructions from their cycling federation.

Greg Oravetz (Coors Light-ADR) outsprinted Michael Engleman (Wheaties-Schwinn) in front of 300,000 spectators to win the 1989 event. Oravetz took home $25,000 of the $110,000 prize list. LeMond finished 10th.

America's Best Teams Compete

In 1980 Panasonic-Shimano was America's only professional racing team. Ten years later USPRO reported six teams and 135 licensed racers.

Coors Light and 7-Eleven came to the starting line in 1990 ready to claim the right to be called the best professional team in the United States. Defending champion Coors Light brought 1988 winner Roberto Gaggioli, Alexi Grewal, Michel Zanoli, David Farmer, and world and Olympic champion Guintautas Umaras to the race.

Jim Ochowicz, the manager of 7-Eleven, wanted to win the CoreStates team championship, adding to victories in 1985, 1987, and 1988. Training for the Tour de France influenced his team's roster. Ochowicz brought Andy Bishop from Europe to join Davis Phinney, Frankie Andreu, John Tomac, Norm Alvis, and 1987 winner Tom Schuler.

In the end Mother Nature proved more powerful than either Coors Light or 7-Eleven. Heat, humidity, and the steep climb up the Manayunk Wall reduced the field from 92 starters to just 52 by the 9th lap. The heat and humidity claimed riders from Coors Light and 7-Eleven. Both teams failed to catch a three-man breakaway group including Paulo Cimini (GIS), Laurent Jalabert (Toshiba), and Kurt Stockton (American Commerce). Cimini edged Jalabert at the line, with a record-setting time of 6:01:54 in the 156-mile race. The first American finisher was not a member of Coors Light or 7-Eleven. Kurt Stockton of American Commerce put on the stars-and-stripes jersey of the best American professional racer.

In the five years since the first CoreStates, performances of the riders had improved significantly. Despite the sweltering weather conditions, Cimini's winning time was almost 3 minutes faster than the previous record set by Tom Schuler in 1987. He averaged 25.86 mph versus Schuler's 25.66. More evidence of the improvement of professional racers could be found in the final finishing list. Tom Schuler's 1987 course record was bettered by the top thirty-five riders in the 1990 event.

1990 AMERICAN PROFESSIONAL TEAMS

Amore Vita/Tommasini
American Commerce National Bank
AC Pinarello
7-Eleven
Spago
Coors Light

As the professional riders' skill, experience, and endurance increased, the winning margins became much closer. The seventh edition of the CoreStates in 1991 ended with a pack sprint. Race officials announced that Dutchman Michel Zanoli slipped past Davis Phinney at the line and would take home the $25,000. Nonetheless, after six tries, Phinney finally won the right to wear the stars and stripes. Coors Light won the team competition, with Chevrolet-L.A. Sheriff 2nd and Motorola 3rd.

The First Solo Victory

The pack sprint finish of 1991 was followed a year later by Bart Bowen's 1:20 solo victory. With less than two years of professional racing experience, Bowen (Subaru-Montgomery) broke away from the pack 12 miles from the finish. An eight-rider chase group failed to close the gap.

At the start of 3 finishing loops, Bowen had a 60-second lead. Aware of the lead Bowen had established, an estimated 100,000 spectators roared their approval. Bowen's win was the third fastest and the first solo victory in the eight-year history of the race. Once again 90-degree heat played a role in the race. Only sixty-four riders finished. Davis Phinney, the defending U.S. champion, finished 46th.

The Million-Dollar Man

In 1993 Lance Armstrong and his Motorola teammates were interested in more than just the CoreStates $110,000 prize list. The CoreStates race was the third leg of the International Cycling Production's Triple Crown. Armstrong won the first two events, the Thrifty Drug Classic and Kmart West Virginia Classic. A win in Philadelphia would reward Armstrong with a $1 million prize.

The 156-mile course began with two 1-mile loops, followed by ten 14.4-mile laps that included the legendary Manayunk Wall and its steep 17 percent grade. The race ended with three 3.3-mile finishing loops. Every year the Manayunk Wall cracked several professional riders. In 1993 Lance Armstrong used the Wall to catapult himself into an insurmountable lead.

At the start of the race, Coors Light riders maintained a lead pack breakaway for almost 100 miles. Although the time gap reached 9 minutes, a strong Motorola team reeled in the break. Riding in team time trial formation, Lance Armstrong, Phil Anderson, Sean Yates, Andy Bishop, and Frankie Andreu closed in on the leaders.

Dave Mann, a member of Coors Light, held a 30-second lead. On Manayunk Wall, Armstrong attacked. Behind him, chaos reigned as riders following his break crashed. Other riders were forced to slow down to navigate through the fallen riders and their bikes.

Armstrong gained a 42-second lead over Saturn's Brian Walton and just over 1 minute on the main pack. On the 9th lap the main pack trailed Armstrong by 3:13. Six riders shadowed Armstrong throughout the 9th 14.4-mile circuit.

Reaching the Wall for the 10th and final time, the seven leaders held a 2:40 lead. At the steepest part of the climb, Armstrong crushed his competitors by sprinting up the Wall. By the time the six chasers reached the top, Armstrong had a 26-second lead, with 17 miles remaining. Riding hard and motivated by the Triple Crown prize, Armstrong extended his lead to 1:42 when he entered the 1st of the 3 finishing laps. Uncontested at the end, Armstrong found time to blow his mother a kiss. Photographs show Armstrong enthusiastically shouting and pumping both arms in the air as he crossed the finish line.

On the podium Armstrong received a giant cardboard $1 million check. His millionaire status was short-lived, though. The Motorola team chose to accept a $600,000 immediate payment instead of a twenty-year annuity with annual payments of $50,000. After taxes, the remaining $390,000 was divided between Motorola's eighteen riders and support staff.

A Champion for Eighty Minutes

In 1997, when the six-year-old Tour DuPont was abruptly canceled, the CoreStates USPRO championship became the most important and recognizable bicycle race in the United States.

Controversy reigned at the end of the 1997 event. Finishing in 3rd place, George Hincapie, the leader of the U.S.

Postal Service team, earned the right to wear the stars-and-stripes national championship jersey. Eighty minutes later, celebrating with his parents and teammates, Hincapie was stunned when race officials informed him he had been stripped of the victory. Officials claimed that after Hincapie replaced a flat tire 9 miles from the finish, he violated race rules by motor-pacing behind his team car for more than two minutes. Mark Gorski, general manager of U.S. Postal, protested the ruling, and the unusual lag time before the ruling was announced, without success. Instead of following teammate Eddy Gragus for a second consecutive U.S. Postal victory, Hincapie lost the champion's jersey to Bart Bowen, the 1992 winner. Riding for Saturn, Bowen finished 8th and became the first rider with two CoreStates victories.

One year after his controversial disqualification, Hincapie stood on the winner's podium once again. Not only did Hincapie earn the right to legitimately wear the stars-and-stripes jersey, he also took home the $30,000 check for the overall winner. His highest previous placing in the U.S. championship was 10th in 1995.

In 1998, after a bank merger, the USPRO's title sponsorship moved to First Union; another merger would change the title sponsor to Wachovia. The USPRO championship continued to grow in reputation and stature.

More Teams, More Riders

In 2002 the powerful U.S. Postal Service team was expected to lead George Hincapie and Fred Rodriguez to the podium. Rodriguez, the defending champion, was forced to withdraw after a battle with bronchitis.

Instead riders from Navigators and

Prime Alliance set the pace. Less than 2 miles from the finish, Prime Alliance's Danny Pate attacked. Chann McRae (U.S. Postal) responded and was surprised to see that Hincapie had not followed the break with him. Navigator's Mark Walters joined Pate and McRae. Representing three different teams, the trio raced for the finish. Walters and McRae followed inches behind Pate until the final sprint. Pate faded and Walters won. McRae, in 2nd, won the USPRO champion's jersey.

After nine previous USPRO races, Saturn's Mark McCormack finished 4th in 2003, 10 meters behind a frantic sprint photo finish between Stefano Zanini of Saeco and Uros Murn of Formaggi Pinzolo. The lead riders had to wait until the officials reviewed the finish line photos before they could declare a winner.

In 2004 Spaniard Francisco Ventoso of the Prodir-Saunier Duval team took home the $35,000 1st-place check. Rodriguez, the first American, finished 4th and became the first racer in the twenty-year history of the USPRO championship to win the stars and stripes three times. Raced in uncharacteristic 60-degree weather, the 2004 race was the second fastest on record. The first 44 finishers across the line received the same time: 5:53:13, averaging 26.5 mph.

2005: A Year of Change

When the first CoreStates USPRO championship was held in 1985, the list of American professional riders was a short one. Twenty-one years later 163 Americans raced professionally all over the world. Although 200 racers on twenty-three teams entered in 2005, the year brought change for teams, riders, and the USPRO championships.

In a major break with two decades of tradition, the 2005 USPRO championships would be the last held in Philadelphia. In November 2005 USA Cycling's CEO, Gerard Bisceglia, announced a three-year agreement naming Greenville, South Carolina, as the site of the U.S. professional cycling championship beginning in 2006. USA Cycling, the governing body for American racing, also changed the international flavor of the race. Beginning in 2006 USA Cycling awarded the national championship stars-and-stripes jersey in a race limited to American riders. The Philadelphia race also lost its title sponsorship when Wachovia's management decided they no longer needed the race to build name recognition.

Fred Rodriguez came to the race in 2005 looking for his fourth national championship. Bobby Julich, who claimed victories at the Paris-Nice* and Criterium International in March, came to

*Julich was the first American to win Paris-Nice.

Philadelphia with his CSC team to win the stars-and-stripes jersey. With growing lists of personal achievements and the support of talented teammates, Chris Horner, Danny Pate, Mark McCormack, Tyler Farrar, former champion Chris Wherry, and Discovery Channel's Antonio Cruz were all mentioned as potential winners.

The 2005 edition of the Wachovia USPRO challenged the riders with the customary 90-degree heat and energy-sapping humidity. For the first time in four years, American riders occupied all steps of the podium. (In 2001 Fred Rodriguez, Trent Klasna, and George Hincapie created an all-American top-three finish.)

Less than 3 miles from the finish Chris Wherry (Health Net-Maxxis) sprinted ahead of Danny Pate (Jelly Belly-Pool Gel) and Chris Horner (Saunier Duval). Wherry's move created a 10-second gap that Horner and Pate couldn't close. The three riders raced to the end of the 156-mile race with a blazing 35-mph sprint. Arms raised, Wherry held off the charging pair and won the final jersey awarded in Philadelphia. Wherry collected $40,000 for the win. Pate received $15,000, Horner $13,000. The prize money reached the 40th rider, although $325 does not go very far. Health Net-Maxxis, the top team, split $3,000 among the riders.

In August 2006 the USPRO championships moved to Greenville, South Carolina. The new race, called The Cliffs USA Cycling Professional National Championships included the inaugural USPRO time trial championship. America's top teams were represented in the starting field, including Discovery Channel, Toyota-United, Navigators, UCI CT, Jittery Joe's, Kodakgallery.com-Sierra Nevada,

and Health Net-Maxxis. The European squad CSC was also represented.

At the request of the title sponsor, the out-and-back 20-mile route wound through "The Cliffs" subdivisions. The last 5 kilometers of the course were located inside a gated community. The technically demanding finish played a crucial role in determining which rider emerged victorious.

David Zabriskie, who rode the course the day before to scout landmarks, transition points, and changes in elevation, left the start house 4th from last. He posted the day's fastest time at the turnaround and maintained his pace to finish in 41:49:69, averaging 28.5 mph. Defending time trial champion Chris Baldwin of Toyota-United was the last rider on the course. An enthusiastic event announcer tracked Baldwin's mile-by-mile progress. At the turnaround he had bested Zabriskie by almost 8 seconds.

Rising to a fever pitch, the announcer informed local spectators and racing fans listening to a live streaming audio broadcast that Baldwin was clearly on pace to post the best time. Anticipation turned to shock when Baldwin failed to negotiate one of the final turns. Riding aggressively, he entered an uphill, right-hand turn too fast. When he tried to compensate, his rear wheel locked up and Baldwin slid off the road into a ravine. He scrambled back to the road and replaced his damaged bike with a new one. The uphill restart hampered Baldwin's ability to quickly reach top speed. Despite the crash and flustered nerves, Baldwin still finished 2nd. At the point of the crash, just 400 meters from the finish, he had an 11-second lead. He finished 32 seconds behind Zabriskie.

The twenty-second USPRO championship road race was held two days later.

The 120.5-mile course featured five 21.8-mile laps and three 3.7-mile finishing circuits in downtown Greenville. George Hincapie, a resident of Greenville, used the crowd's support to ride an aggressive race and win the first USPRO championship contested with an Americans-only field. Hincapie also won the road championship in 1998.

Temperatures in the 80s, high humidity, and the blistering pace set by the leaders reduced the field to thirty-one finishers. The pace of the race was aggressive from first lap to last. Levi Leipheimer, Zabriskie, and Hincapie used the 3-mile, 1,000-foot Paris Mountain climb to fracture the field and send pretenders to the sidelines. Leipheimer was riding his final race with Gerolsteiner before moving to Discovery.

On the 2nd lap, a group of eight riders formed the lead group. Joining Hincapie and Leipheimer were Phil Zajicek and Burke Swindlehurst (Navigators), Andrew Bajadali (Jelly Belly), and three from Toyota-United: Chris Baldwin, Justin England, and defending national champion Chris Wherry.

In a race of attrition, Hincapie's challengers fell behind one by one over the next 2 laps. When Hincapie, Leipheimer, and Bajadali entered the final three 3.7-mile circuits, the future teammates attacked, first Hincapie, then Leipheimer. Bajadali cracked. On the final lap Leipheimer caught Hincapie but failed to match his final attack 1 kilometer from the line. Leipheimer finished 16 seconds back and Danny Pate of TIAA-CREF took 3rd, 1:20 behind.

Wachovia Liberty Classic

In 1994 the women's Liberty Classic was added to the annual USPRO championship racing schedule in Philadelphia.

2006 USPRO CHAMPIONSHIP: TOP TEN FINISHERS

1. George Hincapie, Discovery Channel
2. Levi Leipheimer, Gerolsteiner, at 0:16
3. Danny Pate, TIAA-CREF, at 1:20
4. Burke Swindlehurst, Navigators Insurance, at 1:25
5. Chris Wherry, Toyota-United, at 1:38
6. Andrew Bajadali, Jelly Belly, at 1:49
7. Ben Jacques-Mayne KodakGallery.com-Sierra Nevada, at 2:39
8. Phil Zajicek, Navigators Insurance, same time
9. Blake Caldwell, TIAA-CREF, at 2:51
10. Will Frischkorn, TIAA-CREF, at 9:15

Held the same day as the men's road race, the Liberty Classic attracted the best professional teams, including T-Mobile and Saturn. From 1999 to 2001 the Liberty Classic was listed as a world cup race, and the course was lengthened to 72 miles to meet world cup standards.

In the race's fourteen-year history, Germany's Petra Rossner dominated her competition, winning seven times, including five consecutive victories from 1998 to 2002. Rossner competed with Saturn, the German national team, and the Nurnberger team. In 2003 Canadian Lyne Bessette (Knowlton's) interrupted Rossner's five-year winning streak. In 2004 thirty-seven-year-old Rossner won the $52,000 Wachovia Liberty Classic for the seventh time in nine years, averaging 23.7 mph over the 57.6-mile course.

With Rossner no longer in the field, a new champion was named in 2005. At the start line were U.S. national champ Kristin Armstrong, four-time U.S. national champ Kimberly Baldwin, and former world champion and Olympic silver medalist Mari Holden. In the final sprint Rossner's countrywoman Ina Teutenberg (T-Mobile) outraced American Laura Van Gilder and Germany's Regina Schleicher.

In 2006, when the USPRO championships moved from Philadelphia to Greenville, South Carolina, the women's race, renamed the Commerce Bank Liberty Classic, remained on the Philadelphia racing calendar. Regina Schleicher and Ina Teutenberg reversed 2005's order of finish and kept a German on the winner's podium for the second consecutive year. American Tina Pic finished 3rd.

No American woman has ever won the Liberty Classic.

LIBERTY CLASSIC WINNERS
1994 - Marianne Bergland
1995 - Clara Hughes
1996 - Petra Rossner
1997 - Edita Pucinskaite
1998 - Petra Rossner
1999 - Petra Rossner
2000 - Petra Rossner
2001 - Petra Rossner
2002 - Petra Rossner
2003 - Lyne Bessette
2004 - Petra Rossner
2005 - Ina Teutenberg
2006 - Regina Schleicher

The Tour de Trump

In Europe classic races like the Paris-Roubaix, Giro d'Italia, Tour de France, Tour of Switzerland, and Vuelta a España had long traditions and storied histories. Until the Coors Classic, the United States had nothing to compare. Creation of an American tour was the elusive dream of cycling's promoters.

As the Coors Classic wound down, USCF officials approached Mike Berg of Jefferson-Pilot Teleproductions about starting an American version of the Tour de France. In 1987, at the Pan Am Games in Indianapolis, Billy Packer, a well-known basketball analyst with ties to Berg and Jefferson-Pilot, had breakfast with Mike Plant and Jerry Lace from the USCF. While the trio dined, Packer pitched his idea for the Tour of Jersey, a race from Manhattan to Atlantic City. One of the most important stage races in the United States started with a question—"What if we . . . ?"—and moved to scribbled notes on the back of a napkin.

Searching for financial support, Packer approached Donald Trump. After Trump agreed to spend $750,000 on the event, the name of the race changed to the Tour de Trump.

The first running of the Tour de Trump in 1989 featured nineteen teams—including PDM, Europe's top-ranked team, and 3rd-ranked Panasonic. Eight pro and eleven amateur teams were entered. LeMond himself was there. Over ten days, riders from fifteen countries rode through 150 communities and 129 police jurisdictions in five states. Race director Mike Plant and his staff managed the smallest of details in an attempt to make the race safe for competitors, interesting for spectators, and visible for sponsors. The details included 35,000 orange traffic cones, 40,000 feet of snow fence, and 2,500 "follow the sign" directional arrows.

Behind Trump's courtship of the media, NBC and ESPN broadcast almost eight hours of race coverage. At the end of the ten-day event, Dag-Otto Lauritzen of 7-Eleven took home the winner's jersey and a $50,000 check. LeMond was virtually missing from the results— although he would go on to win his second Tour de France later that summer.

Founded with the financial support of Trump and later sponsored by one of the largest chemical companies in the world, the Tour de Trump/Tour DuPont would last for eight years. The world's best riders came to the East Coast in early May to compete for large purses and reputations. For American teams, this was their chance to race their international competitors on home turf. By 1996 the UCI ranked the Tour DuPont as a Category 1 stage race, on the same level as the Tour of Switzerland.

When the Coors Classic ended late in 1988, American riders were left without a major domestic race. The Tour de Trump filled that void and, at least for a time, became "America's Tour."

The Tour DuPont

America's Tour, 1989 to 1996

The inaugural Tour de Trump featured six road races, three individual time trials, a circuit race, and a criterium. The rider with the lowest total time after 837 miles received a $50,000 1st-place prize. The competitors split an unprecedented $250,000 purse.

INAUGURAL TOUR DE TRUMP

May 5: Albany prologue time trial, 2 miles

May 6: Albany to New Paltz, 110 miles

May 7: New York City to Lehigh Valley, 123 miles

May 8: Lehigh Valley to Harrisburg, 120 miles

May 9: Gettysburg to Winchester, 107 miles

May 10: Front Royal to Charlottesville, 114 miles

May 11: Richmond time trial, 9 miles

May 12: Arlington circuit race, 68 miles

May 13: Baltimore criterium, 51 miles

May 14: Atlantic City to Brigantine time trial, 24 miles

Greg LeMond entered the race, drawing the attention of spectators and media to the event. Still recovering from a series of physical setbacks, LeMond finished the first two stages far behind the leaders, placing 54th in the 110-mile first stage and 58th in the 123-mile second stage. LeMond rode for the recently introduced Coors Light-ADR team. Alexi Grewal, the 1984 Olympic road race gold medal winner, was also part of that team. The 7-Eleven team was packed with talented riders including Ron Kiefel, Davis Phinney, and Andy Hampsten, the first American to win the Giro d'Italia.

Eight stages went by before an American managed a victory. Phinney won the eighth-stage Arlington circuit race in a pack sprint. Belgium's Eric Vanderaerden and Phinney crossed the finish line simultaneously on opposite sides of the road. After reviewing the finish line photos, Phinney was declared the winner with a 1-inch margin of victory. Phinney won the next day's criterium as well. Phinney's teammates Ron Kiefel and Dag-Otto Lauritzen added two more stage wins, helping 7-Eleven to 1st place in the team competition. The Coors Light team did not play a role in the first running of the Tour de Trump. Greg Oravetz, Greg LeMond, and Alexi Grewal finished out of contention.

Lauritzen (7-Eleven) held the lead for most of the race. Before the 24-mile Atlantic City time trial held on the tenth and final day, Lauritzen had a 28-second lead over Dutchman Henk Lubberding and 50 seconds over Eric Vanderaerden of the Netherlands. Vanderaerden made a costly mistake that ensured Lauritzen would remain in 1st place. Closing in on the turning point of the out-and-back course, Vanderaerden became confused and followed a motorcycle off course. The 500-meter detour cost him any chance of capturing the stage and the Tour. Kiefel won the 24-mile final stage in 51:27. Lauritzen won the inaugural ten-day Tour de Trump (his time was 33:22:28) without winning a stage. He received a check for $50,000 and the right to wear the winner's multicolored jersey.

The race was a Federation Internationale Amateur de Cyclisme (FIAC)–sanctioned amateur race, but professional riders and teams dominated.

America's answer to the Tour de France received unprecedented television coverage. NBC broadcast four hours of Tour de Trump race coverage and ESPN added another three and a half hours. The first Tour received more coverage than CBS scheduled for the Tour de France.

Once again, in the 1990 Tour, the $50,000 individual 1st-place prize was the richest in the country. The top team shared a $10,000 prize. Mexico's Raul Alcala captured the $50,000 1st prize, 43 seconds in front of Atle Kvalsvoll of Norway. Alcala's Netherlands-based PDM team won the team title with a commanding 31-minute lead over the American AC Pinarello team.

American riders, fueled by enthusiastic spectators, performed well in the international field. Nine Americans finished in the top twenty. Clark Sheehan, Bryan Miller, and Michael Carter were members of the 2nd-place AC Pinarello team. For the second consecutive year, Greg LeMond struggled. He placed 78th, his cumulative time 1 hour and 40 minutes behind Alcala.

Facing a financial crisis in other parts of his empire, Donald Trump relinquished the title sponsorship after the 1990 event.

New Sponsor, New Name

DuPont, the giant chemical company, was already involved in professional bicycle racing. In addition to manufacturing racing apparel and signing Greg LeMond to endorsement contracts, the company signed a one-year agreement to take over the Tour de Trump and its $4.5 million operating budget. The contract included a three-year option. In 1991 the Tour de Trump officially became the Tour DuPont. In addition to changing the name, the race organizers changed the leader's jersey from pink to yellow. An eagle on the leader's jersey and a mountain goat on the climber's version added a little home-country flair.

While unable to match the Tour de France's $400,000 prize, the $50,000 1st-place check still brought a field of more than one-hundred professional and amateur racers to the starting line. Four amateur teams, including the Soviet and U.S. national squads, entered the race. The names of the world's top riders could be found on the general classification list. Greg LeMond, Alexi Grewal, and Erik Breukink of Holland brought international stature to the field. Alcala did not return to defend his title, opting to race in the Tour of Spain.

Davis Phinney captured the first stage and the overall sprinters' prize at the end of the Tour. Breukink (PDM) narrowly defeated Norway's Atle Kvalsvoll on the final day. The winning margin was 12 seconds. Once again Greg LeMond finished out of contention.

LeMond's Last Victory

Greg LeMond's participation in the Tour de Trump and Tour DuPont helped legitimize the race and drew other elite riders and teams to compete. In 1992 Gatorade of Italy, the top-ranked team in the world, arrived with their leaders, Gianni Bugno and Laurent Fignon.

Hampered by nagging injuries, LeMond's performances in the previous editions of the Tour de Trump/Tour

DuPont didn't reflect his stature as America's top racer. LeMond returned to form in early 1992. He reminded the field of his prowess by winning the prologue time trial in record time. Atle Kvalsvoll, LeMond's teammate and a strong contender for the top spot in the first two events, rode in support of LeMond over the final stages of the Tour. Going into the last day, LeMond wore the yellow jersey by the thinnest of margins. Kvalsvoll trailed by 0.13 seconds, Phil Anderson of Motorola by 10 seconds, and Coors Light rider Stephen Swart by 14 seconds.

LeMond's expertise and experience held each competitor at bay. He finished ahead of all three. The 1992 Tour DuPont victory was the last major win of his career and his first on U.S. soil since the 1985 Coors Classic.

Lance Armstrong Arrives

Mike Plant, the race director, expanded the 1993 course to include mountain stages in North Carolina. Large crowds of enthusiastic spectators at each stage motivated city officials throughout the region to ask Plant to route the Tour through their towns.

The winner of the 1990 Tour de Trump, Raul Alcala, battled twenty-one-year-old Lance Armstrong throughout the 1,100-mile race in 1993. Alcala, riding for WordPerfect, won the race for the second time by a record-setting 2:26 margin, receiving a $40,000 check and a new Saturn automobile. As a first-year professional, Armstrong made a strong showing, finishing less than 2 seconds behind Alcala in the prologue time trial. Armstrong won the fifth stage and was in 2nd place, 19 seconds behind Alcala, at the start of the final stage.

Starting the 36.7-mile individual time trial 2 minutes behind Armstrong, Alcala

passed him with 16 miles remaining. But then Alcala flatted and fell behind by 25 seconds. He recovered, caught Armstrong again, and won the time trial in 1:14:16. Young Armstrong finished the final stage in 4th place and maintained 2nd overall, 2:26 behind Alcala.

The seven-member Chevrolet-L.A. Sheriff team shared a $5,000 prize for winning the team competition. Coors Light had been expected to challenge for individual and team honors. Although Ron Kiefel won a stage, a virus swept through the team, handicapping their performances.

The 1994 Tour DuPont began on May 4 in Wilmington, Delaware, and finished 1,060 miles and twelve days—and four states—later in Winston-Salem, North Carolina. For the second consecutive year, Lance Armstrong finished 2nd overall. In 1994 it was Viatcheslav Ekimov who denied Armstrong the winner's jersey. A decade later "Eki" would prove to be a powerful ally for Armstrong in the Tour de France.

Other than Coors Light rider Scott McKinley taking 3rd in the first stage, Armstrong was the only American to stand on the podium during the 1994 Tour DuPont.

1995: Armstrong's First Win

Winning the 1993 American and world road racing championships put Armstrong at the top of his profession. Finishing 2nd in the 1993 and 1994 Tours DuPont to riders from Mexico and Russia added extra incentive at the start of the 1995 race.

It wasn't close. Armstrong won three stages and the yellow rested on his shoulders for the last eight. At the start of the last stage, a 30-mile time trial, he held a commanding 3:55 lead over

Motorola teammate Andrea Peron of Italy. The 1994 winner, Ekimov, was just over 4 minutes back. Winning a second consecutive Tour DuPont was a long shot for Ekimov—it would require an inspired time trial from him and a time-consuming crash or mechanical problem for Armstrong.

The riders blasted out of the start house at 2-minute intervals. Motorola team managers kept Armstrong informed of Ekimov's progress. The Russian won the time trial with an average speed of 29.63 mph. Armstrong crossed the line in 5th, 2:04 behind Ekimov on the day but still holding a 2-minute lead. For his first Tour DuPont win Armstrong earned $40,000, added $5,000 as the mountain leader, and took home $5,100 more for winning three stages. Motorola's second consecutive team title added a little more to the pot.

The peloton set a record for the fastest average speed in the seven-year history of the Tour. Over twelve days eighty-four riders covered 1,100 miles, averaging 24.32 mph.

Another American, Clark Sheehan, riding for Montgomery Bell, put his name in the Tour DuPont history books in 1995. Sheehan and Novell rider Djamolodine Abdoujaparov, legendary sprinter of the European peloton, broke away from the pack early in stage eight. At one point the unlikely duo led by more than 15 minutes. On the final climb Sheehan sprinted away from Abdoujaparov and crossed the line with a 4-second lead. The pair's 115-mile break was the longest in Tour DuPont history.

Armstrong, surrounded by his Motorola teammates, became the first to win the Tour DuPont in consecutive years. Armstrong again dominated the 1996 Tour, taking the overall lead on the

second day and winning a record five stages, including both time trials. On the final stage, a 9.1-mile time trial, Armstrong beat 2nd-place rider Daniele Nardello (Mapei-GB) by an impressive 28.2 seconds.

LANCE ARMSTRONG'S TOUR DuPONT RECORDS

Ten days wearing the yellow jersey
Five stage wins in one year
Ten stage wins in his career
Largest margin of victory
Fastest average speed in time trial

Packer v. Plant

The race was a success and at the height of its popularity. But the Tour DuPont ended abruptly in December 1996 when a legal battle between race director Mike Plant and Billy Packer, the original race promoter, triggered DuPont's decision to end its sponsorship with another year left on the contract.

It was Billy Packer who envisioned an American version of the Tour de France and made the original pitch to Donald Trump. Packer then enticed Plant to leave his executive position with the USCF to become race director for the Tour de Trump.

Plant formed a firm called Medalist Sports and managed the race successfully through 1996. When DuPont became title sponsor, the company paid Plant a fee for services and assumed responsibility for race-related expenses. In his lawsuit Packer alleged that Medalist Sports generated more than $1 million in profits that were not shared with him. Plant made two $50,000 payments, claiming them as a generous bonus for supporting the race similar to another $100,000 in bonuses awarded to the staff.

Packer claimed that all profits from the Tour de Trump and the Tour DuPont that followed should have been split evenly. In response, Plant claimed that Packer was never an equal partner. Before the case went to trial, Plant and Packer reached a settlement, in which Packer became sole owner of the Tour DuPont and Tour of China events.

With the change in ownership formalized, DuPont exercised a clause in its contract that allowed it to discontinue sponsorship if Plant wasn't involved in the event. The company's announcement read that it was withdrawing as sponsor "due to the fact that commercial obligations have not been met as a result of a lawsuit between the event's owners."

Once again, American riders were left without a tour of their own.

The Pros in the '90s

Earning a Living in 1990

Two months after winning the closest Tour de France in the history of the event, Greg LeMond signed a $5.7 million, three-year contract to race for the French Z team. The contract was reported to pay him $1.8 million in 1990, $1.9 million in 1991, and $2 million in 1992. He was clearly the highest paid professional racer in the world; his fellow competitors earned far less than him for their labors.

In 1990 there were fewer than 150 professional bicycle racers in the United States. Their average salary was approximately $30,000. For instance, the AC Pinarello team paid its riders a $12,000 base salary and offered another $12,000 to $15,000 in prize money earned at races. On 7-Eleven the salaries ranged from $20,000 to $75,000. Making a living as a professional bike racer wasn't necessarily the best way to fame and fortune.

In April 1990 Jack Simes, one of the founders of USPRO, introduced the DuPont Pro Cycling Series, promoted as the first American professional criterium championship. The first race was held in Washington, D.C. on April 27, 1990. On a 1.2-mile course that passed in front of the Capitol, six professional teams competed: 7-Eleven, Coors Light, AC Pinarello, Spago, Amore Vita, and American Commerce. Thirty thousand spectators came to see Greg LeMond race in his world championship rainbow jersey.

Points were awarded to the first twenty riders in each of the three races in the series, and a leader's jersey was given to the rider with the most points at the start of each race. The rider with the most points after the completion of the series would be named the U.S. professional criterium champion and would receive $2,500 and the use of a Porsche 944 S2 for one year. It was quite a carrot to dangle in front of a struggling pro field.

Coors Light riders Chris Huber and Roberto Gaggioli led nine other riders away from the pack on the 10th lap. At one point the lead break included riders from all six teams. On the final laps Coors Light and 7-Eleven battled for position. David Farmer (Coors Light) prevailed to win the first race in the series. LeMond, battling a persistent virus, abandoned after 29 laps. Farmer would go on to win the series.

America's Best Women Struggle for Support

Women represented just 8 percent of the USCF's membership at the end of 1988. In 1989 more than a third of the USCF's districts reported no female competitors at the district championship level. In 1990 there were still fewer than 2,600 licensed female riders.

Despite a significantly smaller number of licensed racers compared to their male counterparts, American women achieved success at home and abroad. At the 1989 Tour de Feminin, six of America's best female racers excelled. Inga Thompson finished 3rd and Susan Elias 4th. Katrin Tobin and Bunki Bankaitis-Davis each won a stage, and the United States took the team title. Three American riders finished in the top ten.

The biggest challenge American women faced wasn't from elite racers from other countries. Instead, inconsistent corporate sponsorships whipsawed the riders' earning power from season to season. At the beginning of 1990, six major women's teams folded. After eight years 7-Eleven canceled its sponsorship of a women's team and put all its resources behind the men's team. Lowrey's, Lycra, Sundance, Team USA, and Mazda also ended their backing, leaving Weight Watchers as the only remaining major sponsor—which only lasted until October 2, when the diet company announced the end of its eight-year-old team. The loss of women's events like the Coors Classic and Seafirst Crown reduced the type of opportunities for media coverage that corporate brand managers coveted.

In the face of economic challenges, women's racing would survive and at times thrive. Promoters and companies that were committed to women's racing tempered the canceled corporate sponsorships. In August 1990 Jim Rabdau launched the Women's Challenge, a seventeen-day stage race that was the longest and richest women's-only race in American history.

The Women's Challenge

 In 1984 interest in bicycle racing was booming across the country. Women received as much attention and opportunity to race as their male counterparts. That summer American women would make history with strong appearances at the Coors Classic and Los Angeles Olympics, where the first women's road cycling medals were awarded.

Founded by Jim Rabdau, the Ore-Ida Women's Challenge became one of the most important stage races in American and international racing. A former Army Green Beret, Rabdau started thinking about a women's race when he watched cyclists racing in the Italian Alps. In 1984 he brought the idea to life. Rabdau, manager of Ore-Ida Foods' general support services, convinced the company's president that sponsoring a women's race would be good for business.

Fifty-two women raced over 180 miles of Idaho's dry deserts and steep mountains, competing for a prize purse of $7,430. Rebecca Twigg won the first event, and then capped a successful summer by winning the silver medal in the Olympic cycling road race. In 1985 she beat Inga Thompson by just under 2 minutes at the Women's Challenge.

In 1986, despite a crash, Twigg won her third consecutive Women's Challenge. By the third year the race had grown to an eight-day, 260-mile race ending with the hour-long Park Center criterium in

Boise, Idaho. At age twenty-two, Twigg battled Madonna Harris and Susan Ehlers, members of the Centurion-Texas Metros racing team. The Metros did capture the team title, but Twigg survived a collision and crash with just 2 miles to go in the final stage. She recovered, finished the race, and protected her lead. Twigg finished in 9:05:19. Madonna Harris followed 1:15 behind. Twigg's 7-Eleven team finished 3:38 behind the Centurion-Texas Metros.

As the race became more established and his reputation for race organization spread, Rabdau expanded the number of stages and course mileage and, most important to the entrants, increased the prize purse.

In 1987 the Challenge covered more than 300 miles in eight days. Inga Thompson's winning margin over Katrin Tobin was a narrow 27 seconds.

The next year, the Challenge featured ten races over nine days and 329 miles. The entry list grew to twenty-three teams and ninety-two riders. The 7-Eleven team did not compete in 1988, preferring to focus on preparations for the Seoul Olympics. The 1988 event included two new stages to increase the spirit of competition. Rabdau added a 3.25-mile time trial that paired racers with similar race performances. The racers left the starting line in pairs 30 seconds apart and received bonuses for finishing more than 5 seconds ahead of their competitor or for catching a rider from a pair already on the course. A points competition was also added to give sprinters and climbers incentives. The Challenge awarded Queen of the Mountain and Hot Spot Sprint titles to the riders with the most accumulated points.

Katrin Tobin turned a close loss the year before into a narrow victory, beating Jane Marshall by 31 seconds in the longest Ore-Ida Women's Challenge to date. The riders endured temperature swings from freezing to triple digits.

Five years after the first race, the prize purse grew to $28,000. In 1989 many of the world's top riders opted to travel to France to race in the Tour de Feminin instead of returning to Idaho. The Challenge still drew eighty starters who fought for a piece of the prize purse in ten stages over nine days.

1989 TEAM LIST

Lowrey's
Weight Watchers
Dave's Bike Sport
Lycra
Raleigh
Aussie-Suntour
Team USA
Designer Floors/Gore Tex
Kinetic Systems
Alfalfa's/Zinn/Mavic
Manukau Cycling Club
Serac/U.S. Masters
Puget Sound
Suntour/Marin
British Columbia
Club Solo
Continental Tradewinds
Cannondale
Bicycle Link

Although the Ore-Ida Women's Challenge earned a worldwide reputation, race organizer Jim Rabdau struggled with the Federation Internationale Amateur de Cyclisme (FIAC) to have the event officially recognized and placed on the 1990 international racing calendar.

Despite a track record of seven successful years, the UCI failed to grant the Challenge the Hors National Tour for Women Category B status Rabdau wanted. The UCI's criteria for awarding the designation stipulated a maximum length of fifteen days. The race organizers also had to provide lodging, a car, and expense money for visiting teams.

Andy Bohlmann, the USCF's director of technical services, informed Rabdau that the FIAC had rejected his application. The reason: The Challenge dates conflicted with a French race and some of the stages exceeded the FIAC's mileage regulations. The organizers responded to the snub by printing and wearing "Let's Get Excessive" T-shirts. Disappointment with the decision was tempered by the status the event reached in 1990. The Ore-Ida Women's Challenge offered $60,000 in prizes, becoming the richest and longest women's race in history. The seventeen-stage race covered 663 miles in stages ranging from 2.65-mile sprints to 80-mile road races. Overall, the riders climbed more than 20,000 feet in fifteen days.

Thompson, who had competed in the Tour de France Feminin, rode for the Cal-Neva/Reno Wheelmen, her hometown sponsor. In the individual time trial, Thompson used a custom-built carbon fiber bike. The four-pound frame was equipped with SunTour Superbe Pro components and a Wolber bladed-spoke front wheel and rear disc. Thompson finished the 2.65-mile flat course in 5:54, eight seconds ahead of Ruthie Matthes of team Oh! Idaho.

A team time trial followed. Thompson's Cal-Neva team included Marion Clignet and national team time trial champions Phyllis Hines and Jeanne Golay. Cal-Neva crossed the line more than 90 seconds ahead of 2nd-place Oh! Idaho.

Inga Thompson wore the leader's jersey for all but two stages. Her winning time of 27:19:46 edged Ruthie Matthes by 1:16. Thompson finished 2:08 ahead of Lisa Brambani, the defending champion, and received $2,590 for her 1st-place ride.

In 1991 France's Jeannie Longo came out of retirement to enter the Ore-Ida Challenge. Longo registered as Jane Ciprelli to avoid the media's glare. Longo won the race, beating Dede Demet by 44 seconds. The Lithuanian national team also entered, before their country was recognized as its own nation separate and independent from Russia.

As with many races around the country, Rabdau relied on corporate sponsorships to finance race operations. Securing long-term sponsorship partnerships was the difference between hosting the race one more year and adding the event name to a long list of short-lived races.

A Bump in the Road

In February 1993 race organizers issued a press release announcing that the Idaho Women's Challenge would be canceled. When the 1992 race came to a close, Ore-Ida, the title sponsor since 1984, told race organizers to look for a cosponsor.

Rabdau refused to fold the event and four months later hosted a smaller, leaner race called the Idaho International Women's Challenge. The five-day, seven-stage event covered 232 miles and

offered a $25,000 prize list. Jeanne Golay, who had competed in seven previous races, finally won the individual title. Golay shocked her competitors by finishing the first stage with nearly a 5-minute lead. She wore the leader's jersey for the rest of the Challenge. Her winning time of 8:41:18 was 3 minutes faster than Eve Stephenson. The U.S. Cycling Team/EDS won the team title.

After eight years of financial support form Ore-Ida, Rabdau tenaciously searched for a new title sponsor. In 1992 and 1993 the name was changed to the Idaho International Women's Challenge, and organizers reduced the number of stages and shortened the course to control costs and keep the race financially viable.

In 1994 Rabdau received a three-year commitment from PowerFoods, the owner of the PowerBar. Still shorter than previous events, the 1994 Challenge featured six stages in five days. The race schedule included two individual time trials, a criterium, two road races, and a circuit race. Clara Hughes took the Challenge title home to Canada.

With a new title sponsor in place, the Challenge began to grow again. In 1995 the UCI officially recognized the Women's Challenge. Dede Demet's individual title was the last for an American rider.

The Richest Race in the World

In 1997 computer giant Hewlett-Packard assumed the role as title sponsor. An international field of teams from Russia, Lithuania, Australia, and New Zealand joined American teams from Saturn, Klein, and Saeco-Timex in the nine-stage event. The prize purse increased to $100,000—more than double the amount offered by any other race based in the United States. Rasa Polikeviciute, a member of the Lithuanian national team, won the overall title and a 1st prize of $5,500.

In November 1998 Hewlett-Packard announced its intention to extend the title sponsorship agreement through 2000. Part of the sponsorship negotiation included changing the name to the HP LaserJet Women's Challenge. Now sixteen years old, the Challenge offered a $125,000 prize list, the largest road-racing purse in the Western Hemisphere. The 1999 event was added to the UCI's North American schedule.

Each year the quality of the competition rose to match challenges added to the course. In 1999 the 693-mile course included almost 14,000 feet in elevation gains in thirteen stages over twelve days. France's Jeannie Longo returned to win her second Women's Challenge. The NBC television network covered the race.

A Growing Influence

Lance Armstrong's victory in the 2000 Tour de France introduced more Americans to the sport of bicycle racing, and new enthusiasts called for more coverage. ESPN2 broadcast a one-hour summary of the eleven-day 2000 HP LaserJet Women's Challenge that reached 68 million American homes and more than 150 million more internationally. The program was aired several times prior to the Sydney Olympics.

Performances in the Women's Challenge influenced the selection decisions of the U.S. Olympic Committee. The large field of experienced international talent helped U.S. coaches evaluate talent and performances against the best in the world. In 2000 organizers created two stages to imitate conditions the riders would encounter in Sydney.

The 2000 Sydney Olympic Games featured five of the last seven HP LaserJet Women's Challenge champions: two-time winner Anna Wilson of Australia, France's legendary Jeannie Longo, 1997 champion Rasa Polikeviciute of Lithuania, and 1994 champion Clara Hughes of Canada. American riders Mari Holden, Nicole Freedman, Karen Kurreck, Alison Dunlap, Ruthie Matthes, and Erin Veenstra-Mirabella also achieved success in the Women's Challenge.

In September 2000 Hewlett-Packard extended the title sponsorship agreement through 2002. Germany's Judith Arndt won what turned out to be the final Women's Challenge race. At the end of the race, Hewlett-Packard announced its decision to relinquish the title sponsorship.

Over nineteen years the Women's Challenge became the world's premier women's stage race. It was formally recognized by the UCI in 1994, and riders from twenty-nine different countries including Korea, China, South Africa, and Lithuania came to compete for more than $1 million in prize money awarded during its run. The names on the list of winners—Twigg, Thompson, Tobin, Longo—represent the best female racers of their generation.

In January 2003 race organizers announced that the Women's Challenge was canceled. ConAgra Foods, which had considered assuming the title sponsorship, withdrew its financial support.

LeMond's Third Victory

In July 1990 Greg LeMond captured his third and final Tour de France yellow jersey. Throughout the race LeMond battled Claudio Chiappucci and Miguel Indurain for the lead. Before the final time trial, LeMond had narrowed Chiappucci's lead from 2:24 to just 5 seconds. In three earlier head-to-head time trials against the Italian rider, LeMond had dominated. His winning margins of 22, 38, and 9 seconds corresponded to a race pace almost 1 kph faster than Chiappucci.

Temperatures hovering near 100 degrees didn't hamper LeMond in the final time trial. By the first official time checkpoint, LeMond had an 11-second lead over Chiappucci. LeMond won his third Tour de France with a 2:21 winning margin. He shared his $360,000 1st-place award with his teammates.

For the first time all nine members of the 7-Eleven team finished the race. Andy Hampsten, in 11th place, was the team's highest finisher.

Changes at the USCF

In the summer of 1990, while Greg LeMond was winning his third and last Tour de France, the USCF canceled its Elite Athlete Program. Founded in 1988 in response to a disappointing Olympic performance, Team USA folded in the face of inadequate funding and increased competition for top riders by corporate teams.

As one team came to an end, another was formed. Subaru of America, one of the USCF's major corporate sponsors, joined with Montgomery Securities to create the amateur Subaru-Montgomery racing team. Coached by Eddie Borysewicz, the former national and Olympic team coach, the team roster included six former Olympians and thirteen 1990 U.S. national team members. Known as Montgomery-Avenir in 1989, the team included Leonard Nitz, a four-time Olympian; Steve Hegg, Olympic medalist; and Thurlow Rogers, Jay Vonderahe, and Kevin Peck. In 1990 Borysewicz added 1988 Olympians Jim Copeland, Mike McCarthy, Ken Carpenter, Lance Armstrong, John Stenner, Jonas Carney, Jim Pollak, Bart Bowen, Greg McNeil, Nate Reiss, and Zack Copeland.

The 1990 national championships were held over ten days in late July. Temperatures in the high 90s greeted entrants in the 100-mile men's road race. The 161-rider field included 9 members of Subaru-Montgomery, including top riders Nate Reiss, Bart Bowen, and Mike

McCarthy. Bob Mionske, riding without a team, kept pace with the group that chased down a three-rider breakaway. Still fresh, he powered forward on the final quarter-mile uphill finish and captured the stars-and-stripes jersey.

Steve Hegg was the fortieth rider to leave the start gate in the time trial but had to wait four hours before learning that his 50:28.40 time would hold up for 1st place. Riders who started later in the day were hampered by gusty winds on the course.

Ruthie Matthes, who finished 2nd in the Ore-Ida Women's Challenge and in the 1989 women's road race, finally put herself on the highest step of the national podium in 1990.

The End of 7-Eleven

In late September 1990 the Southland Corporation announced the end of its ten-year sponsorship of the 7-Eleven team. Shortly afterward, Jim Ochowicz announced that he had agreed to terms with a new major

In September 1990 the Southland Corporation announced that it was ending its ten-year sponsorship of the 7-Eleven team. A force at the Coors Classic and the first professional team to race at the Tour de France, the 7-Eleven team brought new fans to American bicycle racing.

sponsor. The shrewd team manager had started discussions with Motorola on August 7, and less than a month later a $3 million, one-year sponsorship was in place. John Vande Velde, a former pro track rider, made the initial contact with Motorola to pitch a proposal for a six-day race. The proposal was turned down, but Vande Velde went to Motorola again seven months later when he heard 7-Eleven was in need of a new sponsor.

Motorola announced its official sponsorship at a press conference on October

Jim Ochowicz (standing), team manager of the soon to be defunct 7-Eleven team, negotiated a new multiyear sponsorship package with Motorola.

19, 1990, in Italy. Dag-Otto Lauritzen modeled the only blue and red Motorola team jersey in existence. The next day the 7-Eleven team made its final European appearance at the Tour of Lombardy.

The new Motorola team's first roster included eight Americans: Norman Alvis, Frankie Andreu, Andy Bishop, Andy Hampsten, Ron Kiefel, Scott McKinley, John Tomac, and Davis Phinney.

Peace at Last (Almost)

After years of acrimony, the ongoing struggle between the USCF and the USPRO reached another turning point in early 1991. An agreement between the two feuding organizations transferred USPRO's existing affiliation with the Fédération Internationale de Cyclisme Professionnel (FICP) to the USCF. The move allowed the USCF to become the sole American representative to the Union Cycliste Internationale (UCI), the international governing body of amateur and professional cycling.

The March issue of *Cycling USA* published a statement from
USPRO's Jack Simes: "Our new relationship with the USCF ensures
that the future growth of cycling in the United States will move in a
unified direction. Professional cycling in the United States will now be
governed by the USCF. However, the organizational structure of
USPRO has been preserved to manage the professional sector. It is a
milestone that will have positive effects on our sport for decades."

America's Tour

In 1991 the Tour de Trump transferred its title sponsorship to the
DuPont chemical company. The $50,000 1st prize attracted one
hundred racers from around the world. PDM rider Erik Breukink
captured the victory on the last day with a narrow 12-second winning
margin. DuPont officials carefully tracked media coverage. Broadcast
coverage by CBS and ESPN placed DuPont's brand in front of 200
million people around the world.

After the demise of the Coors Classic in 1988, promoters worked
to re-create the excitement generated by the American team's historic
performance at the 1984 Olympics and the fourteen-year run of the
Coors Classic. Other than the Tour DuPont and events like the Tour of
Somerville and Longsjo Classic, opportunities for domestic racing were
becoming increasingly limited.

In 1991 Michael Aisner introduced the U.S. Bicycle Classic as the
first major international amateurs-only stage race in this country since
the 1984 Coors Classic. Once again politics played a role. Preparations
for the new race paralleled rising tensions in the Persian Gulf. The U.S.
State Department, concerned about the safety of international teams
traveling to the race, advised Aisner to cancel the event. He followed
their guide, but just a week after the announcement, President Bush
declared the war was over. Sponsors initially interested in supporting
the race had already moved funds to other projects, and Aisner was
unable to proceed.

CHAPTER EIGHT

The Lance Armstrong Era

A Rising Star at the 1991 National Championships

Lance Armstrong, riding for Subaru-Montgomery, withstood a late charge by Steve Larsen of Team Ritchey to win the senior national road championship in 1991.★ Held near Park City, Utah, the course climbed 700 feet each lap and provided little level terrain for rest and recovery. Ninety-degree temperatures limited breaks, and the race became a war of attrition as rider after rider succumbed to the heat. Only 30 of the 112 starters finished the race. At nineteen, Armstrong covered the 168-kilometer course in 5:06:36.

In the women's race Inga Thompson dominated. On the 54-kilo-meter course, she passed Maureen Manley on the 4th of 7 laps and rode to the finish with an almost 60-second lead. Defending champion Ruthie Matthes finished 2nd. Thompson also captured a second stars-and-stripes jersey by winning the individual time trial.

Armstrong and Thompson earned positions on the Pan American team but neither accepted the invitation.

At the end of 1991, Lance Armstrong and Janie Eickhoff were named "Athletes of the Year" by the USCF. Eickhoff was honored for a silver and bronze medal at the world championships. She also captured her third national championship and broke Twigg's individual pursuit record at the Marymoor velodrome.

---

*The 1991 U.S. national championships also included a criterium in addition to the road race and time trial. Lance Armstrong's Subaru-Montgomery teammate Jason Carney beat him to the line to win the 80-kilometer criterium. With 8 laps remaining in the women's criterium, a crash involving fifteen riders stopped the race. Three riders, Maureen Manley, Patti Lightfoot, and Laurie Brandt, were transported to the hospital with minor injuries. The race was restarted, and Shari Rodgers (Bridgestone AVCT) won the race.

In addition to winning his first senior national road championship, Armstrong became the first American to win Italy's Settimanna Bergamasca stage race in 1991. The spotlight, however, had not quite found him yet.

Corporate Teams

In the early 1990s professional teams raised the visibility of American bicycle racing. Teams like Motorola and the new domestic Saturn squad became the focus of corporate advertising and energetic public relations campaigns.

In March 1992 Saturn (a division of General Motors) announced the formation of an American amateur cycling team. The thirteen-rider team of eighteen- to twenty-nine-year-old men competed in the 1992 national race circuit. The roster included two-time Olympian Bob Mionske, 1992 Olympic pursuiter Matt Hamon, and 1992 national champions Chann McRae and Dave McCook.

The Saturn team was featured in a major advertising campaign launched during the Barcelona Olympic coverage. At domestic events Saturn promoted the team with a 35-foot GMC tractor-trailer that functioned as a rolling billboard. The truck also had a workshop for the team mechanic; bunks, showers, and a washer and dryer for riders; and a fold-down tent for promotions. For the next twelve years Saturn would become one of the most important domestic teams in the United States. Saturn's support of bicycle racing would grow to include both men's and women's professional and amateur teams, as well as sponsorships of single-day races and series.

Public relations campaigns may have raised the public's awareness of the teams, but winning races captured the attention of the American press. In that regard the Motorola team was a cut above. The 1992 Motorola team needed just three and a half months to win its first major race in Europe. On May 9 Andy Hampsten won the fourth stage of the Tour de Romandie and claimed the overall title the next day. Of the seventeen riders on Motorola, only seven were American.

In the spring of 1993, three days before the Tour of Flanders, Motorola executives announced that the company would pull the plug on its sponsorship of its highly successful team at the end of 1993. Two years after Jim Ochowicz managed the team's transition from 7-Eleven to Motorola, he was searching for a new corporate sponsor willing to fund an estimated $5 million team budget. The announcement was made early in the year to give Ochowicz time to approach new sponsors. The team, however, would go on to have such a successful season that Motorola decided to renew its sponsorship.

Races of the Early '90s

LeMond's Last Gasp

After three Tour de France victories, Greg LeMond was the most recognized bicycle racer in the United States in 1992. Although his competitive career was in its final stages, his appearances at events like the Tour DuPont were guaranteed to attract more media coverage and spectator support. In the first two editions of the Tour de Trump/Tour DuPont, LeMond's race performances did not put him into contention. In 1992 LeMond defeated 105 other riders to win America's Tour. It was the last major victory of his career.

Andy Hampsten, a leader on Motorola, was seen as a possible heir apparent. Seventy-five miles into the fourteenth-stage climb to Alpe d'Huez at the 1992 Tour de France, Hampsten led a breakaway. As the climb progressed, rider after rider fell behind Hampsten's pace. With 1 mile to go Hampsten pushed forward, dropping Miguel Indurain to become the first American to win that legendary stage. His performance moved him into 3rd place overall. At the end of the Tour, Indurain wore the yellow jersey and Hampsten finished 4th.

For the first time in his Tour de France career, Greg LeMond abandoned the race, on the second day in the Alps.

From Barcelona to San Sebastian

The American cycling team continued to carry the specter of the 1984 Olympics on their shoulders. The level of international competition increased every year, but the public, whose interest in cycling competition spiked on Olympic years, expected to see American cyclists with medals around their necks.

In 1992 in Barcelona, the team could deliver only two bronze medals. Armstrong, expected to contend for gold in the road race, ended his amateur career with a 14th-place finish in a 121-mile race in Sant Sandurni d'Anoia, Spain, finishing 35 seconds behind Fabio Casartelli of Italy, a future teammate.

Armstrong turned his competitive attention to the Motorola professional racing team. Seven days after the Olympics ended, Armstrong entered his first pro race at the 1992 Classico San Sebastian, a race he would win some years later. He finished in 111th and last place. Miserable conditions caused dozens of riders to abandon. Forty-eight hours later, at the Tour of Galicia in Spain, Armstrong won the 99-kilometer fourth stage; the next day he finished 2nd in the final stage. Armstrong also competed in the 1992 world championship professional road race. Still in contention with 40 miles to go, he crashed into a fan who moved into the road to snap pictures, and was forced out of the race.

After the disappointing results in Barcelona, the USCF reorganized the organization's coaching hierarchy. Former Olympic sprint champion Mark Gorski was named national team director. Chris Carmichael was promoted from head coach of the road racing team to the newly created position of director of athletes and programs. His goal, like others before, was to bring home the gold. With the Atlanta Olympic Games just a few years away, Carmichael moved quickly to institute his vision. In late December the UCI announced a decision that would have a significant impact on Carmichael and racers all over the world—professional cyclists would be allowed to compete in Olympic events for the first time in history in 1996.

Racing's Million-Dollar Prize

Early in the 1993 racing season, Thrift Drug and promoter International Cycling Productions announced that any professional racer who won all three events in the Thrift Drug Triple Crown of Cycling would receive a check for $1 million.* It was the largest prize in the history of professional racing.

The Thrift Drug Classic, a 120-mile road race in downtown Pittsburgh, was the first race in the series. Armstrong won for the second consecutive year. When Armstrong captured the second installment of the Triple Crown—the six-day, 500-mile Kmart Classic stage race in West Virginia—media attention skyrocketed.

Riding for Motorola, Armstrong won the final leg, the CoreStates USPRO cycling championship. Late in the race Armstrong led by over 2 minutes. On the podium he received a large replica check and held it high in the air. After choosing a lump sum payment over the twenty-

---

*One year earlier Scott Moninger (Coors Light) captured the first Thrift Drug Triple Crown. Moninger received a $25,000 1st-prize check.

year payment option and paying taxes, Armstrong split the remaining funds with his Motorola teammates.

Armstrong's First Tour

Shortly afterward, Motorola team manager Jim Ochowicz took his squad to the 80th Tour de France. In his first exposure to the Tour, Armstrong finished the first stage in 86th place, 22 minutes after the leader. Gaining experience with every stage, Armstrong gave the peloton a glimpse of his future potential by sprinting past Raul Alcala to win the eighth stage. Ochowicz pulled Armstrong out of the race three stages later.

Motorola finished the 1993 Tour by becoming the first team to place two riders in the top ten: Alvaro Mejia, a Colombian climber, finished 4th and Hampsten finished 8th.

After the massive publicity generated by Lance Armstrong's victory in the Thrift Drug Triple Crown, his first stage win at the Tour de France, and his teammates' historic top-ten ranking in the Tour's final general classification, Motorola officials reconsidered their decision to end the team's sponsorship. Team Motorola survived to race again.

America's Best World Championships

The 1993 world cycling championships were held in Norway in August. For the first time the track championship events used an open format, allowing amateurs and professionals to race side by side. Amateurs captured six medals.

American racers returned home with two gold, two silver, and three bronze medals. The team finished in 2nd place, just 1 point behind Germany, its most successful world championship event since the USCF was founded in 1920.

The final event of the world championships was the 257.6-kilometer men's professional road race. Just twenty-one years old, Lance Armstrong capped off his incredible 1993 racing season by becoming the youngest winner of the race. Conditions in Oslo were treacherous, with dozens of riders falling on a bizarrely slippery circuit. Ten years earlier Greg LeMond was twenty-two when he won the first of two pro world championship races.

Sponsored by Fresca, the 1993 national road cycling championships were held in Dublin, Ohio. Rebecca Twigg captured national championship honors in the criterium and time trial. Scott Mercer finished 1st in the individual and team time trial.

The track championships were held at the Major Taylor Velodrome in Indianapolis. The competitors raced for ten national championships in seven track events. Erin Hartwell won his fifth consecutive national kilometer title. Janie Eickhoff and Lucy Vinnecombe each won two event championships. Eickhoff recaptured her 3,000-meter pursuit title and added the points race. Vinnecombe won the women's kilometer and match sprint.

The Fight for Control of Professional Racing

The USCF ended 1993 by negotiating a four-year sponsorship contract with Electronic Data Systems. The sponsorship called for more than $1 million annually. The funding included information technology and financial contributions. At the time it was the largest sponsorship deal in the history of the Federation.

In 1994 the UCI insisted that the USCF and USPRO reach an agreement over the control of professional racing in the United States, demanding a single American governing body. After more negotiations the USCF's board met in Seattle on June 12 to 19 to bring the governance of professional racing under the management of the USCF. The operations of USPRO were moved to the Olympic Training Center in Colorado Springs. After years of acrimony the USCF became the internationally recognized governing body for all racing disciplines in the United States: professional, amateur road and track, mountain biking, and BMX.

Three men's professional teams were based in the United States in 1994: Motorola, Coors Light, and Chevrolet-L.A. Sheriff. The teams faced each other in every major event. Motorola swept all three races in the 1994 Thrift Drug Classic Triple Crown. Steve Hegg, riding for Chevrolet-L.A. Sheriff, was the 1st American finisher in the 1994 USPRO championship. Hegg won his tenth national championship ten years after winning a scandal-tinged individual pursuit gold at the 1984 Olympics.

The roster of women's teams continued to change from year to year. In 1994 Bodywise, Chevrolet-L.A. Sheriff, World TEAM, and Shaklee remained strong supporters of women's cycling. Saturn sponsored a three-person team of Jeanne Golay, Julie Young, and Jessica

Grieco. Timex also formed a team. Kahlua and TGI-Friday folded their squads.

1995: LeMond Moves On, Armstrong Moves In

At the 1995 Tour de France, Armstrong captured the second stage win of his career. A few days earlier Fabio Casartelli, his Motorola teammate, was killed when he crashed on a descent from the Pyrenees. Armstrong dedicated the stage victory to his friend.

While Lance Armstrong was earning his first stage wins in the Tour de France, Greg LeMond was receiving rewards for his three overall victories, and bowing out. LeMond announced his retirement at a Korbel "Night of Champions" banquet on December 3, 1994. In July 1995 he signed a long-term licensing agreement with the Trek Bicycle Corporation in Wisconsin. The agreement called for LeMond to assist in the design and creation of a line of road bikes and accessories that carried the LeMond brand name. Trek would continue to support professional racing and in a few years would make a significant contribution to Lance Armstrong's Tour de France performances.

With Armstrong winning the Tour DuPont and Saturn's Norm Alvis capturing the CoreStates USPRO championship, men's professional racing was flourishing in the United States. In support of women's racing, the CoreStates introduced the Liberty Classic. The $27,500 prize list was one of the richest one-day purses ever offered.

On the amateur side of racing, the American national team won a record-setting fourteen medals at the 1995 Pan American Games in Argentina.

USA Cycling is Born

On March 29, 1920, the Amateur Bicycle League of America was founded to govern bicycle racing in the United States. In 1975 the ABLA was reorganized and renamed the United States Cycling Federation (USCF). Nineteen years later, in 1995, USA Cycling was born. USA Cycling was created to serve as an umbrella over four amateur and one professional racing division: the National Bicycle League, the National Collegiate Cycling Association, the National Off-Road Bicycle Association, the United States Cycling Federation, and the United States Professional Racing Organization. At the end of 1995, USA Cycling served 35,000 members and 1,000 cycling clubs and groups.

Trouble on the Horizon

In 1996 interest in bicycle racing was reaching a new peak. Fueled by the public relations efforts of corporate sponsors, professional racing was successful on many fronts. Although the Coors Light team folded after winning more than 500 races from 1989 to 1994, there were still eight American professional teams: Motorola, U.S. Postal Service, Saturn, Shaklee, Chevrolet-L.A. Sheriff, Plymouth, NutraFig-Colorado Cyclist, and The Bike Shop-Peaberries. Entering its ninth year, Shaklee was the longest-running national team sponsorship since 7-Eleven's eleven-year campaign. The top women rode for Saturn, Chevrolet-Klein, Shaklee, Vanwood, and Bodywise.

Four years after entering its first sponsorship agreement, Saturn became the official sponsor of the 1996 U.S. road and track cycling nationals and Olympic cycling trials and other events. Looking to the future, Saturn renewed its sponsorship of the Saturn team for two more years, through 1998.

For the first time in twelve years, the Olympics were coming to the United States. Based on the highly publicized efforts of Project '96, expectations for cycling gold were very high. In addition to investing millions in state-of-the-art training and bicycle design technology, USA Cycling was also building a team of the best American riders. On April 27, 1996, Lance Armstrong became the first American professional to qualify for the Olympic road racing team.

As 1996 unfolded, promoters, racers, fans, and corporate sponsors found reasons to be concerned about the future. In May, after the ninth stage of the Tour DuPont, Motorola announced that the company would not renew its sponsorship of the team in 1997. Despite the news, Armstrong went on to win his second Tour DuPont and became the first American to be ranked number one in the world UCI rankings. His Motorola team was ranked 2nd in world cup standings and 6th in the world.

Motorola's final appearance at the Tour de France did not end with Lance Armstrong riding into Paris with his teammates. On the sixth of twenty-one stages, Armstrong, struggling with a bad cold and sore throat, signaled team manager Jim Ochowicz that he needed assistance. A Tour official removed Armstrong's No. 61 badge, and his Tour was over.

Americans in the Tour de France

 The world's most recognized bicycle race started in 1903. Except for disruptions caused by the World Wars, the Tour de France captivated the attention of European bicycle racing enthusiasts every year.

For decades America's best racers stayed home. The U.S. cycling governing bodies downplayed the importance of international racing events and provided little financial or logistical support for the handful of American racers who wanted to test their skills against the best in the world.

Year by year the legends of the Tour de France grew. For three weeks in July, racing enthusiasts from France, Belgium, Italy, and Spain would turn their focus to the flatlands of France and the Alps and Pyrenees mountains. The greatest riders of their time raced in the Tour. Two French riders, Jacques Anquetil and Bernard Hinault, won five yellow jerseys. They shared that record with Belgium's Eddy Merckx and Spain's Miguel Indurain.

Seventy-eight years passed before the first American rider entered the Tour. Eighty-three years passed before an American took a yellow jersey home from France. In 2006, 33 Americans stood with the peloton on the first day. One hundred years after the Tour de France began, an American racer matched the performances of Anquetil, Merckx, Hinault, and Indurain. And he would not stop there.

The story of America's slow rise to success in the Tour de France begins almost thirty years ago. In May 1977 twenty-one-year-old Jacques (Jonathan) Boyer signed his first professional racing contract with the French BP-Lejeune team. Boyer, who earned $400 per month, joined Mike Neel as the second American racing in Europe.

Henri Anglade, the director of BP-Lejeune, considered Boyer too young to compete in the long 1977 Tour de France. Twenty-two-year-old Bernard Hinault received the same instructions. Both riders were entered in shorter European races to learn race strategy and gain stamina.

In 1978 Greg LeMond added his name to the cycling history books by winning the gold medal in the road race, silver in the pursuit, and bronze in the team time trial at the junior world championships. His performance attracted the attention of Cyrille Guimard, director of the French Renault-Gitane racing team. Two years later Guimard traveled to the United States to sign nineteen-year-old LeMond to a one-year contract. Reportedly, Guimard paid LeMond a salary of $50,000, the largest ever offered to a new pro rider. LeMond joined two other Americans racing in Europe: Jacques Boyer, who switched to the French Puch-Campagnolo team in May, and George Mount, who signed with Italy's San Giacomo-Benotto. LeMond's contract marked the first time three Americans were members of European racing teams in the same year.

Guimard also hired Boyer, bringing him on to help LeMond's transition to European racing. Despite Guimard's best intentions, Boyer's and LeMond's personalities didn't mesh.

The First Americans in the Tour de France

In 1981 Boyer became the first American to race in the Tour. Finishing 32nd, he started a journey that would take American riders and teams from strangers in France to record-setting champions.

Boyer improved and finished in 23rd place in 1982. He was 44:09 behind winner Bernard Hinault in the general classification. The twelfth stage featured two difficult climbs in the Pyrenees. At the summit of the 1,700-meter l'Aubisque, Boyer joined a group of eighteen riders who made the first significant breakaway of the 1982 Tour. Boyer finished the stage in 13th place and moved from 43rd to 19th in the general classification.

LeMond continued his rise to the top of the international cycling world. In 1983 he won the world professional road race championship and received the Super Prestige Pernod award as the season's top-ranked cyclist.

Organizers of the Tour de France sent a formal invitation to the USCF in early 1984, but American officials declined to send an amateur team to the Tour. Ed Burke, USCF technical director, said the cost of fielding a ten-rider team for the three-week Tour was too expensive—the top priority was the Olympics.

In 1984 Bernard Hinault left Renault-Gitane to start his own La Vie Claire team. His teammate LeMond stayed with Renault-Gitane, sharing the team leadership with Laurent Fignon. LeMond received a seven-year, $180,000 contract, earning more than Fignon, an older and more experienced racer.

Despite the excitement, the first two weeks of LeMond's Tour debut were miserable. At the prologue time trial, he rushed to the platform and arrived without a moment to spare, and a loose toe strap hampered his start. A strong time trial rider, LeMond rode aggressively and finished 9th. A case of bronchitis slowed him down and prevented him from challenging teammate Fignon and La Vie

In 1977 Jacques (Jonathan) Boyer signed his first professional contract with the French BP-Lejeune team. He earned $400 per month. Four years later he became the first American to race in the Tour de France. He finished 32nd.

Claire's Hinault for the yellow jersey. As the weeks progressed, LeMond recovered physically and climbed through the general classification. Over the last six stages, LeMond reduced his time gap on every rider except the eventual winner, Fignon.

When the 1984 Tour arrived in Paris on July 22, LeMond was in 3rd place. It was the best finish by an American since the Tour was founded in 1903. Standing on the podium wearing the white jersey awarded to the best first-year Tour rider, LeMond brought legitimacy to American racing. Jacques Boyer finished his fourth consecutive tour. Riding for Skil-Sem, Boyer recovered from a midrace crash and finished 31st.

Before the 1985 Tour Hinault pursued Fignon and Stephen Roche to help him win a record-tying fifth Tour victory. Both riders, bound by long-term contracts with their current teams, turned him down. La Vie Claire co-owner Bernard Taupie and Hinault turned to LeMond and offered him a three-year, $1 million contract. Guimard was unable to match the offer, and the Renault-Gitane team folded one year later.

America's First Yellow Jersey

The 73rd Tour de France started in Paris on July 4, 1986, Independence Day in the United States. The 1986 Tour would mark

Before the 1985 Tour de France, the La Vie Claire team signed Greg LeMond to a three-year, $1 million contract. He rode in support of Bernard Hinault that year.

America's ascendance to the top of the most important bicycle race in the world. Over the next twenty-three days and across 4,100 kilometers of flat French countryside roads and steep mountain climbs in the Pyrenees, a race unfolded with drama, intrigue, tightly wound emotions, and single-minded passionate competition.

The American-based riders' record-setting performances started the first day. The 7-Eleven team became the first American professional team entered in the Tour. Cameras from CBS Sports tracked Alex Stieda as he rolled down the prologue's time trial ramp. Stieda, a Canadian riding for 7-Eleven, wore a body-hugging red, green, and white skin suit. Riding a Murray-branded bike with a disk rear wheel, Stieda accelerated through the 4,600-meter hexagonal course. He averaged 49.71 kph and finished in 5:33. His time remained unchallenged for an hour. By the end of the day, Stieda finished 21st. His 7-Eleven teammate Eric Heiden matched his time.

Not content to just finish the Tour, 7-Eleven made history on the first stage of the race. Alex Stieda finished 5th in the first road stage and accumulated enough bonus points to wear the leader's yellow jersey, polka dot climber's jersey, green points jersey, and combination jersey, all at the same time. The accomplishment was short-lived. In the team time trial later that day, 7-Eleven finished 20th of twenty-one teams and Stieda fell from 1st to 116th in an afternoon.

In 1985 Greg LeMond became the first American to win a Tour de France time trial. Davis Phinney added another American first in 1986, when he outsprinted the pack to win the third stage by just inches. The team continued to perform well, with Ron Kiefel taking 2nd in the seventh stage and Alex Stieda matching his 2nd place one day later. Over the remaining stages the 7-Eleven team lost ground, losing riders to illness, injuries, and fatigue. Five members survived the Tour: Bob Roll, Raul Alcala, Jeff Pierce, Alex Stieda, and Ron Kiefel. Team

Ron Kiefel was a key member of the 7-Eleven racing team. Kiefel was one of only five members of the 7-Eleven team to finish the 1986 Tour.

Ron Kiefel attacking the legendary Alpe d'Huez stage at the 1986 Tour de France.

7-Eleven's first appearance in the Tour was covered extensively in American media, but the inch-high bold headlines were dedicated to Greg LeMond.

In 1985 Hinault rode to his fifth Tour de France victory with LeMond at his side supporting him from opening stage to the final day. LeMond tempered his own competitive drive to support Hinault. He finished 2nd, trailing Hinault by just 1:42. Standing victorious on the podium, Hinault thanked LeMond and made a public promise to help his teammate and friend wear the yellow jersey in 1986.

At the start of the 1986 Tour,

Hinault's proclamation to ride for LeMond wavered. A chance to win a record-setting sixth Tour caused Hinault to question his loyalties to his team and think of his own legacy. Hinault was racing in the Tour for the eighth time, motivated by the chance to separate himself from two other Tour legends with five victories. LeMond, who held his own ambitions in check in 1985, was hungry to prove to the world that he was capable of beating Europe's best and winning the Tour.

After ten stages of the 1986 Tour, LeMond was in 8th place overall. The peloton entered the mountains on the twelfth stage. On the first day in the mountains, the peloton began to separate into competitors and pretenders. A lead pack of twenty-three, including Hinault and six La Vie Claire teammates, pushed up the mountain. Ninety-one kilometers from the finish, the lead pack was averaging 36 kph. Hinault launched an aggressive attack with Spain's Pedro Delgado, and they dropped their competitors one by one. Delgado won the stage but Hinault opened a 4:36 lead over LeMond, who finished 3rd.

Instead of supporting LeMond, Hinault had raced for the yellow jersey. In the general classification after the twelfth stage, Hinault led LeMond by over 5 minutes. Surprised, hurt, and under heavy questioning from French and American reporters, LeMond publicly questioned his role on the La Vie Claire team. The split between Hinault and LeMond dominated the rest of the Tour.

The next day Hinault and fifteen other riders led the pack to the summit of the 8,000-foot Tourmalet. Once again the French rider called "the Badger" leaped forward with an aggressive attack on the descent. Flying down the mountain at speeds close to 100 kph, Hinault reached the valley 100 seconds ahead of the chase group. Thirty kilometers from the finish, his lead grew to nearly 3 minutes.

Before the Tour American Andy Hampsten was hired by the La Vie Claire team to support Hinault and LeMond through the difficult mountain stages. Hampsten, LeMond, and Swiss rider Urs Zimmerman worked together to narrow the gap to Hinault. On the last 1,160-meter climb of the day, Hinault cracked. Hampsten, Zimmerman, and LeMond caught and passed him unchallenged.

Hampsten pushed the pace, dropping Zimmerman and launching LeMond to race the last 5 kilometers alone and in the lead. Hinault finished 4:39 behind LeMond. The previous day's insurmountable lead had been reduced to just 46 seconds.

On July 20, 1986, LeMond started the seventeenth stage 34 seconds behind Hinault. When the stage ended at the top of the Col due Glandon, Greg LeMond became the first American to wear the yellow jersey. Hinault faltered again, finishing 13th in the stage and losing more than 3 minutes to LeMond.

With the yellow jersey on his back, LeMond expected Hinault to drop his quest for a sixth title and live up to his promise to help LeMond win. July 21, the final day in the Alps, was the legendary 165-kilometer stage to the ski resort at Alpe d'Huez. Hinault and LeMond broke away on the descent after crossing the summit. The pair, responding to the cheers of thousands of spectators lining the course, screamed down the mountain, reaching 110 kph at one point. Side by side the five-time champion and his young rival rode the final 130 kilometers alone. At the finish the tension of previous days seemed to disappear. Just meters from the line, Hinault grabbed LeMond's hand and thrust it over his head. LeMond, still deferential to his former team leader, pushed Hinault forward to give him the stage win.

LeMond held a 2:43 lead three days before the final stage. The twentieth stage, a 58-kilometer individual time trial, offered Hinault one last opportunity. LeMond and Hinault were the last riders on the course. Hinault started three minutes before LeMond and at 16 kilometers posted a time 37 seconds faster than any of the previous riders. LeMond responded and reached the 16-kilometer point 9 seconds faster than Hinault. By 31 kilometers LeMond's lead was 4 seconds. The race announcer's next message stunned the spectators. Racing hard through St. Chamond, LeMond failed to negotiate a tight right-hand corner and crashed. Up off the ground immediately, he continued for 3 more kilometers before brakes damaged in the crash forced him to stop and exchange bikes. At the next time check, 5 kilometers after getting a new bike, LeMond learned that he trailed Hinault by 30 seconds. Hinault strained to maintain his pace as LeMond charged back. With 6.7 kilometers remaining LeMond had cut the lead to 16 seconds, but could get no closer. No matter—at the day's award ceremonies, LeMond's name was still at the top of the general classification.

On July 27, 1986, Greg LeMond rode through Paris wearing the leader's yellow. After 6 laps around the Champs Elysées, LeMond crossed the finish line and became the first American to win the Tour de France. More than 150,000 spectators lined the boulevard to celebrate the historic achievement.

Returning to Paris 4,100 kilometers from the start, LeMond finished the 1986 Tour in 110:35:19. The Badger was 3:10 behind. Urs Zimmermann of Switzerland was 3rd. Andy Hampsten, LeMond's La Vie Claire teammate, finished 4th and received the white jersey awarded to the best first-year rider.

LeMond's victory received unprecedented attention from newspapers, magazines, and television and radio stations in the United States. The *New York Times, Boston Globe, USA Today, Time,* and CBS Radio featured stories about his breakthrough. Bill Wilkinson, deputy director of the Bicycle Federation of America, called LeMond's win "the biggest thing that's happened in U.S. cycling this century."

Increased interest from corporate sponsors would support the growth of professional bicycle racing until the end of the decade, and LeMond's own earnings would grow exponentially.

A Legacy Interrupted

On March 14, 1987, during the second stage of the Tirreno-Adriatico stage race, Greg LeMond crashed and broke his wrist. Unable to race, he returned to Lincoln, California, to recover. On April 20, just three days before his planned return to the European racing circuit, Patrick Blades, his brother-in-law, accidentally shot LeMond during a turkey hunt.

A CHP helicopter transported LeMond to the UC-Davis Hospital in Sacramento. The Tour champ was suffering from two broken ribs, a collapsed right lung, and internal injuries. Surgeons worked for two and a half hours to remove buckshot from his liver, small intestines, lungs, and diaphragm. When LeMond left the hospital six days later, he had lost fifteen pounds. An appendectomy in July further hindered his recovery. LeMond did not race again in 1987.

7-Eleven Makes Tour History

Andy Hampsten, drained by the turmoil surrounding LeMond, Hinault, and the La Vie Claire team in 1986, accepted a $200,000 contract to join 7-Eleven for the 1987 season. The contract was signed before LeMond was shot. With Hinault retired and out of the Tour field, Hampsten would have been the leader of the La Vie Claire team. Instead, he set out to lead the weaker and inexperienced 7-Eleven team to the podium.

At the 1987 Tour 7-Eleven continued to improve, winning three stages.

Although he failed to finish the Tour for the second consecutive year, Davis Phinney captured his second stage victory. The twelfth stage was a final flat stage before the peloton entered the mountains. Beginning in Brive-la-Gaillard and finishing in Bordeaux, the 228-kilometer stage was a fight between Belgian and Dutch teams who were not expected to challenge in the climbing stages.

In the last turn Phinney trailed six riders. Previously in these situations in the Tour, Phinney had been pinned against the fence and was unable to fight through to challenge the leaders. This time Phinney found space on the right side of the road and accelerated. On the other side two riders bumped shoulders. They recovered, but two other riders touched wheels and crashed, creating chaos in the finishing sprint. Phinney finished 1st.

Two days later another 7-Eleven rider, Dag-Otto Lauritzen, won the most difficult stage up to that point in the Tour. Lauritzen chased down a three-man break and dropped them, conquering the climb to the Luz Ardiden ski area 7 seconds ahead of the next rider. By the end of the '87 Tour, 7-Eleven had won three stages. Six of nine riders survived the entire race. Raul Alcala, in 10th place, was the top finisher for the team and won the competition for the white jersey.

7-Eleven Stalls

The 1988 Tour de France started three weeks after Andy Hampsten's historic Giro d'Italia victory. Arriving in France, 7-Eleven—Hampsten, Alcala, Lauritzen, Phinney, Ron Kiefel, Jens Veggerby, Nathan Dahlberg, Bob Roll, Jeff Pierce, and Roy Knickman—had high expectations. With LeMond sidelined with injuries for a second consecutive year, 7-Eleven carried America's hopes in the Tour.

It was not to be. The team struggled and finished the 1988 race without a stage win. Andy Hampsten in 15th was the highest-placed American. Phinney finished the Tour de France for the first time and placed 2nd in the points competition, but could not repeat his stage-winning performances of the last two Tours. Seven riders finished, and the team moved from 3rd to 2nd in the final team competition standings.

Andy Bishop rode his first Tour as a member of the Dutch PDM team and finished in 135th place.

The Closest Finish in the Tour's History

Greg LeMond missed the 1987 season recovering from gunshot wounds and an appendectomy. The next summer he aggravated a tendinitis condition that required surgery to repair. Beginning 1989 with PDM, LeMond switched to Belgium's ADR for a $350,000 base salary and lucrative bonuses built into the contract. The All Driving Rental team negotiated a partnership with the American Coors Silver Bullet team that increased LeMond's salary to $500,000 and offered opportunities for him to race in Europe and the United States with a single team.

With business issues resolved, LeMond focused his energies on returning to the podium. By 1989 his professional ranking had dropped from number 2 to number 345 in the world.

Twenty-seven months after being shot in the hunting accident, LeMond returned to the Tour de France. Laurent Fignon, who won his first Tour in 1984, was looking for his second. Fignon and LeMond passed the yellow jersey back and forth. Fignon won the tenth stage. LeMond pushed him back into 2nd place by finishing the fifteenth-stage time trial 47 seconds faster. During the time trial LeMond rode with his aerodynamic Scott handlebars. The uphill course didn't show off the design's potential—that would come on the final day.

On the steep Alpe d'Huez climb, LeMond slipped back into 2nd place, 26 seconds behind his French rival. The next day Fignon attacked again, winning the stage and extending his lead to 50 seconds with three stages to go.

The second-to-last stage was a flat course from Versailles to Paris with little opportunity for a sustained breakaway. LeMond beat Fignon in the final sprint and won the stage to Aix-les-Bains. Riding hard, the group of leaders including LeMond, Fignon, and Pedro Delgado finished 2 minutes ahead of the peloton. Fignon's lead remained unchanged.

The day before the final stage, LeMond trailed Fignon by such a substantial margin that French newspaper reporters had already written their stories about Fignon's Tour victory. Traditionally, the Tour ended with a road stage to allow the leader to celebrate on the way to Paris. The 1989 Tour would be decided in a 24.5-kilometer time trial. Although LeMond had a well-earned reputation as a strong time-trialist, most observers felt the 50-second lead was out of reach.

LeMond left the start gate at 4:12 p.m., Fignon two minutes later. Most riders left at one-minute intervals, but the top twenty riders started two minutes apart. LeMond rolled down the start ramp using a new aerodynamic profile that included tri-bars, an aerodynamic helmet, and wraparound sunglasses. Looking for any possible edge, LeMond tested the aerodynamic potential of the Scott aero bars by riding next to team-

COR VOS

Greg LeMond used revolutionary aero bars to defeat Laurent Fignon on the last day of the 1989 Tour de France. Trailing Fignon by 50 seconds at the start of the final time trial, LeMond finished 8 seconds ahead of his rival. The 8-second margin is the closest in Tour de France history.

mate Janusz Kuum while Kuum was using traditional bars. Boone Lennon, the inventor, offered the handlebars to PDM and Panasonic, but there was no interest from the European teams. A simple question of aerodynamics would prove vital to the outcome of the race.

Positioned along the course, team managers provided the riders with precise timing information. After the 5-kilometer mark, LeMond said he didn't want to know—he wanted to focus all his energies, mental and physical, on reaching the finish line. At the midway point LeMond was 24 seconds ahead of Fignon. Riding hard until he reached the finish line in 26:57, LeMond returned to the line to watch the digital clock and await Fignon's arrival.

The night before, Fignon was anxious and irritable. French television showed him spitting at the cameras. Sunday morning he complained about saddle sores and shortened his warm-up ride.

With the last rider on the course, 500,000 spectators used the electronic clocks and loudspeakers to track his progress. Fignon started fast, but at the 5-kilometer mark, team director Cyrille Guimard informed him he was already 6 seconds behind LeMond's pace. Unable to match LeMond's ride, Fignon slipped further behind. At 11.5 kilometers the gap grew to 21 seconds, and it kept growing—to 24 seconds after 14 kilometers, 35 seconds after 18, 45 after 20.

Officially, Fignon lost the race 50 meters from the line. At that moment he trailed LeMond by 50 seconds, the margin he started the day with. Eight seconds later Fignon crossed the line to bring the 1989 Tour de France to an end. After three weeks and 2,025 miles, twenty-eight-year-old Greg LeMond won his second yellow jersey by just 8 seconds, the smallest margin in the eighty-six-year history of the Tour.

Five weeks later LeMond won the world championship road race in Chambery, France. In 1989 LeMond's financial rewards included $250,000 from the Tour, a $500,000 base salary from ADR, and a $350,000 bonus for winning the Tour and world championship. LeMond charged a $10,000 appearance fee to attend a series of criteriums between the Tour and worlds. After his world championship triumph, the fee rose to $30,000. Endorsement offers poured in along with an invitation to the White House.

In September 1989 LeMond signed a three-year, $5.7 million contract with Roger Zannier, owner of the French Z team. In the flurry of negotiations leading up to the announcement, 7-Eleven and Toshiba offered six-figure contracts. Reportedly, Toshiba offered $6 million, but LeMond felt a connection with Roger Legeay, the coach of the Z team, who had recruited him before his 1989 Tour win. The Z team also agreed to ride on LeMond bikes marketed by his father. Finally, in a move to address difficulties LeMond had faced getting paid in full from teams of the past, the contract was also guaranteed by Credit Lyonnais, one of France's major banks.

COR VOS

LeMond followed his dramatic 1989 Tour de France victory by winning the world championship road race in Chambery, France.

Number Three

LeMond returned to the 1990 Tour de France with the Z team. His experience and skill in the individual time trials was key to his second consecutive victory. LeMond finished 2nd in the prologue time trial and 5th in three other time trial stages.

LeMond chased Italian Claudio Chiappucci throughout the three-week Tour, finally taking a commanding lead on the stage twenty 45.5-kilometer time trial. LeMond finished 5th, 57 seconds behind the winner, Erik Breukink, but 2:21 ahead of Chiappucci, to seal the victory. LeMond won his third Tour without winning a single stage. Hampsten was the highest-placed rider for 7-Eleven, which finished 9th in the team competition.

Years of Transition

In September 1991 the Southland Corporation announced the end of its ten-year sponsorship of the 7-Eleven team. Jim Ochowicz, the team's general manager, reached an agreement with Motorola to become the new title sponsor. The familiar green, white, and red of 7-Eleven would no longer grace the Tour de France. Motorola made its Tour de France debut in 1992.

LeMond failed in his attempt to win three consecutive Tours, finishing 7th in 1991. After twelve stages of the 1992 Tour, LeMond was 4th in the general classification, but his training had been affected by a variety of ailments, and he would not finish the race. It was his first time to drop out of the Tour.

A momentous passing of the torch took place on the strenuous mountain climbs of the '92 Tour. On July 19 Hampsten attacked the Alpe d'Huez stage more than two hours from the finish. He

1990 TOUR DE FRANCE PRIZE LIST
Total
$1,831,536
Overall winner, general classification
$363,636
Winner, mountain competition
$145,455
Overall points winner
$27,273
Best young rider, overall winner
$5,455
Team, general classification winner
$21,818
Stage winner
$9,091
Prologue winner
$4,545
Team time trial winner
$9,091
Final Champs Elysées sprint
$1,818

led the peloton up the legendary twenty-one-turn ascent, 3 minutes ahead of Claudio Chiappucci and Miguel Indurain, and maintained that lead until the finish. Hampsten, leader of the new Motorola team, was the first American to win the daunting Alpe d'Huez stage and moved into 3rd place overall behind his two chasers on the day. Hampsten finished the Tour in 4th place. LeMond, who started the stage 41st in general classification, did not finish the climb.

Meanwhile, Lance Armstrong entered his first professional race, the Classico San Sebastian, and finished dead last.

The Armstrong Era Begins

Millions of racing fans, both rabid and casual, know about Lance Armstrong's legendary streak of seven consecutive wins at the Tour de France. His first Tours were not as successful.

Armstrong's first Tour in 1993 introduced him to the rigors of the Tour and revealed the emotional highs and lows experienced during the three-week event. His general manager, Jim Ochowicz, wanted Armstrong to experience the Tour, but did not intend for his young protégé to finish the race.

His first Tour lasted twelve days. On his best day, Armstrong won the eighth stage from Chalons-sur-Marne to Verdun. Showing the grit and tenacity that would come to separate him from the field in coming years, Armstrong outsprinted Stephen Roche, the 1987 Tour champion. At twenty-one, he was the youngest rider to win a Tour stage that year.

Armstrong's stage victory left him 12th in the overall standings, 2:32 behind race leader Johan Museeuw of Belgium. Three other Motorola riders, Hampsten, Frankie Andreu, and Andy Bishop, were also in the top twenty. On that day Motorola led the team competition.

Entering the Alps, Armstrong experienced the other end of the emotional spectrum. In the first mountain stage, he finished 22 minutes behind the winner, Tony Rominger of Switzerland. The next day he fell farther behind, finishing 97th. His ranking in the general classification dropped from 12th on the day of his stage victory to 62nd. Armstrong finished so far behind that he missed his team car at the finish and had to continue pedaling until he reached the hotel. Miguel Indurain of Spain was the overall winner that year.

Tragedy Strikes the Tour

In 1995 Armstrong completed his first Tour after three attempts. The achievement was bittersweet. He finished in 36th place and captured the eighteenth stage under the saddest of conditions.

Motorola rider Fabio Casartelli crashed into a concrete barrier at high speed on the descent from the Port d'Aspet and suffered massive head injuries. An emergency medical team airlifted him, but Casartelli died at the hospital. The racers paid tribute to the fallen rider. On the next day the riders rode at a somber pace. Near the finish line the 119 riders in the peloton let the Motorola team cross the line first.

After a two-day pause, racing returned. Armstrong pushed ahead of a breakaway lead group and, crossing the finish line to win the stage, reached his hands to the sky to pay personal homage to his friend and teammate.

Motorola's Frankie Andreu was the only American to finish the 1996 Tour. He finished 111th of 129 riders. His American teammates, George Hincapie and Lance Armstrong, withdrew. Bjarne Riis of the Netherlands was the overall winner. As a member of both 7-Eleven and Motorola, Andreu reached Paris in each of the five Tours he entered.

America's performance in the Tour de France had reached a plateau. The excitement of Greg LeMond's three victories had faded, and observers debated over who would replace him. In 1986 Andy Hampsten had finished 4th and worn the white jersey awarded to the best new rider, but he would never fulfill expectations by standing on the podium at Tour's end.

U.S. Postal's First Tour

The U.S. Postal Service cycling team became the second American team to race in the Tour de France when general manager Mark Gorski received a wild-card invitation to join twenty-one other teams at the start of the 1997 Tour. All nine members of the team finished their first Tour. Only two other teams matched that performance.

"Postal" was a collection of riders from the United States and Europe. Gorski's first squad included three Americans. In 69th place, Tyler Hamilton was the top American overall. Marty Jemison came in 96th. George Hincapie finished 5th in the final stage and 104th overall. France's Jean-Cyril Robin, the Postal Service's highest-placed rider, finished 15th. Riding Saeco-Cannondale bikes in its first year, Postal finished 10th in the team competition.

Other Americans competed in the 1997 Tour as members of the French Cofidis team. Finishing 17th, Bobby Julich, who assumed the role of team leader after Cofidis and Lance Armstrong parted ways, was the highest-placed American rider in the race. Kevin Livingston in 38th and Frankie Andreu in 79th joined Julich with respectable positions in the general classification.

In 1998 Julich became the first American since Greg LeMond to stand on the Tour podium. Julich arrived on the podium's 3rd step, his time 4:08 behind the *maillot jaune,* Marco Pantani. Julich started a streak of eight consecutive years with an American in the top three.

The U.S. Postal Service Team Delivers

In the next seven years, Lance Armstrong changed the face of the Tour de France. Beginning with the U.S. Postal Service team and ending with the Discovery Channel team in 2005, Armstrong turned the race for the yellow jersey into a tightly focused personal mission.

Training to peak in July, the team worked with bike designers and exercise physiologists and visited a wind tunnel to fine-tune Armstrong's riding positions to gain any incremental aerodynamic advantages. Armstrong and other Postal team members went to France to ride the most critical stages of the Tour to get a first-hand understanding of potential obstacles and competitive opportunities.

The single-minded approach to the Tour embraced by Gorski; Johan Bruyneel, the team's directeur sportif; and Armstrong showed dividends in 1999. Returning to the Tour after a remarkable recovery from cancer, Armstrong made a statement by winning the prologue, beating time trial specialists Alex Zulle and Abraham Olano, the world time trial champion.

The Tour started on July 4, and the second of three individual time trials was held on Sunday, July 11. Months earlier Armstrong had reconned the course several times. When he rolled down the ramp, the experience paid off. Bobby Julich, who raced the course for the first time the day of the stage, crashed on an unfamiliar turn. His injuries forced him to abandon the race. Armstrong recaptured the yellow jersey.

The next day the miserable wet and cold conditions seemed to affect the other competitors more than Armstrong. Supported by Hincapie and Andreu, he strategically attacked on the last 6 kilometers of the climb to Sestriere and finished 1st for the second consecutive stage. His lead over Zulle, thought to be his strongest rival, reached 6 minutes. The yellow jersey remained securely on his back until the peloton reached Paris. Armstrong was in the lead on fifteen of the twenty stages.

His dominance in the 1999 Tour continued in the next-to-last day's 57-kilometer Futurescope time trial. Although his lead was secure, Armstrong did not settle for anything less than victory.

The next day, surrounded by his Postal teammates, Armstrong became the second American to win the most famous cycling event in the world. The achievement was definitely all-American. Armstrong was the first American to win the Tour while riding for an American team on an American-made bike.*

The Tour records also show Armstrong became the first American, and only the fourth rider ever, to win three time trial stages in the same Tour. Listed next to Eddy Merckx, Bernard Hinault, and Miguel Indurain, Armstrong's performances would eventually surpass each of these Tour legends.

In 2000 two former Tour de France winners, Germany's Jan Ullrich and Italy's Marco Pantani, joined Armstrong in the starting field. Neither offered any real challenge. Pantani abandoned the race and Ullrich finished 2nd, 6 minutes behind. In the final, 58.5-kilometer time trial, Armstrong set a new Tour record by averaging 53.986 kph (33.525 mph). Armstrong captured his second consecutive Tour de France, holding the yellow jersey on twelve of the twenty-one stages.

In 2001 Armstrong's competitors found no weaknesses. Surrounded by a strong team of riders who served just one master, Armstrong won two mountain stages, the hill climb time trial, and the stage nineteen time trial. The climb to Alpe d'Huez signified Armstrong's performance in the 2001 Tour.

One of the most famous and legendary stages in Tour history, the 209-kilometer stage ending at the summit of

Alpe d'Huez features three climbs rated "beyond category" by course officials. As the peloton rose up the 19.9-kilometer Glandon climb and the 24.8-kilometer climb that followed, Armstrong was not in the lead pack. Team radios crackled up and down the mountain, debating if Armstrong was losing it. The Telekom team tested him by pushing the pace. The result was that his Postal teammates were relieved of their usual chore of setting the pace. On the last climb to the Alpe d'Huez, Armstrong easily threaded his way through the pack.

Reporters, media commentators, and casual observers still debate the way Armstrong passed Jan Ullrich that day. Passing rider after rider who struggled up the 8 percent grade, Armstrong caught Ullrich, then moved quickly past. When he was several bike lengths ahead, Armstrong came out of his saddle, turned back to assess Ullrich's condition, and powered forward, leaving his rival unable to match his attack. The gap between Armstrong and Ullrich in the general classification increased to an unambiguous 6:42. Some observers interpreted the look Armstrong shot back at Ullrich to be a challenge or "dis." Armstrong later denied it, but the media-created legend persists to this day.

By the end of the 2002 Tour of France, the spectator excitement and media frenzy surrounding Lance Armstrong and the Postal team had grown to new levels. Before the champagne was poured to celebrate Armstrong's fourth Tour win, speculation about his chances to win a fifth consecutive Tour and put his name next to Anquetil, Merckx, Hinault, and Indurain was rampant. Indurain's streak of five consecutive wins from 1991 to 1995 offered one more incentive for the

---

*The Trek OCLV 5200.

Americans to succeed. Already exceeding Greg LeMond's three Tour wins, Armstrong was hungry for more.

The U.S. Postal team was filled with riders specifically selected to support Armstrong. Russia's Slava Ekimov, Pavel Padrnos from the Czech Republic, Colombia's Victor Hugo Pena, Benoit Joachim from Luxembourg, and two riders from Spain, Roberto Heras and Jose Luis Rubiera, joined Americans George Hincapie and first-year pro Floyd Landis.

The Other Americans

By 2002 Lance Armstrong had become an American brand. Even the most casual sports fan knew his name and accomplishments. Outside of the media spotlight that shone on him, other Americans tried to make a name for themselves in the Tour.

Levi Leipheimer left Postal to ride with Rabobank as a team leader and potential Tour winner. Bobby Julich, who finished 3rd in 1998, was joined by Kevin Livingston on the Telekom team—Livingston was another defector from the "Blue Train" of U.S. Postal. Jonathan Vaughters, yet another ex-Postal rider, raced with Credit Agricole but was vexed by crashes and other mishaps that forced him to abandon two Tours. Tyler Hamilton signed on to lead Denmark's CSC. Freddy Rodriguez rode for Vini Caldirola-So.Di but was dropped from the Tour in 2003 for finishing outside a time limit.

After Tyler Hamilton joined Postal in 1997, he rode in support of Jean-Cyril Robin, the team's first leader, and protected Armstrong through three Tour victories. At the end of 2001, Hamilton decided it was time for a change. Instead of always being a loyal lieutenant, Hamilton wanted his own opportunity to wear the yellow jersey. He negotiated a contract with Denmark's CSC team.

Hamilton won the fourteenth stage of the 2002 Giro and started the 2003 season with another American milestone. Reinforcing his reputation as a strong rider regardless of conditions, Hamilton finished 12 seconds ahead of Spain's Iban Mayo to win Liege-Bastogne-Liege, one of the most prestigious one-day races. More than half the riders abandoned the course, unwilling to compete in the cold rain.

At the start of the 2003 Tour de France, Hamilton was mentioned as one of Armstrong's challengers. The start of Hamilton's seventh Tour was memorable, but more nightmare than dream. Thirty-five riders were involved in a crash at the finish of the first stage, and Hamilton suffered a broken collarbone.

Expected to withdraw and return home, Hamilton stayed with his team and completed the remaining nineteen stages. Not content to ride protected in the peloton, Hamilton raced to win. Eighteen days after the crash, Hamilton took his first stage win in seven Tour appearances. Stage sixteen was the final mountain stage, traversing six climbs. Hamilton went off on a solo breakaway. Forty kilometers from the finish, the closest rider was 5 minutes behind. He averaged 39.5 kph and finished almost 2 minutes ahead of the pack. When the Tour ended four days later, Hamilton ranked 4th in the general classification, 6:17 behind Armstrong.

Hamilton became the sixth American to win a Tour de France stage. At that point the stage win list included seventeen for Armstrong, four for LeMond, two for Phinney, and one each for Jeff Pierce, Hampsten, and Hamilton. The tally would continue to grow in the next three years.

Number Five

U.S. Postal searched to find any competitive edge that would give Armstrong an advantage in his quest for a fifth consecutive yellow jersey. Technology played a key role throughout his streak.

In 2003 Trek's designers and engineers designed and built new bikes in five months, less than half the normal twelve- to fourteen-month development time. Responding to Armstrong and team officials' requests, Trek created two specially designed bikes, one for the road stages, the other for the time trials. The Madone 5.9 used state-of-the-art carbon fiber technology to produce a lightweight and aerodynamic frame. Trek's engineers tested the Madone frame at the Oran J. Nicks Low Speed Wind Tunnel at Texas A&M University. The tests found the new frame would save Armstrong ten watts of energy. Translated into racing terms, the savings amounted to a 1-minute reduction in time over a 200-kilometer stage.

In the end the centennial Tour de France of 2003 was a measure of Armstrong's will to win and the strength of his U.S. Postal team. So dominant in his first four Tours, Armstrong needed significant contributions from his team to build and secure his yellow jersey.

The fourth stage marked the return of the team time trial. Directeur sportif Johan Bruyneel selected Victor Hugo Pena, Hincapie, Landis, Ekimov, and Armstrong to race against the clock and twenty-one other teams. Twice before U.S. Postal had finished behind Spain's ONCE team. In 2003 the five riders trailed ONCE by 14 seconds at the first time check and narrowed the lead to just 6 seconds by the second. In preparing his riders for the 68-kilometer race against the clock, Bruyneel had called for maximum effort in the last 20 kilometers. Over the last 10 kilometers, the team responded and finished in 1:18:27, 30 seconds ahead of their rival ONCE. The victory moved Armstrong into 2nd overall.

Four days later on the eighth-stage climb to Alpe d'Huez, Armstrong struggled. Unable to match the attacks of the lead riders, he finished 3rd, 2:12 behind winner Richard Virenque. Although he did not win the stage, he took over 1st place overall and kept the yellow jersey until the end of the race.

Armstrong was never challenged in his first four victories—his margin of victory was always at least 6 minutes. The 100th running of the Tour de France ended much closer. Jan Ullrich, the leader of the Bianchi team, was within striking distance at the start of the last time trial. Riding aggressively, Ullrich crashed near the end of the 49-kilometer course. Lance Armstrong matched Miguel Indurain by winning his fifth consecutive Tour, finishing just 1:01 ahead of Ullrich. The team shared more than $440,000 from the $2 million prize purse.

. . . and a Little Luck

In seven years Armstrong finished more than one hundred stages over thousands of miles in conditions ranging from cold wind-driven sheets of rain to energy-draining humidity and 90-degree temperatures. Though he was protected and supported by fiercely loyal teammates, a close reading of stage history shows Armstrong also had Lady Luck on his side to guide him safely through calamities, crashes, and potential Tour-ending disasters.

Other Americans didn't fare as well. In a crash near the end of the first stage in 2003, Tyler Hamilton cracked his collarbone. Although he bravely continued and finished 4th, he rode in pain all the way to Paris. Levi Leipheimer, who was involved in the same crash, fractured his hip and left the Tour on the second day. Armstrong was also involved in the thirty-five-rider crash, but his injuries did not prevent him from continuing. Bobby Julich's crash on a rain-slicked time trial stage in 1999 put him out of the Tour one year after he finished 3rd.

Jonathan Vaughters left two Tours due to injuries sustained when his fast-moving bike and body hit the pavement. Possibly the strangest cause for abandoning a Tour befell Vaughters in 2001. In his third Tour Vaughters and his Credit Agricole teammates used a third-week rest day for a training ride. Stung by a wasp under his right eye, Vaughters suffered an allergic reaction. The swelling closed his eye and hampered his vision. A trip to the doctor added another disappointing twist. Officials at the UCI, citing anti-doping laws, refused Vaughters's appeal to have the sting treated with cortisone under a doctor's supervision. Vaughters could not see well enough to safely navigate the course and was forced to leave the Tour.

Lady Luck intervened to save Lance from potential Tour-ending disasters at least three times in seven years. In reality, the number is probably much greater, but a trio of stories shows how close Armstrong's streak came to being interrupted.

On July 2, 1999, Lance Armstrong and George Hincapie were scouting the prologue route. A long line of team cars was parked at the base of a hill on the circuit. While Lance was looking down at his drivetrain, a Telekom team director pulled his car out into the road. Startled, Armstrong tried to avoid a collision. The car's rear-view mirror smacked him and sent him tumbling to the ground. He brushed himself off, accepted the nervous driver's apology, and continued the training ride. And went on to his first Tour victory.

Armstrong showed his bike-handling skills on and off road on Monday, July 14, 2003. Chasing ONCE rider Joseba Beloki down the steep, twisting ninth stage, Armstrong watched Beloki's bike somersault over him after Beloki slid out on a strip of melted road tar while braking. With only one way to avoid a similar fate and avoid running over the fallen Beloki, Armstrong left the asphalt and crossed a rocky dirt field filled with scrub grass. Staying upright across the field, Armstrong got off his bike, climbed down a short hill, and returned to the course. Once again, he continued safe and sound. Beloki broke his femur, wrist, and elbow in the crash.

Disaster struck again nineteen days later. On the last climb of the fifteenth stage, Iban Mayo, Jan Ullrich, and Armstrong were challenging for the lead. When Mayo attacked, Armstrong followed. Just moments later it was Armstrong who was attacking, with Mayo out of the saddle and matching his pace. While the pair rode perilously close to the cheering crowd, a spectator's bag caught on Armstrong's handlebars, twisting his bike and throwing him to the ground. Mayo, tight on his rear wheel, tumbled over him.

Jan Ullrich, unaffected by the mishap, seemed to show true sportsmanship and competitive honor by slowing his pace to allow the pair to recover—although some would argue that he only slowed after Hamilton motioned for him to do so. Two years earlier Armstrong had offered a similar gesture when Ullrich crashed. Shaken but undaunted, Armstrong worked his way back to the lead group. Regaining his composure, he attacked and took the stage win by 40 seconds. In the general classification, Ullrich finished 1:01 behind Armstrong in the record-tying fifth consecutive win. The winning margin was the smallest of the seven victories.

Armstrong Stands Alone at the Top

Lance Armstrong arrived in France for the 2004 Tour de France standing shoulder to shoulder with legends of the past. All four of the other five-time winners had attempted to win a sixth career victory, but none was successful. Jacques Anquetil did not finish in 1965. Bernard Hinault came close, finishing 2nd when Greg LeMond took his first win in 1986. Miguel Indurain finished far from the podium in 1996, in 11th place.

In 1975 Eddy Merckx made his first of two attempts to win the elusive number six. At the start of the fourteenth stage, Merckx held a 1:30 lead on France's Bernard Thevenet. Three hundred meters from the finish, a fan staggered onto the course and delivered a vicious punch to the leader's side. Doctors treated Merckx's bruised kidney with a blood-thinning medication that affected his performance the following day. Fighting each day to stay in contention, he suffered a broken jaw in another crash. At the end Merckx finished 2nd, 2:47 behind Thevenet.

Prior to the 2004 Tour, Johan Bruyneel, Postal's directeur sportif, shuffled the makeup of the team to create the best opportunity to win an unprecedented sixth race. The final roster of nine included Americans Armstrong, Hincapie, and Landis. They were joined by a collection of international riders: Ekimov, Pavel Padrnos from the Czech Republic, Portugal's Jose Azevedo, and Spaniards Manuel Beltran, Jose Luis Rubiera, and Benjamin Noval.

Armstrong's tenth Tour started at 7:08 p.m. on July 3. Riding with an aerodynamic helmet decorated with a red and white star of Texas and a skintight body suit, he finished the prologue 2 seconds behind Switzerland's Fabian Cancellara but held a first-day lead over rivals Ullrich, Hamilton, Mayo, and Ivan Basso.

The strength of the team was revealed early in the Tour. At the end of the prologue, four Postal riders ranked in the top twenty. On the fourth-stage team time trial, the team faced challenges from Hamilton's Phonak team and Ullrich's T-Mobile, but finished 1st for the second consecutive year.

At the start of the twelfth stage, Armstrong trailed France's Thomas Voeckler by 9:35. With the peloton entering the mountain stages, the lead would not last. The 197.5-kilometer stage crossing the Tourmalet ended any speculation about Armstrong's ability. Although Ivan Basso captured the stage win, Armstrong extended his lead over other rivals like Ullrich and Andreas Kloden. Voeckler's lead was cut almost in half, and the 5:24 gap would not hold.

By the end of the fifteenth stage, the yellow jersey was on Armstrong's back. He protected it well, winning the next day's Alpe d'Huez time trial and taking a third consecutive win on the seventeenth stage. He added one more footnote to the Armstrong legacy by winning the final time trial for an unmatched sixth time.

BThe 101.5-mile final stage on July 25 ended with eight 3.8-mile laps around the Champs-Elysées. Armstrong rode cautiously in the pack, concerned more about the riders zipping in and out hoping to get their picture taken with Lance than any rival. Armstrong finished the last

COR VOS

Lance Armstrong, riding for the U.S. Postal Service team for the last time, celebrates his record-setting sixth Tour de France victory.

Discovery's First Tour, Armstrong's Last

On April 18, 2005, thirty-three-year-old Lance Armstrong announced he would retire from professional bicycle racing after that year's Tour de France. Armstrong made the announcement at a press conference with Johan Bruyneel, who had guided Lance's career since 1998, sitting at his side.

On July 4 Armstrong finished the Tour prologue 2 seconds behind David Zabriskie, an American rider for Denmark's CSC team. A moment's distraction with a pedal may have cost him the win. As it had the year before, the 2nd-place finish placed him significantly ahead of pre-Tour rivals like his former teammates Landis and Leipheimer. George Hincapie finished 4th, just under a minute behind. Landis finished 6th.

Changing the name on the jerseys of Armstrong's teammates had no effect on their performance. The Discovery Team charged through the 67.5-kilometer fourth-stage team time trial. Zabriskie, still wearing the yellow jersey, put his CSC team into the lead before crashing in the finishing stretch. The Discovery riders, who trailed CSC throughout the course,

stage officially in 114th place. After covering 3,391 kilometers in 83:26:2, Lance Armstrong stood alone at the top, above the Tour de France's all-time greats.

With the record sixth jersey in hand and the celebrations still lingering, his team began to change. After a successful nine-year run, the U.S. Postal Service ended its sponsorship. This time there was little trouble finding a replacement. One day before the end of the 2004 Tour, the Discovery Channel signed a three-year sponsorship contract estimated at $30 million. The contract included a stipulation that Lance Armstrong ride at least one Tour wearing the blue and silver Discovery Channel jersey.

Levi Leipheimer and Floyd Landis, finished with their roles as Armstrong's protectors, left to lead their own teams. Landis joined Phonak and Leipheimer became the leader of Gerolsteiner.

2005 DISCOVERY TEAM

Lance Armstrong (USA)

Jose Azevedo (Por)

Manuel Beltran (Esp)

George Hincapie (USA)

Benjamin Noval (Esp)

Pavel Padrnos (Cze)

Yaroslav Popovich (Ukr)

Jose Luis Rubiera (Esp)

Paolo Savoldelli (Ita)

finished 2 seconds ahead. The stage win, the third team time trial victory in a row for Armstrong's team, put him in the yellow jersey.

Once again the mountain slopes separated the peloton into leaders and chasers. Armstrong didn't win the first mountain stage. Racing to the finish with Alejandro Valverde, Armstrong intentionally held back in the final sprint. More important than the win, his 2nd-place finish extended his lead over Kloden, Ullrich, Landis, and Ivan Basso.

Hincapie's Reward

There was never a question about the hierarchy of riders on the U.S. Postal and Discovery Channel teams. Eight riders suppressed any personal ambitions to support Armstrong every kilometer of every stage.

Until July 18, 2005, Armstrong was the only member of the team to win a Tour de France stage. George Hincapie had been a member of every team since the six-race streak began. On the fifteenth-stage ascent to Pla d'Adet, Hincapie and thirteen other riders broke away from the field. Without any threat to the general classification, the group rode away unchallenged. Bruyneel, communicating with Hincapie through an earpiece radio, told him to go for the win. One by one the group fell off the pace. Only Oscar Pereiro stayed with Hincapie until the end. The finishing sprint began 300 meters from the finish, and Hincapie had little trouble passing Pereiro and winning the stage. Lance Armstrong had much to celebrate. In addition to his friend's first Tour de France victory, Armstrong continued to gain time on his competitors.

Lance Armstrong ended the 2005 Tour de France with a statement of his dominance in the time trial. After finishing 2nd

in three stages, Armstrong picked the final individual time trial to win his final stage victory. He finished 23 seconds ahead of T-Mobile's Jan Ullrich, staking a claim as the best time trial rider in the history of the Tour de France. For the seventh and final time, Lance Armstrong stood on the winner's podium wearing the yellow jersey, listening to "The Star-Spangled Banner" play in Paris.

COR VOS

In 2005 the Discovery Channel replaced the U.S. Postal Service as the sponsor of Lance Armstrong's team. The agreement included a requirement that Armstrong ride with the team one more year. Armstrong won his unprecedented seventh victory wearing a Discovery jersey. When Armstrong retired, George Hincapie was expected to take the lead. In February 2007, Discovery officials announced their sponsorship would end after the 2007 racing season.

Le Tour Feminin

In the early 1980s American women were making a name for themselves. World championships and top finishes at the Coors Classic were not flukes but evidence of a strong and thriving American field.

The first Tour de France Feminin was held from June 30 to July 22, 1984. Since the dates overlapped with the Coors Classic, the first field did not include many of the world's top riders.

American Marianne Martin, twenty-six, made her racing debut at the 1983 Coors Classic and finished 32nd in the general classification. Suffering from the effects of anemia, Martin failed to make the top ten in any event at the Olympic trials in 1984. With many of the Olympic team riders participating in the Coors Classic, the USCF's Michael Fraysee selected Martin as the last member of the American Tour Feminin team.

Arriving in France, the team struggled with administrative and support issues. Race organizers assigned a Frenchman who spoke very little English to coach the team. Transportation was chaotic, and the team managed without a mechanic for the first week of the race.

The twelfth-stage road race started with a 10-kilometer climb. Martin won her first stage by setting an early pace the other riders couldn't match. She finished 2:40 ahead of Holland's Helen Hage and moved into 2nd place. Another mountain stage win moved her into the overall lead.

Virtually unknown, Martin finished the 1,050-kilometer race in 29:39:02 to become the first champion of the Tour de France Feminin. Teammate Debbie Shumay was 3rd. At the conclusion of the men's Tour de France, Martin stepped up to the winner's podium for a photo-op with Laurent Fignon.

Under international rules at the time, a women's stage race could have no more stages than the longest men's amateur race. Based on that regulation, the Federation Internationale Amateur de Cyclisme (FIAC) came down on the Tour de France Feminin and its long-stage race. The directors responded by creating two separate races under the same overall banner.

In 1986 the FIAC allowed the Tour Feminin to host a prologue and fifteen-stage, 996-kilometer race. The Tour, 371 kilometers longer than the Coors Classic, started five days after the men's Tour and featured a mix of flat stages, time trials, and mountain climbs. The Tour Feminin had its own police escorts, announcers, and commissaries, and a five-minute program on French television.

Throughout the race Maria Canins of Italy, Jeannie Longo of France, and American Inga Thompson competed for the yellow jersey. Twelve of the fifteen stages found one of these riders on the podium's top step. Thompson won the fourteenth-stage time trial to secure her 2nd-place position behind Canins. Thompson, who moved from 7-Eleven to a team called Winning Club, was joined in France by teammates Phyllis Hines, Susan Elias, Carol Rodgers-Dunning, Debbie Stephan, Tamiko Warden, and Betsy King. Racing in her third Tour de France Feminin, Betsy King captured the third stage, beating Canins by 200 meters in an uphill sprint. The Americans finished 3rd in the team competition.

The American team's performance at the Tour de France Feminin was in decline in 1987. Instead of sending the best female riders to France, the USCF scheduled qualifying races for the world championships and Pan Am Games during the Tour dates. The Winning-Peugeot club team represented the United States at the Tour. The Winning squad included six Tour rookies with an average of less than two years' racing experience.

Seven months after winning the American cyclocross championship, Elizabeth Chapman was racing in France. After winning individual and team honors in 1984, American riders could do no better in the '87 Tour than Chapman's 23rd place overall.

The USCF changed direction in 1989.

In response to requests from members of the women's teams to have more international racing exposure, the top riders were sent to Europe to compete. Women's coach Pat Cashman evaluated riders at the Tour of Texas stage race and selected thirteen women from the field to compete in Europe. Seven riders would race in the Tour Feminin, the remaining six in the PostGiro. The European races created a scheduling conflict with the Ore-Ida Women's Challenge, the largest domestic women's stage race, but Cashman felt the team was strong enough to compete at all three events.

The six riders Cashman selected to ride in France had world-class credentials: Bunki Bankaitis-Davis, two-time winner of the Tour of Texas, winner of the 1987 PostGiro, and Olympic team member; Susan Elias, winner of the 1989 Tour of Somerville and 2nd in the Tour of Texas; Phyllis Hines, 1988 national individual and team time trial champion; Inga Thompson, 1988 national road champion and Coors Classic winner; Katrin Tobin, two-time Tour of Texas stage winner and 1988 Ore-Ida Challenge winner; and Sally Zack, Olympic team member and two-time national criterium champ. (Linda Brenneman was also invited but declined, preferring to concentrate on the Ore-Ida Challenge.) Coach Cashman had three goals: win the team event, win the overall jersey, and win as many stages as possible.

At the end of the Tour, the American riders had achieved two of the three objectives.

Bankaitis-Davis won the third stage, Tobin the fourth. And Thompson finished 3rd overall. All six riders were in the top twenty and three finished in the top ten. Susan Elias won the points jersey without winning a stage. Elias placed in the top

ten in every stage except one. The U.S. team fulfilled their goal of winning the team competition.

The Tour Feminin struggled at the end of the '80s. Suffering from financial strains and competing events, the Tour was not held in 1991. New promoters relaunched the race in 1992 as the Tour Cycliste Feminin.

In 1996 Alison Dunlap became the first American to win a stage in the race since 1989. The 155-kilometer sixth stage was the longest of the Tour that year. Dunlap was having a rough day. Near the end of the stage her teammates Mari Holden and Kim Langston had to drop back and tow Dunlap back to the lead group. But in the finishing stretch, Dunlap outsprinted Zita Urbonaite of Lithuania to win the stage by three bike lengths.

After the turn of the century, the name changed again to the Grande Boucle Féminine Internationale. Over its long history and different titles, the women's edition of the Tour de France has been one of the premier cycling events in the world. Americans performed well when the powers that be in U.S. cycling sent the country's best riders.

After Lance: The Coming of Floyd

On April 18, 2005, Armstrong announced that the 2005 Tour de France would be his last race. On the last day of the Tour, Armstrong kept his promise and formally retired from professional racing. Johan Bruyneel's team thus shifted instantly from the perennial preordained Tour winner to an unproven squad of experienced support riders.

At the edges of the bright media spotlight that followed Armstrong, another set of riders hoped to take his place. After long careers supporting

Armstrong, George Hincapie, Levi Leipheimer, and Floyd Landis became leaders of their own teams.

COR VOS

After serving as one of Lance Armstrong's lieutenants on the U.S. Postal Service team, Floyd Landis left in 2004 to become the leader of the Phonak team.

Floyd Landis started his racing career on the dirt. In his second year as a mountain bike racer, Landis won the 1993 national junior championship. Two years later, after he finished 11th at the National Off-Road Bicycle Association (NORBA) finals, *Mountain Bike* magazine named him 1995 Rookie of the Year.

Landis captured the 1997 under-twenty-three national championship and switched to road racing the next year. In 1999 Landis joined the professional Mercury team. His 3rd-place finish in the Tour de l'Avenir caught the attention of

U.S. Postal scouts and earned him a spot on Postal for 2002. Serving beside Armstrong in three Tours, Landis earned a reputation as a relentless climber in mountain stages.

During a training ride in January 2003, Landis crashed and fractured his hip. Surgeons inserted three titanium screws to repair the damage. He recovered and in July helped Armstrong win his fifth Tour, the second of three that Landis would finish with U.S. Postal.

At the end of the 2004 Tour, Landis felt he had earned a chance to compete for his own yellow jersey and joined Tyler Hamilton on the Phonak team. In 2005—as leader of the team after Hamilton was fired—Landis finished 9th.

In 2006 Landis made his bid to become Lance Armstrong's successor. After winning the Amgen Tour of California, Phonak entered the 63rd annual Paris-Nice race. Landis took the lead after the third stage and defended his position through four more stages. At the end of April, Landis continued to dominate the spring racing season by winning the Fräbel glass trophy, awarded to the 1st-place finisher of the Tour of Georgia stage race.

Although Landis was generating the most media buzz, other American riders were also performing at the highest levels. At the seven-stage Critérium du Dauphiné Libéré, one of the major races used as preparation for the Tour, American riders took the first 4 places in the third stage. David Zabriskie followed his prologue victory with a 1st-place finish in the third-stage time trial. Landis, Levi Leipheimer (Gerolsteiner), and George Hincapie completed the American sweep. More importantly, Leipheimer finished the Dauphiné in 1st place, joining LeMond, Hamilton, and Armstrong as the fourth American to win the race.

As the 2006 Tour de France approached, race fans, team directors, and media observers put Landis's name on the list of racers thought to have a strong chance to win the first post-Armstrong Tour. Any list of contenders also included Hincapie and Leipheimer.

The First Post-Lance Tour de France

The starting field of the 93rd Tour included eight Americans. Riding for five different teams, the Americans included potential contenders for the yellow jersey and journeymen working to support their team's designated leader.

George Hincapie, riding for U.S. Postal and the Discovery Channel, was the only team member to ride with Armstrong for each of his seven victories. Johan Bruyneel, director of the Discovery Channel team, expected Hincapie to step forward as the team's new leader. After three major victories leading up to the Tour, Phonak's Floyd Landis was ready to race. Levi Leipheimer was also considered a viable contender.

Three of the five remaining riders—David Zabriskie, Bobby Julich (3rd in the 1998 Tour), and Christian Vande Velde—rode for the CSC team. Chris Horner and Fred Rodriguez raced for the Belgian squad Davitamon-Lotto.

Scandal Strikes the Tour

Twenty-four hours before the scheduled start of the 2006 Tour de France prologue, the field was shattered. Spanish authorities announced they had uncovered a blood doping ring, allegedly operated by Spanish doctor Eufemiano Fuentes. The investigation implicated T-Mobile's Jan Ullrich, CSC's Ivan Basso, and seven other riders from five teams.

Following the explosive announcement, officials from all twenty-one teams met in an emergency closed-door meeting to discuss how to move forward. The teams followed UCI regulations that banned any rider under investigation for blood doping from competing in the race. With the start of the prologue just hours away, the officials also agreed to prohibit the affected teams from adding last-minute replacement riders.

Shocked by the news and proclaiming their innocence, Basso and Ullrich, both experienced leaders of strong teams, were out of the Tour. Landis and Hincapie suddenly moved into serious contention to follow Armstrong to the podium.

Eight Americans in the Tour

After the dust settled, the 93rd Tour de France started with the traditional prologue time trial. American riders faced high expectations to match the skill and speed Lance Armstrong displayed in his Tour time trial performances. After 176 riders completed the 7.1-kilometer course, the three Americans finished in the top ten. Still, the competitors felt more disappointment than elation.

Starting his tenth tour, George Hincapie was coronated as the leader of the Discovery Channel team. In that role he was the last rider to leave the start ramp. Hoping to capture his second stage win, he fell 0.73 seconds short of Thor Hushovd's time of 8:17.73. David Zabriskie (CSC), who won the first-stage time trial in 2005, finished 4 seconds behind.

As he approached the start ramp, Phonak team director John Lelangue noticed a small cut on the rear tire of Landis's bike. Instead of risking a disastrous, time-consuming flat tire on the course, race mechanics scrambled to replace the wheel. The delay cost Landis precious seconds, but he raced aggressively to finish 9th.

The race for the yellow jersey can be measured in the smallest units of time. Frustrated by finishing less than a second behind the leader the first day, Hincapie took the yellow jersey at the end of the first road stage, a 183-kilometer flat course conducive to a chaotic mass sprint finish. Watching his competitors closely, Hincapie captured a 2-second bonus in the last intermediate sprint, 7.5 kilometers from the finish. He finished safely in the pack, but the bonus gave him the overall lead. Zabriskie was in 3rd.

Hincapie relinquished the yellow to Hushovd just twenty-four hours later and slipped to 4th, 10 seconds behind the leader. In the second road stage, Fred Rodriguez crashed after hitting a pothole, and his injuries forced him to abandon. Finishing 33rd in the sixth stage, Hincapie remained the highest-placed American, trailing Tom Boonen by 25 seconds. Landis followed in 8th place, 36 seconds back.

The next day's time trial marked a significant shift in the fortunes of the American competitors. Landis survived a potentially disastrous mechanical problem with his handlebars that forced him to switch bikes midrace, and placed 2nd behind Ukrainian rider Sergei Gontchar. The ride vaulted Landis from 8th to 2nd in the general classification.

David Zabriskie placed 13th in the time trial, moving him into the top ten overall, but the rest of the Americans had little cause for celebration. Bobby Julich left the Tour after smashing his wrist in a crash. Hincapie's and Leipheimer's mediocre showings damaged their chances to lead the race. Discovery could not match the time trial dominance of

their now retired teammate and failed to place a single rider in the top fifteen.

On July 12, 2006, Landis finished 3rd in a mountain stage and climbed into the yellow jersey, becoming the fifth American ever to wear it.* Levi Leipheimer made a dramatic reversal, finishing 2nd in the stage and jumping to 13th in the general classification, 5:36 behind Landis.

Landis surrendered his lead to Spain's Oscar Pereiro at the end of the thirteenth stage and reclaimed it in stage fifteen. Supported by a weaker team than Armstrong relied on, Landis rode with Andreas Kloden of T-Mobile up the twenty-one-turn climb to Alpe d'Huez. Finishing 4th, Landis moved 10 seconds ahead of Pereiro and more than 2 minutes ahead of his other competitors. A 10th-place finish in the stage moved the resurgent Leipheimer into the top ten.

Floyd Falters

Ten kilometers from the finish of the most difficult mountain stage in the 2006 Tour, Landis failed to respond to an attack by the lead group. At the finish he found himself out of the lead, trailing Pereiro by a disastrous 8:08. He was no longer even the top American. Leipheimer, 9th overall, ranked 2 positions higher than Landis at the end of the day.

Race commentators, media observers, and hard-core racing fans furiously debated Landis's chances to recover from his horrible sixteenth stage. Outdoor Life Network's Tour commentator Phil Liggett gave the American little chance of getting back in the race. Landis attended a hastily scheduled press conference to address his performance. At the end, a deeply disappointed rider talked unconvincingly about fighting back. The reporters would have to wait until the next day to find the truth in those words.

*LeMond, Zabriskie, Armstrong, and Hincapie are the others.

THE HIP FROM HELL

Professional bicycle racing can be a dangerous profession. In 1986 soaring insurance premiums forced the USCF to require all riders in sanctioned events to wear hard-shell helmets. The helmet rules spread to the UCI after a few ugly incidents in international races, including crashes, injuries, and protests by European racers who did not want to wear helmets. Despite their initial resistance and brief peloton-wide protest at the Tour de France, the racers accepted the decision.

Unfortunately, helmets can't prevent most types of injuries suffered by racing cyclists. Eddie Merckx broke his jaw. Joseba Beloki broke his femur and various other things. Greg LeMond's broken wrist forced him to stop racing and return to California—where he was shot in a hunting accident. Racing to catch the pack after repairing a flat tire, Davis Phinney slammed into the back of a parked team car and needed dozens of stitches on his face. Tyler Hamilton snapped both collarbones in the same crash. Bobby Julich abandoned the 2006 Tour when a time trial crash broke his wrist.

In mid-January 2003 Floyd Landis left his home in Murrieta, California, for a training ride. At the intersection of Calle Vista Lejos and Sunset Terrace, Landis hesitated for an instant deciding which way to go: straight ahead or turn right. The smallest decision, made thousands of times on other rides, had long-lasting effects. Leaning into the right-hand turn, Landis lost control when his front tire hit loose pebbles on the asphalt road. He slammed to the ground and slid for 30 feet.

At the hospital surgeons inserted three titanium pins into his hip to repair the damage. Landis recovered in time to ride for Lance Armstrong and U.S. Postal in their fifth Tour victory.

His injury was diagnosed as avascular necrosis, a condition that reduced blood flow to the top of his right femur. Without normal circulation, the blood vessels in the hip and ball joint failed. Instead of the smooth mechanical rotation found in a healthy hip, Landis's bones painfully ground against each other.

The hip weighed heavily on Landis's mind when he left U.S. Postal and signed a $700,000, three-year contract with Phonak. In November 2004 Landis endured another surgery. Called decompression, the procedure involved surgeons drilling small holes in the bones to reduce pressure and improve blood flow. Just ten days later he met with Phonak team doctors in Zurich for a preseason physical. Nervous and apprehensive, Landis survived the perfunctory examination. He continued to race in pain throughout the 2005 season, mastering the discomfort enough to finish 9th in the Tour de France.

From the beginning Landis kept information about his injury private. His few confidants were sworn to secrecy. But a news posting on bicycling.com and a long feature article in the Sunday, July 16 edition of the *New York Times*

continued

Magazine publicized his plight. Landis held a press conference on the Tour's rest day to answer questions and try to describe riding at an elite level with a hip socket that needed to be replaced.

The damaged hip affected his pedaling style and his aerodynamic position on the time trial bike. He experimented with different seat and handlebar configurations until he found a setup that caused the least amount of pain and met UCI regulations. His doctors received official UCI approval to treat him with cortisone shots to reduce the pain.

On September 27, 2006, Landis's damaged hip was repaired in a two-hour operation performed by orthopedic surgeon Dr. David Chao. As the surgery progressed, the surgeon reported the hip was in much worse condition than expected. Instead of a full replacement of the hip joint, surgeons used a state-of-the-art technique to cut away the damaged portion, and replaced it with a metal ball. At home the following day, Landis began a six-week recovery regimen. Time will tell if he will have speed and endurance to win a second Tour de France yellow jersey.

Floyd's Fantastic Finish

Instead of accepting the pessimistic predictions of the melee surrounding him, Floyd Landis created a new legend in Tour de France history. Averaging 37.2 kph over the 182-kilometer seventeenth stage from Le Bourg-d'Oisans to La Toussuire, Landis attacked on the first of five climbs, broke away from the peloton, and, as cycling fans looked on in amazement at what was clearly a historic achievement, crossed the finish line more than 5 minutes in front of the 2nd-place rider.

After trailing Oscar Pereiro by 8 minutes at the start of the stage, Landis reduced the gap to just 30 seconds. In 3rd place with three stages remaining, Landis was back in contention for the yellow jersey. The negative media buzz of the previous day paled in comparison with the excitement created by his performance. Crowds surrounded the Phonak trailer, and headlines around the world announced that the American was once again in the race. Race commentators spent the next twenty-four hours analyzing both sides of his dramatic story. Why had he cracked and how had he responded so well? The debate about his recovery would continue far after the last day of the Tour.

Another American milestone fell almost unnoticed in the reports of his dramatic comeback. Landis became the ninth American to win an individual stage at the Tour de France. In the twenty years since LeMond's first stage win, Jeff Pierce, Phinney, Hampsten, Hamilton, Armstrong, Hincapie, and Zabriskie also earned that honor.

The Final Time Trial

Pereiro's lead over Landis remained at 30 seconds at the start of the nineteenth-stage time trial. But three other riders—Carlos Sastre, Andreas Kloden, and Cadel Evans—were also within striking distance. The course required speed, endurance, and the ability to flick the bike back and forth through a series of ten sharp turns in the first kilometer.

Team directors and the riders in contention used three time checks to gauge their riders' performances. Sergei Gontchar set the pace for the other riders to chase. With the final three riders, Landis, Pereiro, and Kloden, on the course, the only question left to be answered was where they would stand on the podium.

At the first time check at 16.5 kilometers, Kloden matched Gontchar and Pereiro trailed by 10 seconds. Landis moved through with the fastest time of the day, 1 second better then Gontchar. Landis continued his aggressive pace and narrowed Pereiro's lead with every passing kilometer. Near the halfway point, 36 minutes into his ride, Landis became the leader of the 2006 Tour de France. Landis covered the 57-kilometer course in 1:07:45. After a fast start, he faded over the second half but still managed to turn a 30-second deficit into a 59-second lead.

The Ride to Paris

In a Tour that started with two of its top riders banned and under investigation for doping, no clear leader emerged until the final time trial. Over twenty stages, seven different racers wore the yellow jersey.

American prerace contenders Hincapie and Leipheimer failed to live up to the expectations placed on their shoulders.

Leipheimer did improve dramatically in the second half, moving from 58th to finish 13th overall. Hincapie, Armstrong's heir apparent on the Discovery Channel team, was not a factor after the first stages and did not finish the race. The team found itself in transition, the void left by Armstrong's retirement unfilled. Chris Horner (Davitamon-Lotto) finished 64th. David Zabriskie started strong but faded to 74th.

On the ride to Paris, Floyd Landis found himself in the position Lance Armstrong had enjoyed for seven years. After recovering from a seemingly insurmountable time gap, thirty-year-old Landis was about to extend America's Tour winning streak to eight years. Averaging 40.7 kph over the 3,657-kilometer course, Landis finished in 89:39:30, ahead of Oscar Pereiro by 57 seconds.

Three days later the international cycling world was stunned when news reports announced that Landis had tested positive for illegal levels of testosterone. Even more disheartening, the urine sample under question was taken at the end of Landis's dramatic stage seventeen climb back into contention. After a second test confirmed the original finding, the Phonak team fired Landis. Aggressively proclaiming his innocence, Landis started a lengthy and controversial appeals process.

Lance Armstrong's Saga

Lance's World Crumbles

By the end of the summer of 1996, Jim Ochowicz was still struggling to find a corporate sponsor to replace Motorola. As independent contractors, members of the team were forced to look in other directions for the 1997 racing season. For the first time in a decade, the starting fields of European events did not include an American pro team.

In September the French Cofidis team signed Armstrong to a two-year, $2 million contract. Cyrille Guimard, the team director, was Greg LeMond's first European coach. With a contract for the coming season secured, Armstrong's attention turned to rest and recovery. The long professional season takes a toll on a racer's body. When the racing calendar comes to a close, riders look forward to letting their aching legs and backs rest and heal.

Armstrong had been bothered by a sore groin. When he started coughing up blood and experiencing dizzy spells, he checked with his doctor. As a precaution, Armstrong was sent to the hospital for ultrasounds and X-rays. Talking with the doctor, Armstrong mentioned that he was experiencing pain in one of his testicles. By day's end, instead of being diagnosed with working too hard on his bike, Armstrong was diagnosed with testicular cancer. Within twenty-four hours surgeons had removed a malignant testicle. Armstrong received more bad news when doctors found the cancer had spread to his lungs and abdomen. Discovery of lesions on his brain followed. One of the top ten riders in the world was fighting for his life. On October 8 Armstrong held a press conference and stunned the cycling community with his news.

Racing Struggles

Two Americans with long, storied careers, Connie Paraskevin-Young and Andy Hampsten, retired from racing in 1996. Paraskevin-Young won eleven national championships, eight world championships, and a bronze medal in the match sprint at the Seoul Olympics; she was a three-time Olympian and won a gold medal in Pan American Games competition. As a member of the 7-Eleven team, Hampsten marked his professional European debut with a stage win at the 1985 Giro d'Italia. In 1986 he rode in support of LeMond and Hinault as a member of the great La Vie Claire team; he later became the first American to win the Giro.

The sudden absence of these two fixtures on the racing scene was emblematic of the struggles of American bicycle racing in 1996. With the cancellation of the Tour DuPont, the demise of the Motorola team, the poor performances at the Atlanta Olympics, and Lance Armstrong's difficult struggle with cancer, American bicycle racing hit a plateau.

The news wasn't all grim. Domestically, the Saturn team moved to the forefront in terms of visibility, performance, and spectator support. Six seasons after its first sponsorship agreement, the 1997 Saturn team was one of the top teams in the United States. In the previous year the team competed in 230 events and captured almost 100 victories. Saturn sponsored eleven men, including top riders like Bart Bowen, Steve Hegg, Mark McCormack, Frank McCormack, Fred Rodriguez, Norm Alvis, and Chris Wherry. Alvis, Bowen, and Hegg were former national road champions, winning their titles in 1995, 1992, and 1994. Saturn also sponsored a six-member women's team.

In 1997 USA Cycling had 75,000 members and an operating budget over $10 million. Acknowledging the United States' growing role in international racing, the UCI appointed a record-setting ten Americans to the organization's commissions and committees in 1997. Jim Ochowicz, former head of the Motorola team, and Lisa Voight, USA Cycling executive director, were named to the UCI road commission. Other appointments were made for the marketing, track, and BMX commissions.

Instead of falling into obscurity as in earlier decades, bicycle racing in the United States would recover from its setbacks and reach new heights.

Lance Returns

On October 2, 1996, Lance Armstrong was stunned with a diagnosis of testicular cancer. Twenty-four hours later he endured the first of two surgeries. Doctors cut through his skull to treat lesions on his brain. Three rounds of debilitating chemotherapy followed. Dr. Craig Nichols, anticipating that Armstrong would want to return to competitive racing, used a treatment alternative that protected his lungs. In the short term the option ravaged Armstrong's body.

During his recovery the professional racing landscape had changed. The Motorola team disbanded, a legal dispute ended the Tour DuPont, and Armstrong's $2 million contract with Cofidis was canceled. Ranked Fifth in the world when he received the diagnosis, Armstrong's name fell to the bottom of the list. His recovery forced him to miss the 1997 season, but in October he received the best possible news. His doctors declared his cancer was in remission and he was cleared to race.

Still looking for a team, Armstrong approached Thom Weisel, the owner of the Subaru-Montgomery team he rode for in 1990-91. He signed on to Weisel's team, which was now sponsored by the U.S. Postal Service. In September 1997 Armstrong called a press conference at the Interbike trade show to announce his intention to return to top-level competition.

The Founding of the U.S. Postal Service Team

The U.S. Postal team holds a venerable place in the history of American bicycle racing. Led by Lance Armstrong, Postal transformed from a team struggling against European competition into one of the most dominant squads in racing history.

U.S. Postal was founded in 1996, but its roots were planted eight years earlier. In 1988, frustrated by organizational politics, Eddie Borysewicz resigned from his post as the coach of the U.S. national team. With the financial support of Sunkyong, a Korean electronics firm, Borysewicz started his own amateur team. The team folded after just one season, but Eddie B.'s relationship with Thom Weisel opened new doors. A few years prior, Weisel had hired Borysewicz to help him prepare for an age-group world championship. Following Eddie B.'s program, Weisel won three masters world championships and five national titles between 1989 and 1991.

In 1988 Weisel hired Borysewicz to coach his newly formed pro-am team sponsored by Subaru and Weisel's company, Montgomery Securities. Armed with an operating budget approaching $600,000, Eddie B. assembled a fifteen-man team of top riders that included Bart Bowen and 1984 Olympic gold medalist Steve Hegg. Two years later eighteen-year-old Lance Armstrong joined. In 1991 Armstrong won the U.S. national amateur road race and Weisel, team owner and teammate, set a world masters record in the kilometer. The team lost Armstrong in 1992 when Jim Ochowicz convinced him to come to Motorola.

Subaru's sponsorship support neared $2 million in 1992, and Borysewicz recast the team in an attempt to earn a spot in the 1993 Tour de France. In early 1993 Subaru-Montgomery ranked 24th in international standings. The top fourteen teams in the computerized ranking received automatic positions in the Tour; six more wild-card spots completed the field. Although Eddie B. received one of the invitations, there was reason for disappointment. Tour officials wanted Subaru-Montgomery's entry to be combined with the French Chazal team—the combined team would consist of four from Subaru–Montgomery and five Chazal riders. Seeing little opportunity to make a statement with its own performance, Subaru–Montgomery declined the invitation.

After investing more than $5 million of his personal fortune, Weisel was still committed to building an elite team that could compete for the yellow jersey. With that goal in mind, Weisel hired Mark Gorski, former director of corporate development for USA Cycling and 1984 gold medal winner. Gorski convinced marketing officials at the U.S. Postal Service to become the title sponsor, and in 1996 Subaru–Montgomery became the United States Postal Service Pro Cycling Team. Gorski used a $3.5 million budget to assemble the support staff, tech wizardry, and racers that would produce the best rider and team in the history of the Tour de France.

Turned away by Cofidis after his illness, Armstrong found little interest from other European teams. He contacted Thom Weisel and discussions about joining Postal began. Initially, Weisel was skeptical and reluctant, recalling his perception of Armstrong as brash and self-centered. An honest dialogue between the two racing enthusiasts changed his opinion.

In January 1998 Armstrong joined the fifteen-rider U.S. Postal Service team for three weeks of training in the California hills. In February, for the first time in sixteen months, Armstrong entered a professional race. After the second stage of the Ruta del Sol in Spain, he was tied for 55th place. At the end of the five-day race, he finished 15th, 1 minute behind the winner.

At his second race, Paris–Nice, Armstrong placed 23rd in the opening time trial. The next day he unexpectedly dropped out, packed up his equipment, and returned to his home in Austin. While his body was returning to form, the mental aspects of traveling, living out of suitcases, and preparing for racing wore on him. He returned to Austin questioning his motivations and plans for his racing comeback.

After ten days of training rides with his friend Bob Roll and conversations with his coach, Chris Carmichael, Armstrong was motivated to race again. In late April he entered the Outdoor Life Network Grand Prix in Atlanta and finished with the pack, in 52nd place out of seventy riders.

At the end of May, Greg LeMond and Miguel Indurain came to Austin to offer Armstrong encouragement and help him raise money for cancer research. On May 22 the two legendary retired racers watched as Armstrong captured the 56-kilometer Sprint Criterium, his first victory since returning to racing. Cheered on by a hometown crowd, Armstrong accepted his $10,000 1st-place check.

Armstrong continued his comeback, racing in longer events against the best riders in the world. In early June he finished 2nd to teammate Frankie Andreu in the 91-mile First Union Invitational in Lancaster, Pennsylvania. A few weeks later he conquered the Tour of Luxembourg, winning his first international race since his victory at the Fleche Wallonne Classic in April 1996. At the beginning of July, Armstrong led U.S. Postal to victory at the seven-day Rheinland-Pfalz Rundfarht event in Germany. He started the second stage in 9th place, 23 seconds behind the leader. By the end of the stage, he had vaulted into 1st place with a 39-second margin.

With four victories for the year, the Tour de France temporarily slowed his momentum. Armstrong and team officials agreed he wasn't ready to take on the hardest race in the world. Instead, he served as a color commentator for ABC on the final two days of the race. U.S. Postal came to the Tour for the second year with four Americans on their nine-man roster: Andreu, Hincapie, Hamilton, and Marty Jemison. All nine members of the team finished the race and U.S. Postal finished 3rd in the team competition. With much of the media attention on Armstrong and the U.S. Postal team, Bobby Julich of Cofidis captured his own headlines by becoming the first American since LeMond to finish in the top three.

When Armstrong resumed racing, he won the Cascade Classic in Oregon and rode in support of George Hincapie in the 1998 USPRO championship. In October he celebrated his second year of recovery by finishing 4th in the twenty-three-day, 2,348-mile Vuelta a España. At the end of the final day, he trailed the 3rd-place rider by just 6 seconds. He ended his remarkable season at the world championships in the Netherlands. Though he was still not at his physical peak, Armstrong's performance there let the world know he was back in contention. He finished 4th in both the time trial and the 162-mile road race.

The Beginning of a Legend

Thirty-three months after being diagnosed with cancer, Lance Armstrong returned to the Tour de France.

In three previous Tour performances, the U.S. Postal squad had performed well in the early stages but faded in the mountains. The fourth appearance ended much differently. Armstrong set the tone by winning the prologue. It was the first stage victory, and first yellow jersey, for U.S. Postal.

By the end of the 86th Tour, Armstrong had captured four stages—three time trials and a mountain stage. He became the second American racer to win the yellow and the first to do so with an American-based team. After failing to finish in three earlier Tours, Armstrong secured his victory with a record-setting average speed of 40.2 kph.

He captured his first *maillot jaune* unchallenged. Alex Zulle (Banesto) finished almost 8 minutes behind. At the afternoon awards ceremony, Armstrong received flowers, the distinctive blue vase presented to each winner, and a check for $350,000. From cancer patient to Tour de France winner, Lance Armstrong became the centerpiece for hundreds of newspaper, magazine, and television reports around the world. Companies willingly paid millions of dollars to have their products associated with Armstrong and the U.S. Postal team. Shortly after the race, he signed a $400,000 book contract to tell his life story. In the years to come, there would be much more to write about.

American Winners

Saturn continued to post impressive numbers in domestic events. In 1998 Team Saturn had ninety-four 1st-place, sixty-four 2nd-place, and fifty-one 3rd-place finishes. Deeply committed to cycling events as a marketing tool, Saturn became the title sponsor of the USPRO cycling tour in early 1999. The fifteen-race series offered more than $600,000 in prize money and an additional $100,000 bonus pool. Saturn continued to reinforce its reputation as one of the strongest supporters of domestic racing.

In 1999 USA Cycling and sponsor Visa named Lance Armstrong, Marty Nothstein, Alison Dunlap, and Kent Bostick Cycling Athletes of the Year. Sixteen other riders received the same award, each one recognizing the top rider in all the racing disciplines supported by USA Cycling. Each recipient received a plaque and $1,000 prize.

Armstrong and Karen Dunne received the award for their road racing performances. Marty Nothstein and Erin Veenstra were the country's best track racers. Road and track received much of the media attention, but BMX and mountain bike racing had their own audiences. Marie McGilvary and Danny Nelson were best in BMX. Alison Dunlap and Eric Carter captured the elite mountain bike awards.

Seven

Every July from 1999 to 2005, Lance Armstrong became the focus of American media and sports fans. For three weeks in midsummer, hardcore and casual fans alike would debate the question—would he win again? How much longer would the streak continue? Armstrong answered those questions by shattering the existing record of five wins and going on to capture two more.

With each victory, more companies lined up to throw money at Armstrong and the team. In 2001, despite complaints that a government agency shouldn't be involved in sports marketing, the U.S. Postal Service agreed to a three-year, $25 million extension. By 2004 the team had sponsorship agreements with Jif peanut butter, Allsport sports drink, Clif energy bars, and Bissell floor cleaning products. In 2004 AMD, a provider of computer processors, became the "Official Technology Partner of Lance Armstrong and the United States Postal Service Pro Cycling Team, which is presented by Berry Floor." The long list of sponsors also included Nike, AIM Funds, Bristol-Myers Squibb, and American General Financial.

Trek Bicycles negotiated a contract with Armstrong in 1997 when he was still recovering from cancer. Photographs of the Trek logo on Armstrong's bikes had a halo effect over Trek's complete line of bicycles. In 2003 Trek built almost a million bikes, more than twice as many as its closest competitors.

On April 23, 2004, officials from the U.S. Postal Service announced the end of their eight-year sponsorship. Less than two months later, team officials signed a three-year agreement naming the Discovery Channel the title sponsor of the former U.S. Postal team beginning with the 2005 racing season. The new sponsor received written assurance from the champion that he would lead the team in at least one more Tour.

At a press conference at the Tour of Georgia in April 2005, Armstrong announced that he would retire from professional racing on the last day of the 2005 Tour, win or lose. Not everyone believed him. True to his word, Armstrong ended his career on July 24 in the silver and blue of Discovery Channel, not long after winning his seventh Tour de France.

The Next Keeper of the Yellow?

Armstrong's retirement left cycling fans worldwide to ponder an astonishing career and to wonder when, if ever, an American racer would again conquer the world's greatest riders in the world's greatest race. The question was answered—or so it seemed—just one year later in the 2006 Tour. Floyd Landis, once an unassuming right-hand man for Armstrong, came back from what most observers believed to be an insurmountable deficit to take the yellow jersey, continuing American dominance of the French national tour. He did it the only way it could possibly have been done—with an epic solo breakaway in the mountains. His historic ride, one of the most impressive in Tour history, erased much of the deficit. A blazing-fast final time trial erased the rest of it.

A few days later the elation of Landis and his newfound legion of fans ran headlong into yet another doping allegation, after Landis failed a routine test measuring the ratio of testosterone to epitestosterone in his system. His ratio was far over the limit. As a result, the former mountain bike racer embarked on a roller coaster of allegations, counter-allegations, and appeals as he fought to keep his victory. As 2006 came to a close, Landis was still maintaining his innocence, claiming impropriety and incompetence in the lab that performed the tests. The question mark after his victory has not been removed, and one wonders if it ever will be.

CHAPTER NINE

Racing in the New Millennium

Dark Shadows

BY THE MIDDLE OF THE first decade of the twenty-first century, dark shadows had started to fall across the landscape of professional cycling. Controversies over illicit doping, once confined to debates between team directors and governing body officials, spilled into the mainstream media when some of the best riders in the United States and Europe were accused of using illegal performance-enhancing techniques.

Shortly after winning the gold medal in the individual time trial at the 2004 Athens Olympics, Tyler Hamilton, following official protocol, was tested for illegal performance-enhancing elements in his system. In September, after winning the eighth-stage time trial at the Vuelta a España, he was tested again. The results were devastating. Officials reported Hamilton had tested positive for blood doping. A new type of test performed on his Athens sample also showed indications that he had received a blood transfusion. Since a second test to confirm the results couldn't be accurately performed (due to the lab's freezing the sample by mistake), Hamilton was allowed to keep his gold medal. The owners of Phonak, Hamilton's team, fired him. He lost several appeals and was banned from racing for two years.

As Lance Armstrong's dominance of the Tour de France reached new levels, the French press reported several doping allegations against him. Official investigations in 2002 and 2005 ruled the accusations were unfounded and called into question the integrity of the lab, the press, and cycling's governing bodies. In 2005 Gerard Bisceglia, the chief executive of USA Cycling, released a statement questioning the motives of the accusers and supporting Armstrong. In 2006 the waters were

COR VOS

Tyler Hamilton won the gold medal in the individual time trial event at the 2004 Athens Olympics. Shortly after, Hamilton became embroiled in a blood doping controversy. Fired by his Phonak team, Hamilton was banned from racing for two years.

further muddied when Frankie Andreu admitted to using performance-enhancing drugs while racing on Armstrong's team.

The indictments cast doubt on the validity of a string of American victories and tarnished the hero worship placed on the shoulders of riders like Armstrong, Hamilton, and Landis. While all three professed their innocence, only the accusations against Armstrong remained unconfirmed in official procedures.

 Doping, Drugs, and Scandals: Searching for a Competitive Edge

 Standing atop the winner's podium at a major cycling race is a life-changing event. Cyclists, searching for even the smallest advantage over their competitors, have pursued the most advanced equipment and training techniques in search of any edge at the finish line.

The lure of media glory and financial gain has led a number of riders to experiment with illegal substances. Drug use has tainted the sport of professional bicycle racing and cast shadows over the Olympics and legendary races like the Tour de France, Tour of Italy, and Tour of Spain. Top riders have been suspended, teams disbanded, and reputations tainted. Seven-time Tour de France winner Lance Armstrong constantly defended himself against vocal European and domestic detractors who claimed his performances were artificially enhanced.

Since the six-day races at Madison Square Garden, cyclists have turned to drugs and stimulants to increase endurance, stamina, and speed. A century ago strychnine, cocaine, amphetamines, and caffeine were commonly used to keep the racers alert on the velodrome tracks.

Over time, street drugs have been replaced by more sophisticated blood doping techniques, human growth hormones, and genetically engineered erythropoietin (EPO), which stimulates the growth of red blood cells.

In 1967 tragedy moved cycling's international governing body to take action. On Friday, July 13, Tour de France riders climbed to the 6,200-foot summit of Mont Ventoux. Twenty-nine-year-old Tommy Simpson started the thirteenth stage in 7th place. Five years earlier Simpson was the first Briton to wear a yellow jersey and finish in the top ten in the Tour de France.

Climbing in hot and humid conditions, Simpson fell off his bike 3 kilometers from the summit. Concerned fans helped him get back into the race, but Simpson crashed again a few minutes later. Unconscious, Simpson was airlifted to a local hospital but died later that day. Stunned racers, fans, and team directors received a second shock when Tour officials reported that doctors found evidence of amphetamines in Simpson's blood. Amphetamine pills were also found in his jersey pockets and hotel room.

The UCI responded by banning the use of any performance-enhancing drugs at cycling events. Through the remainder of 1967, fourteen riders received penalties for doping or refusing to take mandatory tests. In September doctors and pharmacologists created the UCI's first list of banned doping substances.

Despite the public pledges to control cheating, top riders still looked for an advantage. At the 1969 Giro d'Italia, officials announced that legend Eddy Merckx had tested positive for amphetamines.

As pressure to win increased, the search for performance-enhancing tools intensified in Europe and the United States. American cyclists had a long record of disappointing results in Olympic events and were not immune to the pressures. With the Soviet Union and Eastern Bloc countries' boycott of the 1984 Olympics, expectations for the Americans were very high.

The American cycling team's unprecedented nine-medal performance at the L.A. Olympics turned the team into media darlings. Corporations clamored to have the medal winners endorse their products. In January 1985 glory turned to shame as reporters uncovered evidence that members of the team had used blood transfusions before the Olympics. Gold medalist Steve Hegg; silver medalists Brent Emery, Pat McDonough, and Rebecca Twigg; and bronze medalist Leonard Nitz received blood transfusions before competing in their events.

The scandal found that national coach Eddie Borysewicz and other team officials had condoned the transfusions and managed the procedures. Following a closely watched and publicized investigation, the USCF suspended Borysewicz and Ed Burke, the federation's Elite Athlete Program director. Mike Fraysee, a former president of the federation, also received a reprimand. Although blood doping wasn't illegal prior to the L.A. Olympics, the USCF formally banned the practice in January 1985.

After the Olympic scandal drug testing became a priority for USCF officials. Rules, testing procedures, and lists of banned substances were expanded and revised annually. The testing, not yet perfected, surprised cyclists with unexpected positives. At the 1986 Coors Classic, Leslee Schenk was disqualified and received a thirty-day suspension for testing positive for pseudoephedrine. She defended herself by noting that the drug was an ingredient in the Nyquil she took to battle a cold.

Behind the scenes, the cat-and-mouse game progressed as governing bodies created new tests and medical professionals found new ways to boost performance and avoid detection. On July 20,1988, Spain's Pedro Delgado, the leader of the Tour de France at that point, tested positive for a masking agent called probenicid, which was used to conceal steroid use. Although illegal, probenicid wasn't on the UCI's banned list. Delgado remained in the race and wore the yellow jersey at the end of it.

Young riders' untimely deaths led to speculation, investigation, and frustration over the inability to link specific drugs to the deaths. Dutch cyclist Johannes Draaijer finished in 20th place in the 1989 Tour de France. In February 1990 a heart attack killed him just days after a medical checkup pronounced him in good health. One death alone was cause for sadness, but Draaijer was the fifteenth racer from the Netherlands to die unexpectedly over the previous three years. The Royal Dutch Cycling Federation launched an investigation to look into rumors of a new drug called EPO. A genetically engineered form of the hormone erythropoietin, originally designed to help people suffering from anemia, EPO was used by cyclists to increase their production of oxygen-enriched hemoglobin. Although the Royal Dutch investigation could not establish a link between EPO and the statistically aberrant deaths of the young racers, EPO became a battleground for detection and deception.

The USOC and USCF administered tests to athletes under their jurisdiction. Hundreds submitted urine tests, but the reporting process was very slow. The International Olympic Committee had accredited only two facilities in the United States, one in Los Angeles and the other at the University of Indiana in Indianapolis.

In 1990 Jeanne Golay received a six-month suspension after testing positive for steroids at the U.S. national cycling championships. Failed drug tests and suspensions were announced in the USCF's newspaper, *Cycling USA.* Without formal rules concerning the publication of results, announcements often followed months after a failed test. Scheduled to compete as a member of the team time trial at the world championship, Golay and Jiri Mainius, the USCF's coach, learned of the suspension just a few days before the event. Alternate Eve Stephenson replaced Golay at the last minute and won a silver medal with her new teammates. Golay steadfastly denied taking steroids. After serving her suspension, she returned to the team and won a gold medal in the individual road race at the 1991 Pan American Games in Havana.

The USCF's drug testing policy was significantly revised in 1990 to address claims from athletes that positive tests were due to unexpected reactions rather than intentional deception. John Siebert, 3rd-place finisher in the Rocky Mountain News Criterium, tested positive for pseudoephedrine. He claimed that Sudafed tablets he took to clear up his sinuses a few days before the race led to the failed test. The new rules announced that "inadvertent use" would no longer be an accepted defense against a positive finding. Siebert's suspension was changed to a warning. The appeals process was also revised. Cyclists who failed a urine test had eleven days to file an appeal. A second test was administered and suspensions were given only when positive results were received from both tests.

Positive drug tests and suspensions rarely reached the front page of daily newspapers. That changed in 1998 when an automobile driven by Willy Voet, the top-ranked Festina team's soigneur was stopped at the border between Belgium and France. On his way to support his team at the start of the 1998 Tour de France, Voet was found with 234 doses of EPO, 80 bottles containing growth hormones, 160 male hormone capsules, and 60 capsules filled with a blood thinner.

Tour de France organizers immediately disqualified all nine members of the Festina racing team. Several riders, including world road race champion Laurent Brochard, admitted to illegal drug use. Bruno Roussel, Festina's coach, and team doctor Eric Ryckaert faced intense scrutiny and questioning.

Four other teams quit the 85th Tour in protest, and on July 25 the peloton went on strike. Claiming they were being unfairly persecuted, the riders delayed the start of the stage by two hours. Only 96 of the 198 starters finished the tour. The Festina doping scandal overshadowed Bobby Julich's 3rd-place finish, the top American finish since Greg LeMond's victory in 1990. Lost in the controversy was the failure of the testing protocols to identify cheaters. The Festina scandal was launched by customs officials, not laboratory technicians.

The risk of public ridicule and scandal didn't stop top riders from using banned substances. In 1999 Marco Pantani, who won the 1998 Tour de France—a race plagued by scandals mostly among European riders—was disqualified at the 1999 Giro d'Italia when tests showed evidence of EPO use.*

Armstrong Defends His Victories

In 1999, on his way to his first Tour de France victory, Lance Armstrong used a skin cream called Cemalyt to treat saddle sores. Since the cream contained corticosteroids, Armstrong received prior approval from Tour medical officials. Trace amounts were later found in Armstrong's urine tests, but the UCI reiterated that the positive result was not illegal. For the next six years, Armstrong was forced to defend his performances in the face of detractors who accused him of using illegal substances.

Armstrong's dramatic recovery from testicular cancer inspired people around the world. Yet some observers used that health scare to question Armstrong's ability to race at the highest levels without artificial help. How could a man so close to death return to dominate professional racing?

In September 2002 the French government called an end to a two-year-old investigation into Armstrong's performance with the U.S. Postal Service team. The investigation was launched in November 2000 after authorities received footage of Postal's support staff disposing of medical waste in a roadside trash bin. The recovered waste included empty packaging for Actovegin. The drug, made from cows' blood products, was not banned, nor did it provide any boost in a rider's performance. The team reportedly used Actovegin to treat road rash injuries suffered during the Tour.

In 2004 the press conference to announce the Discovery Channel's new three-year, multimillion dollar sponsorship of Armstrong's team was interrupted by questions about a new book, *L.A. Confidential: The Secrets of Lance Armstrong.* David Walsh, a columnist for Britain's

---

*Pantani died on Valentine's Day 2004, apparently of a cocaine overdose.

Sunday Times, and Pierre Ballester, a former writer for the French newspaper *L'Equipe,* used interviews with a former Postal Service soigneur to accuse Armstrong of using mysterious syringes during the 1999 Tour. Emma O'Reilly claimed she applied makeup on Armstrong's arms to hide needle marks and traveled to Spain to pick up unidentified medications. Once again Armstrong vehemently denied using any illegal substances and threatened to sue the authors for libel.

L'Equipe continually published controversial articles accusing Armstrong of cheating. On August 23, 2005, *L'Equipe* published "The Armstrong Lie," calling it the first substantiated proof that Armstrong used performance-enhancing substances during the Tour. According to *L'Equipe,* an analysis of Armstrong's urine samples from the 1999 Tour showed six positive results for EPO. Although EPO was on the UCI's banned list since the early 1990s, there was no reliable test to identify its use until 2001. *L'Equipe* reported that the French anti-doping lab had retested samples frozen in 1999, allegedly for scientific study, and that six of Armstrong's samples from that year showed evidence of EPO use. Although the twelve numbered vials contained no names, *L'Equipe* claimed they had matched numbers of Armstrong's drug control forms to the tainted vials.

In response to the explosive claims, the UCI hired Dutch lawyer Emile Vrijman to launch an independent investigation. In June 2006 Vrijman's 130-page report concluded that the laboratory's analysis of the 1999 urine samples was flawed and the claims that Armstrong used EPO were unproven and unsubstantiated. The UCI responded to the report by formally announcing that Armstrong was cleared of any doping violations.

In July Armstrong faced yet another bombshell headline. This time the source of the disputed cheating allegations was much closer to home. Armstrong was involved in a legal dispute with SCA Promotions. Based in Dallas, Texas, the company had offered Armstrong a $5 million bonus for winning the 2004 Tour de France. When doping allegations surfaced, SCA refused to make the payment. Armstrong filed suit and the dispute was placed in front of a three-judge arbitration panel.

Sworn testimony taken during the arbitration leaked to the press. The documents contained transcripts from former friend and Postal teammate Frankie Andreu, his wife Betsy, Motorola teammate Stephen Swart, and Michael Ashenden, an Australian medical researcher. Although these witnesses stated they had never witnessed Armstrong using illegal substances, they did provide extensive anecdotal evidence about EPO use that challenged Armstrong's credibility and ongoing denials.

The suit was settled out of court and SCA Promotions paid Armstrong $7.5 million. Despite attacks from numerous European and American detractors, Lance Armstrong has never failed a drug test.

Protecting Olympic Ideals

Use of performance-enhancing drugs by athletes in swimming, track, and cycling threatened to tarnish the Olympic ideals of fair play in competition. European countries and the United States responded by creating independent organizations to address drug-related cheating.

In early 1999 the International Olympic Committee hosted the World Conference on Doping in Sport. When the conference closed, the Lausanne Declaration on Doping in Sport created an independent international anti-doping agency, the World Anti-Doping Agency (WADA), in time to test athletes competing in the 2000 Sydney Olympics.

The U.S. Anti-Doping Agency (USADA) opened for business on October 1, 2000. Formed by the USOC, the USADA was authorized to conduct a comprehensive anti-doping program. In 2001 the USADA tested 219 cyclists. Four years later more than 500 tests in and out of competition were conducted.

A Tarnished Hero

At the turn of the century, Lance Armstrong's victories at the Tour de France brought new fans to professional bicycle racing. Sponsors hoping to associate their products with the image of elite racers formed new teams. Riders who worked for years to reach the top levels of the sport were finally reaping financial rewards. The pressure to perform was higher than ever.

Although overshadowed by Armstrong, Tyler Hamilton was one of the top racers in the United States. In 2003 he finished 4th in the Tour de France, an accomplishment made even greater by his racing the majority of the stages with a broken collarbone.

When Hamilton won the individual time trial gold medal at the 2004 Athens Olympics, he claimed his share of the media spotlight. But like the 1984 team's, Hamilton's victory celebration would soon turn sour. In late September officials at the Tour of Spain announced that Hamilton had tested positive for blood doping. More bad news quickly followed. Cycling fans learned Hamilton had also tested positive for blood doping at the Olympics.

Hamilton's samples from the Olympics and Tour of Spain showed signs of what the USADA called "mixed populations." The evidence indicated Hamilton had received a transfusion of another person's blood, a process that increases the body's ability to store and use oxygen. His Olympic samples were mishandled and lab technicians were unable to conduct a second test to verify the positive result. Although he was implicated with illegal doping, the lab error allowed Hamilton to keep his gold medal.

Further investigations found that UCI officials had sent Hamilton a letter in June 2004 warning him that recent blood tests showed evidence of possible manipulation. After the suspicious findings the UCI targeted Hamilton for follow-up testing. Tests at the Olympics and Tour of Spain changed speculation to clear evidence.

Prior to the 2004 Olympics test, blood transfusions were impossible to detect. Australian researchers developed a test that scrutinized the sample to look for abnormalities caused by manipulation of the cyclist's blood, and the International Olympic Committee added the protocols to their testing procedures.

Still claiming his innocence in the face of mounting evidence to the contrary, Hamilton was dropped by his Phonak team and received the maximum two-year suspension for a first-time blood doping offense. Hamilton's appeals to the American Arbitration Association and the North American Court of Arbitration for Sport were rejected. As Hamilton's suspension expired, he signed with the Italy-based Tinkoff team and anticipated racing a full season in 2007. But his future is far from certain. As details of yet another doping scandal—the scandal that overshadowed the opening days of the 2006

Tour de France—slowly emerged, Hamilton's name was among the accused. If he is found guilty in that affair, it could result in a lifetime ban from the sport.

Landis's Dream Turned Nightmare

From the moment Lance Armstrong announced his retirement after winning his seventh Tour de France, anticipation for the first post-Armstrong Tour grew stronger with each passing day. Experienced observers and new racing fans alike debated for months who would be the next rider to win the yellow.

Once again, illegal drugs took the focus away from the race. The controversial doping scandals that opened and closed the Tour serve as the legacy of the 2006 Tour de France.

The day before the Tour's scheduled start, race organizers disqualified thirteen riders implicated in a doping ring investigation by the Spanish police. Before the first stage had begun, two of the prerace favorites were on their way home. In 2005 Ivan Basso and Jan Ullrich finished 2nd and 3rd. Ullrich, leader of T-Mobile, and Basso, his counterpart on Denmark's CSC, were prevented from staking their claim to the yellow jersey. Although the banned riders were not formally charged with any crimes, Tour officials and team directors followed international cycling rules that banned any rider involved in a drug or doping investigation, prior to the investigation's conclusion.

The Tour's storybook finish pushed the opening-day scandals into the background. On July 23, after a dramatic comeback performance in stage seventeen, Phonak's Floyd Landis became the third American rider to win the Tour de France. Three days later UCI officials

revealed ominously that a rider had failed a drug test during the Tour. The next day a Phonak spokesman reported that Landis had tested positive for high levels of testosterone after his seventeenth-stage victory. Phonak suspended Landis the following day. The dream finish had turned into a nightmare.

Following Tour drug testing procedures, race leaders are required to submit two urine samples after every stage. Landis fulfilled that obligation at least three times. One of the samples Landis submitted after the seventeenth stage revealed his ratio of testosterone to epitestosterone was abnormally high. WADA established a standard of 4:1. The ratio in Landis's sample was 11:1.

Landis defended his performance, denied taking any illegal substances, and pointed out that he took medicines for hypothyroidism and received medically approved cortisone injections for his damaged hip. Landis also wondered if the beers and Jack Daniel's whiskey he consumed the night before the test might have influenced the results.

His comments were met with skepticism, and observers waited for the results of the second follow-up test. On August 5 the UCI announced that the second test confirmed the abnormally high ratio found two weeks earlier. Additional testing also found evidence of synthetic testosterone.

The results of the 2006 Tour were thrown into chaos. Second-place finisher Oscar Pereiro declared victory, and final results of the 2006 race are conspicuously absent from the Tour's official Web site.

Landis and his representatives continued to profess his innocence as the complicated appeals process unfolded well into the following year. Instead of being recognized as the third American to win the Tour de France, Landis's place in history could be defined by his being the first cyclist to lose a Tour victory because of a failed urine test.

New Sponsors

The End of Saturn, the Rise of Health Net

For more than thirty years, corporate America's financial support of professional bicycle racing kept the sport alive. Some sponsorship contracts ended after just one season; others, like 7–Eleven, Coors Light, Motorola, and Saturn, prospered for years. But these companies were not in the business of selling bikes. Changing economic situations, heightened competition, and slashed marketing budgets led to the teams' cancellations.

Launched in 1992, Saturn's became one of the most recognized cycling programs in the United States. Seventeen riders supported by Saturn competed in Olympic events, eight in 2000 alone. In 2003 Saturn riders had their best year. Mark McCormack won the USPRO championship. Chris Horner finished 1st in the Tour of Georgia and the T-Mobile International in San Francisco. The Saturn women's team was the top-ranked team in the country.

Entering only domestic events, team owner Tom Schuler supported thirteen men and nine women with a $1.2 million budget (Postal's budget was over $8 million). In September 2003 Schuler learned Saturn would be ending its twelve-year sponsor relationship on the last day of the year. Schuler persuaded Quark shoes to become the new sponsor of the former Saturn women's team, but the men's team folded.

One year after Saturn's demise there were twelve professional men's teams competing regularly in American events.★ In 2005, while Lance Armstrong's Discovery Channel team was the top international racing story, Team Health Net was having a landmark season in the United States. The team's Scott Moninger, a veteran of fifteen racing seasons, captured his second National Racing Calendar (NRC) championship. (Thirteen years earlier, riding for Coors Light, Moninger won the series when it was called the Korbel Cup.) During the 2005 season Moninger finished 1st in four NRC stage races and was named *Velonews* North American Male Cyclist of the Year. Health Net ("Presented by

---

*American professional teams in 2004 included Colavita Olive Oil-Bolla Wines, Health Net-Maxxis Pro Cycling Team, Jelly Belly-Aramark Cycling Team, McGuire Pro Cycling Team, Ofoto.com Cycling Team, Sierra Nevada Cycling Team, Sharper Image-Mathis Brothers Furniture, Subway Express Cycling Team, Team Seasilver, Team Monex, The Jittery Joe's Cycling Team, and the Webcor Builder Cycling Team.

Maxxis") was named the North American Team of the Year, winning thirty-one individual NRC stages and one-day races. Five different team members captured nine victories in eleven NRC team stage race events. Chris Wherry won the 2005 USPRO championship, and the USPRO national criterium championship went to teammate Tyler Farrar.

During sixty-three days of competition on the National Racing Calendar, a Health Net rider was missing from the medal podium on only eight days.

Team TIAA-CREF

If winning the Tour de France is the measure of success for professional bicycle racers, American riders arrived at the top of the world. Greg LeMond, Lance Armstrong, and Floyd Landis captured eleven yellow jerseys in twenty years. But LeMond and Armstrong have retired and Landis faces an uncertain future, hampered by hip replacement surgery and doping controversy. In their mid-thirties, other leading Americans —George Hincapie, Levi Leipheimer, and Bobby Julich—are closer to the ends of their careers than the beginning. Where will the next generation of elite American racers come from? Most likely from the dedication of individuals like Jonathan Vaughters, and teams like TIAA-CREF.

In 2003 Jonathan Vaughters ended a ten-year professional cycling career. As a member of the Mercury, U.S. Postal, and Credit Agricole teams, his resume included top-five finishes at Paris-Nice, the Dauphiné Libéré, and the Tour of the Mediterranean. For several years he held the record for the fastest ascent of brutal Mont Ventoux after setting the mark in a Dauphiné time trial. In domestic races Vaughters was a star who often found himself riding alone up the toughest climbs, winning Colorado's Saturn Classic and Bob Cook Memorial Mount Evans Hillclimb. With Postal at the Tour, Vaughters played a key role in the team's winning the team time trial in 2001.

No longer a competitive racer, he did not leave the sport. In 2004 Vaughters dedicated his energies to recruiting, training, and supporting young riders. In April 2004 TIAA-CREF, a national financial services company, became the formal title sponsor of a team of sixteen- to twenty-two-year-old racers who have the potential to become America's next generation of elite cyclists.

Under Vaughters's leadership results came quickly. Colby Pearce finished 3rd in the UCI world cup and Timmy Duggan finished 2nd at the under-twenty-three (U23) national time trial championship. At the 2004 Tour of Georgia, Vaughters experienced one of the most difficult circumstances of leading a team. Craig Lewis was struck by a car and suffered life-threatening injuries. Two years later, after recovering from internal bleeding, two punctured lungs, and forty-seven broken bones, Lewis won the 176-kilometer U23 road race at the 2006 USA Cycling national festival.

Success on the road isn't Vaughters's only mission. With Colby Pearce, a 2004 Olympian and former TIAA-CREF rider, Vaughters is determined to build a four-man pursuit team capable of winning a medal at the 2008 Olympics in Beijing. And, unlike many of his predecessors, he is dedicated to doing it without a doping program.

At the Interbike trade show in September 2006, Vaughters announced that the team was looking for a new title sponsor for 2007. It was a familiar refrain.

New Races

The Tour of California

In the first two months of 2006, two major announcements roused the interest of racing fans still wondering how the post-Armstrong era would unfold.

First, Philip Anschutz, billionaire financier and owner of several pro sports teams, announced his commitment to spend $35 million over five years to create a Tour de France–caliber stage race in the United States.

Amgen, a $12 billion biotech company, was named the Tour of California's title sponsor.* The newest American stage race was sanctioned by USA Cycling and the UCI, and sixteen elite teams entered. On the roster were seven UCI pro teams: Discovery Channel, Gerolsteiner, Davitamon-Lotto, Phonak, Saunier Duval, Credit Agricole, and T-Mobile. Three American-based teams—development team TIAA-CREF, Toyota-United, and California-based Kodakgallery.com-Sierra Nevada—joined the international entries.

One month later, on February 7, 2006, the Toyota-United team was introduced at a press conference. Sean Tucker, a former professional racer turned entrepreneur, secured Toyota's multiyear title sponsorship

---

*In an ironic twist, Amgen is also the primary producer of synthetic EPO (erythropoietin), the hormone illicitly obtained and used by cyclists and other athletes to boost the oxygen-carrying capacity of their blood.

and second-tier sponsorships from *Bicycling* magazine, Cendant Hotel Group, United Bicycles, Easton Sports, Shimano, OS Performance Nutrition, Tifosi Optics, Champion System, and the SockGuy. The sponsorship was Toyota's first entry into professional bicycle racing and was reported to be the biggest sponsorship deal ever for a domestic racing team. In addition, Tucker created a new fan-based membership program that encouraged racing fans to purchase an ownership stake in the team for as little as $100 per year.

Team directors Frankie Andreu and Harm Jansen recruited seventeen experienced riders away from elite domestic and international teams. Toyota-United planned a heavy domestic racing schedule that included the first Amgen Tour of California, the Pro Cycling Tour series, and key races in the seventy-event USA Cycling NRC.

A New American Stage Race

Toyota-United made its debut on February 19, 2006, at the start of the eight-stage Amgen Tour of California. More than one hundred of the world's top riders came to San Francisco for the heavily promoted event and its $150,000 prize purse. The field included Levi Leipheimer, Cadel Evans, and Floyd Landis; all three finished in the top ten of the 2005 Tour de France. Three stage winners were also entered: David Zabriskie, George Hincapie, and Paolo Savoldelli.

Officials estimated 200,000 spectators lined the 1.9-mile course from San Francisco's famous Pier 1 to the Coit Tower at the top of Telegraph Hill to watch Sunday's

The Toyota-United Pro Cycling Team was introduced on February 7, 2006, and made its debut at the Amgen Tour of California.

prologue. Leipheimer, riding for Gerolsteiner, was the third-from-last rider on the course. Motivated by the raucous cheers of hometown fans, he finished faster than 127 others, with a time of 4:53. In a field of top international racers, American riders took the top five positions—behind Leipheimer were Bobby Julich, Hincapie, Landis, and Zabriskie.

Toyota-United's Juan Jose Haedo won the 129.1-kilometer first stage from Sausalito to Santa Rosa. Discovery Channel's Hincapie won the second stage and Phonak's Landis the third-stage individual time trial—the deciding stage of the first Tour of California. Landis finished the time trial in 1st, in 35:58.91, about 30 seconds ahead of Zabriskie. Hincapie, leading at the start of the stage, finished almost 1 minute behind Landis and dropped to 4th overall. Landis kept his lead the rest of the way, and CSC's Zabriskie and Julich followed in 2nd and 3rd. After winning the prologue, Leipheimer slipped to 6th. The jersey for best young rider was awarded to TIAA-CREF's Tom Peterson. Despite winning two early stages, Toyota-United could not maintain the team lead and finished behind T-Mobile in 11th place. Team CSC and Discovery Channel finished 1st and 2nd.

The first Amgen Tour of California drew 1.3 million spectators, making it the largest single sporting event in California's history. In July the Anschutz Entertainment Group (AEG) announced that the Tour would return on February 18 to 25, 2007. Later in July Toyota-United announced less positive news: that it had fired team director Frankie Andreu. A dispute between team owner Sean Tucker and Andreu over his commitments to other business obligations led to the dismissal.

New Heroes

The most recognized names in American bicycle racing started competing as teenagers. The careers of Greg LeMond, George Hincapie, and Lance Armstrong were nurtured and supported by dedicated coaches and team directors when these future stars were unproven youngsters. Often underfunded, the U.S. cycling organizations have helped to add new names to the history of American racing. With long-term, consistent financial support and strategically managed development programs, the United States can bring even more legends to the sport.

Founded on August 17, 2000, the USA Cycling Development Foundation has since awarded more than $3 million in grants to support development programs. The foundation's annual grant awards reached $600,000 in 2003, a 20 percent increase over 2002. The grants provided the financial resources needed to operate development programs like the U23 Endurance European Residence Program, Track Program,

Women's Endurance Program, and U23 Resident Mountain Bike Program. The foundation's Center of Excellence awards $60,000 annually to clubs, teams, and collegiate riders. The Edmund R. Burke Fund for Cycling Development provides junior riders with travel and training grants.

In mountain biking, a relatively new racing discipline that was created on home soil and was once dominated by American riders, Americans fell behind the rest of the world. In February 2004 USA Cycling launched the U23 national mountain bike team to train and support riders who could compete at the highest level. John Devine, Alan Obye, Sam Schultz, and Nick Waite were named to the first team. In September 2004 Obye became the first U23 national cross-country champion, defeating twenty others over a 27-mile Mammoth Mountain course.

USA Cycling also devoted coaching and financial resources to developing young road riders. Formed in 1999, the U23 (also known as *espoir*) national team gave young riders opportunities to race and gain experience in international events. The program was funded by grants from the USA Cycling Development Foundation and managed by U23 national team director Noel Dejonckheere.

The program fulfilled its mission in 2006. At the Tour de l'Avenir, U23 national team members Tyler Farrar and Patrick McCarty delivered the best American performance since LeMond won the race in 1982. McCarty finished 11th overall. Farrar, who won a stage in an earlier l'Avenir, won the second stage and wore the green sprinter's jersey for four days. Saul Raisin ended the l'Avenir with the polka-dotted King of the Mountain jersey on his back. Success also came at the Tour de France. David Zabriskie became the first national team graduate to wear the yellow jersey.

In 2006 USA Cycling sold 57,218 licenses through September, already a 6 percent increase over 2005's total. More than 36,000 licenses were sold for road and track racers and almost 11,000 for mountain bike racers. Interest in racing is strong, but the support racers need to succeed is also growing—the number of licensed clubs reached 1,800 in 2006, 16 percent more than the year before.

More racers means more opportunities for long-term success and the creation of new American bicycle racing heroes. But much more work needs to be done to build a sustainable long-term program to keep America's cyclists at the highest levels in professional racing and Olympic competitions. Lack of racing opportunities for domestic riders, low salaries outside the ranks of marquee teams like Discovery, limited domestic media coverage, and unresolved doping scandals present obstacles to racing's continued rise.

Bicycle racing needs heroes to sustain the interest of corporate sponsors, mass media coverage, and the enthusiastic support of American sports fans. Like Frank Kramer at the turn of the twentieth century, Lance Armstrong created an iconic position at the Tour de France. Between Kramer and Armstrong a long list of racers, whose names are perhaps best known to a small group of hard-core enthusiasts —riders like Greg LeMond, Davis Phinney, Marty Nothstein, Ned Overend, Connie Carpenter, Rebecca Twigg, and Inga Thompson— inspired a new generation of track, road, and mountain bike racers to follow them.

Ten years from now, who will be the new American bicycle racing heroes on the road, track, and trail?

Afterword

Nineteen eighty-six was my first year of riding a bike, watching the Coors Classic, and seeing the world championships in Colorado Springs. Somehow this unknown sport had landed on top of me and become enormous in my little teenage world of suburban Denver. It seemed like cycling was the most important sport in the world that summer. LeMond was winning the Tour de France, all these exotic foreigners were coming to Colorado to race in the world championships, and I was entering my first race. I finished last. My little Celeste Bianchi had failed me, and I figured it was just as all the other sports were: big, popular, and something I wasn't good at.

Happily for me, cycling was different in 1986. It was only popular in the way the Sex Pistols were popular—fanatically so—for the few who loved it beyond true. It was about passion and hard work, not so much about raw physical gifts. Cycling was the sport of the outcasts, geeks, and underdogs in America. In 1986 cycling was a sport that Bill Gates could have been good at (had he trained really hard).

In a funny way all of these elements conspired to make America the most successful cycling nation of the next millennium. It seems clear now; all over America kids of my age were searching for something different, something where they could be unique, and something outside the high school field. Some of these outsiders became the core of Silicon Valley, some became the end of Generation X, and a few became Tour de France riders. The harsh reality of growing up as a constantly teased kid wearing spandex in America proved fertile for producing great champions in a sport that, ironically, many of these same high school peers would take up twenty years later to "fit in." Watching the cultish CBS tapes of the Tour de France and cheering wildly for strange-named heroes in Boulder proved to be just the fertilizer needed to produce a Tour de France–winning vine twenty years on.

It's been a fascinating story to watch unfold from my unique perspective— a few key elements conspiring to produce the perfect storm of success. Now we will have to wait a few more years to see if our sport leaps forward once again. Will my generation have inspired a new group of kids to take on the impossible? Or have we just made cycling more visibly discouraging? I guess we'll have to wait and see.

My guess? Keep an eye on the next crop. Signs are everywhere that cycling is coming to a small town near you, in a big way.

—Jonathan Vaughters
CEO Director Sportif
Slipstream Sports
Boulder, Colorado

Index

About the Author

Lou Dzierzak spent sixteen years in advertising before becoming a full-time writer. His inspiration to follow competive cycling came in the mid-1970s when he attended Milwaukee's Superweek National Championship race. A life-long road rider with an avid interest in history, he wanted to explore the cycling heroes who were racing long before Lance Armstrong captured America's attention.